Filming the City

Filming the City
Urban Documents, Design Practices and Social Criticism Through the Lens

Edited by Edward M. Clift, Mirko Guaralda, and Ari Mattes

Series Editor: Graham Cairns, AMPS

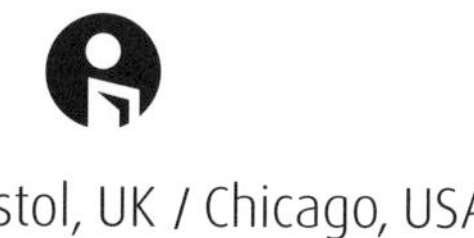

intellect Bristol, UK / Chicago, USA

First published in the UK in 2016 by
Intellect, The Mill, Parnall Road, Fishponds, Bristol, BS16 3JG, UK

First published in the USA in 2016 by
Intellect, The University of Chicago Press, 1427 E. 60th Street,
Chicago, IL 60637, USA

A catalogue record for this book is available from the
British Library.

Copy-editor: Emma Rhys
Cover designer: Gabriel Solomons
Front cover image: *The Limey* (Steven Sodebergh, 1999). ARTISAN PICS /
    THE KOBAL COLLECTION / MARSHAK, BOB
Production managers: Gabriel Solomons and Jelena Stanovnik
Typesetting: John Teehan

ISBN 978-1-78320-554-7
ePDF ISBN 978-1-78320-555-4
ePub ISBN 978-1-78320-556-1

Produced in conjunction with AMPS (Architecture, Media, Politics,
Society)

Printed and bound by Hobbs, UK

Contents

Acknowledgements

The editorial team would like to thank the Brooks Institute for their support on this book series.

Foreword

Graham Cairns

Today, we are perfectly attuned to the ever-present moving imagery of the commercialized urban landscape. We still watch the 'city symphonies' of a new generation of film-makers and constantly see 'the city' as a site, subject and protagonist in cinematic productions from California to Mumbai. Furthermore, we watch TV shows that highlight their spatial locations as key to their allure and intrigue: New York, Los Angeles, London, Tokyo and a seemingly infinite number of other cities, function as labels to both televisual and cinematic production the world over. In the realms of architectural and urban design, filmic-realistic imagery in the presentations of design proposals is standard practice. The computer generated 'fly-through' leads the viewer through the as yet unconstructed proposals of new cities and buildings in ways that echo Sergei Eisenstein's notion of the cinematic promenade.

The fact that film remains, over a century since its invention, a medium fascinated by the city and its architecture, is evident in the wealth of projects and initiatives that can be found mining this interdisciplinary terrain. This book represents one of them. Beyond being an engagement with film and the city however, this book represents part of a much broader and more complicated tapestry represented by Intellect's Mediated Cities series. Both this book, and its associated series, find their roots in the 'Mediated City Research Programme' coordinated by the research group AMPS (Architecture, Media, Politics, Society) and its associated scholarly journal, *Architecture_MPS*. The programme brings together theorists, practitioners and academics from various fields to consider the multiple ways in which the city has become a phenomenon that we understand and interact with in a continually 'mediated' way.

This approach opens the AMPS 'Mediated City Research Programme' to multiple ways of engaging with the urban and is reflected by the three titles it has prepared with Intellect Books to launch this series: *Digital Futures and the City of Today: New Technologies and Physical Spaces*; *Imaging the City: Art, Creative Practices and Media Speculations*; and of course the present volume, *Filming the City: Urban Documents, Design Practices and Social Criticism Through the Lens*. Through this filmic prism, this book brings together film-makers, architects, designers, media specialists and video artists. It offers new insights in three areas of mutual engagement: film as a design practice; film criticism; and film as an arena of architectural/urban theory and analysis. It gives commentaries of particular films and their social and urban relevance; it offers historical and contemporary criticisms of both film and urbanism from conflicting perspectives; and it documents examples of how to actively use the medium of film in the design of our cities, spaces and buildings.

Giving a sense of the diversity of interactions between the medium of architectural-urban design and the medium of film, *Filming the City: Urban Documents, Design Practices and Social Criticism Through the Lens* is ideal for readers from both fields. For those coming from a spatial-design background, the tropes and possibilities of film as a tool and a documentary medium will be explored. For those coming from a film-media background, the multiple possibilities of film as a visual backdrop, narrative theme or conceptual tool will be examined. In this sense, it is typical of the Mediated Cities series and the AMPS 'Mediated City Research Programme', in resisting static discipline categorizations and explicitly overlaying and interlacing ideas and working practices. This then, is a book that seeks to engage with a diversity of scholars and readers.

What it engages those readers with is a series of arguments that, in their unique ways, all indicate that the potential of film as a radical visual language, a medium of communication and as a site of architectural and urban investigation, is far from exhausted. Despite the emergence of ever newer visual technologies as we move forward in the twenty-first century, film is still a medium with the potential to move in new directions. Through its now well-established visual and narrative tropes, it still has the potential to continue instigating thought and debate about our built environments and how we experience, design, build or destroy them.

Introduction

Edward M. Clift

Cities, with their social complexities and vibrant multisensory environments, have always inspired artists. Painters, writers and musicians have long described and celebrated urban spaces and have taken inspiration from the narrative of cities to construct their vision of urban societies. Film-makers today are similarly drawn to cinematic visions that seek to depict the changing urbanscapes appearing in different locations throughout the world. This book provides an overview of the privileged relationship that exists between cities and films while successfully problematizing it through extended case studies, theoretical analysis and historical research.

The editors have grouped the chapters into three separate categories based on the nature of their inquiry. Each section seeks to develop a layered set of perspectives emphasizing varying aspects of theory, research or practice in exploring the complex symbiosis that exists between film and the city as a metaphorical device. The first section, 'Film as Spatial Theory', deals with a complex set of cinematic and spatial theories through the work of various directors like Jonathan Kaplan, Christopher Nolan and Jacques Tati. Following this is a second section, 'Film as Spatial Research and Experiment', which is devoted to film as a type of research into the underlying society that film represents and its spatial affinities. A third and final section, 'Film as Spatial Practice', focuses on film-making itself to uncover particular determinants and outcomes it may have within the larger cultural and design conversation.

In the initial chapter, Ari Mattes describes in detail the ways that the pictorial representation of urban and (sub)urban space in Jonathan Kaplan's *Unlawful Entry* (1992) foreshadowed, to a large degree, the city that Los Angeles was to become. In his reading, the film uses cinematography and a particular visual style to render its theoretical point regarding the pervasiveness of surveillance in suburban contexts. Los Angeles is portrayed geographically as an artificial dystopia that keeps the disorder of its urban population in check through high degrees of surveillance. Mattes equates the panoptic city that emerges from the narrative with contemporary concerns relating to drone surveillance and remote warfare.

Jarrad Cogle examines the fictionalized representation of 'Gotham City' in Christopher Nolan's *Batman* films (2005–12) in order to better understand how cities contribute to the mapping of social order within a postmodern global context. The character of *Batman*, in this interpretation, is a stitching device intended to reintegrate fragmentary perspectives of the city into a new whole. Complicating this Dickensian challenge is the tendency of large blockbusters of this sort to target fractured global audiences with simplified action-oriented sequences. The re-envisioned Gotham of these movies must therefore strike a symbolic balance between the heterogeneous forces of globalization and the homogeneous forces of the city as an integrative transcendent symbol of a singular civilization.

In her analysis of Jacques Tati's 1967 movie *Playtime*, Lisa Landrum explores the quirks of modern cities and modernist architecture. Her chapter positions the film as an example of the disjuncture between an architect's idea of the city and the experience it may provide for urban residents. Landrum seeks out the larger meanings of the film at the same time as she explores Tati's working style in minute detail. It is a fascinating look into the mind of the director and the many ways that film can subvert the dominant paradigm. From the point of view of designers, architects or urban planners, Landrum also shows how film can provide an enormously useful paradigm to understanding cities in a different way, to get closer to the everyday experience that people might have of an urban environment.

Maciej Stasiowski and Joern W. Langhorst provide two separate chapters investigating further the gap between lived experience and its filmic representation. Film in their view could potentially reflect the deeper psychological dimensions of urban design and reveal aspects of life that are often ignored. It can represent the dark side of the city just as easily as an idealized image. However, more often than not, these authors believe that films end up reinforcing the status quo rather than questioning it. Cities depicted on the screen are most typically shown as idealized environments in some way. They are much more homogeneous than in real life; the potential of crafting the perfect scene in fact allows the film-maker to select congruent parts of built environments to describe ideal cities as if they were coherent entities like a character in a plot.

Stasiowski uses two blockbusters from 2012, Pete Travis's *Dredd* and Christopher Nolan's *The Dark Knight Rises*, to detail the process employed by cinematic images to represent the city and its underlying ideologies, within a Deleuzian framework of horizontal and vertical vectors of power. Langhorst examines Spike Lee's documentary films, *When the Levees Broke* (2006) and *If God is Willling and da Creek Don't Rise* (2010), as entry points to explore political debates over the meaning of post-Katrina New Orleans. Issues of representation for a city can become especially acute following a crisis such as that brought on by Hurricane Katrina. In such situations, the representational meanings of the city tend to co-evolve with their filmic counterparts in a fitful and often highly-contested manner.

Section Two of the collection contains four chapters that all explore film as a means of conducting spatial research and experimentation. The films they feature relate to mid-century Los Angeles (United States), early-twentieth-century Guadalajara (Mexico), Berlin (Germany) and the 'Metropolis' or city of the future. Gabriel Solomons begins this section with the empirical observation that mid-century modern architecture in LA is typically associated with villains and other evil-doers in Hollywood film. Significantly, the pattern he identifies through a series of case studies turns on its head the intended meanings of the architectural form. Instead of imbuing the inhabitant of the space with a sense of rational order, the modernism portrayed in film communicates to viewers a suspicious lack of appreciation for all the elements of life.

In contrast, Carmen Elisa Gómez-Gomez shows how film can promote a modernist message through a subtle interweaving of film, desire, cultural tradition and the exotic within an urban setting. The film she selected for her case study is *Guadalajara en verano/Guadalajara in the Summer* (Bracho, 1964), which recounts the experiences of a group of American students studying English in the city. Narrative and editing sequences portray the city as accessible and illustrate activities congruent with the cosmopolitanism it promotes. The author's self-reflective analysis also makes evident film's potential for enabling us to look back in time in a similarly touristic manner.

Ayşegül Akçay Kavakoğlu considers the portrayal of a future architecture to be one of film's most important strengths, as well as a key feature in science fiction narrative. Film, as the historical form of the city symphony montage makes clear, is an experimental conductor that is not limited by physical form or other spatio-temporal constraints. She closely examines the portrayal of cities in *2001: A Space Odyssey* (Kubrick, 1968), *Minority Report* (Spielberg, 2002), *Renaissance* (Volckman, 2006) and *Elysium* (Blomkamp, 2013). In each case, the movie's restructuring of space and time relies on a related transformation of form in the architecture represented.

Graham Cairns investigates the significance of *Lola Rennt/Run Lola Run* (Tykwer, 1998) as an emblem of modern approaches to architecture and their articulation of contemporary urban experience. The narrative of the film revolves around a young woman's anxious quest for money to pay off her boyfriend's debt. Three different renditions of the same story in the film demonstrate how small changes in one's experience of the city can dramatically change narrative outcomes. As such, it disrupts both our cinematic expectations and sense of the city as a coherent space. Cairns proposes that Tykwer's film, like Walter Ruttmann's 1927 *Berlin: Symphonie einer grossstadt/Berlin: Symphony of a Great City*, articulates a view of space and design that resonates with contemporary trends in architecture, especially the work of Rem Koolhaas.

Film can be a productive method of research as much as it can serve as an object of analysis. The four chapters in Section Three, 'Film as Spatial Practice', offer thought-provoking examples of such an approach. Gemma Barton compares and contrasts the working practices of architects and film-makers to pinpoint two distinct approaches to representation. Although both professions share a common desire to imagine future realities or spaces for inhabitation, they enclose space in radically different ways. Film-makers may see space in a much more constricted manner than architects, owing to the presence of the singular narrative. What comes out of this analysis is that understanding these sorts of divergences in representation can foster the growth of hybrid forms and increased collaboration between them.

Alice Arnold, in her chapter '*Electric Signs* Revisited', recounts the making of her own city symphony film showing the particular uses of electric billboards in Hong Kong, Los Angeles and New York. Electric digital billboards are especially bright and facilitate signage that allows for visual movement. Beginning around the turn of this century, electric signs proliferated but their introduction in each of these global cities has been received with varying degrees of openness. Fearing visual pollution, LA residents have sought to limit their display. New York, on the other hand, used zoning to concentrate them in the Times Square district while Hong Kong has largely used them to commercialize public spaces. By placing these different sign-functions side-by-side in a film, Arnold is able to generate insights that might have been unavailable through another mode of inquiry.

Luisa Bravo likewise seeks to use film in order to capture new meanings and recognitions beyond idealized representations of the city. In this chapter, Bravo reports on outcomes from the 'Visioni Urbane/Urban Visions' film competition included in the 2014 festival 'Visioni Italiane' in Bologna. Participants in the competition sought to translate their experiences of the urban environment into different categories like documentary, fiction and experimental. In the process, she realized that film can serve as a kind of conscience of the eye in its ability to capture essential truths of life once that opportunity is afforded.

The ability to see the city in filmic terms opens up a novel approach to the study of social interaction online. As Benjamin Koslowski explains in the concluding chapter, social media has enabled larger and larger numbers of people to essentially treat the city as the visual backdrop of their lives. The urban environment thus becomes self-reflexively understood as the *mise-en-scène* for a multitude of micro-stagings. Social media reconfigures the city into what he calls an 'informational overlay' that can be readily shared through the technologies of virtual space. In this sense, social media continues to play upon the built environment of the city in many of the same ways as film since its invention.

Italo Calvino in his *Invisible Cities* (1997 [1974]) renders different surreal cities, each one representing a human condition or a system of relationships, often sourcing inspiration from real-world settlements. Calvino celebrates cities as a way to reveal the contradictions of contemporary society. He brings the reader into a fictional word where everyday architectures and activities become sources of wonder and amusement when described in exotic terms or settings. The readers are carried away but their fantastic journey is grounded in their own experience of urban environments. In a similar way, the narrative of cities has inspired film-makers and provided the settings for their work, but film-makers have also provided a privileged perspective on cities.

Films provide rich analytical sites in which to examine the multitude of overlapping motifs that exist between our collective lives and the stories we choose to represent them. While other arts build on one's experience of urban environments, films not only immerse viewers in new exciting spaces, but also unravel different perspectives on our cites. As the authors in this book convincingly argue, the cities in which we live even share many of the mediumistic qualities of film. Our everyday experience is edited and represented within the larger narrative provided by the city context. Exploring the interplay of film and the city in this way promises to open our eyes to their common underlying movement in the restless spread of culture.

Section One

Film as Spatial Theory

Chapter 1

Unlawful Entry: The imbrication of suburban space and police repression in Jonathan Kaplan's Los Angeles

Ari Mattes

A great metropolis today absorbs and divides the world in all its diverseness and inequality.

Marc Augé, Non-Places

Now the fat policeman wakens definitely, and feels of his club to see that it is ready for business.

Upton Sinclair, The Jungle

Motherfuck you and your punk-ass ghetto bird.

Ice Cube, Ghetto Bird

Introduction

Jonathan Kaplan's 1979 film *Over the Edge* opens with an image of a signpost, perfectly framed by the screen: 'Welcome to New Granada. Tomorrow's city… today.' The camera tracks back to reveal a panorama of this city of the future. Surrounding the sign is an expanse of arid, vacant lots; a poorly maintained asphalt road stretches towards a background peppered with barely visible outlines of condominiums, the putative message of the sign completely undercut by its squalid surrounds. In sync with a heavy rock guitar riff (Cheap Trick's 'Speak Now'), a caption rolls across the screen making explicit the connection between morally bankrupt hyper-development and urban waste; the film is based on 'true incidents', it informs the viewer, occurring in a community in which city planners overlooked the fact that a quarter of the population were aged 15 or under. The proliferation of sub/urban crime in the United States – such a charged political topic over the next decade – is explicitly linked to an alienation built into the very structure of habitable space. Kaplan's SoCal is an overdeveloped wasteland, its suburbs the 'excrescence of the circulation of capital' (Lefebvre 2003: xvii), the poorly designed and developed SoCal ripped apart by urbanist Mike Davis in *Ecology of Fear* (1999 [1998]: 59–91).

The following scene in the youth centre – the first of the diegesis proper – juxtaposes this dead exterior space with the vitality of life inside the centre, a dialectic that comes

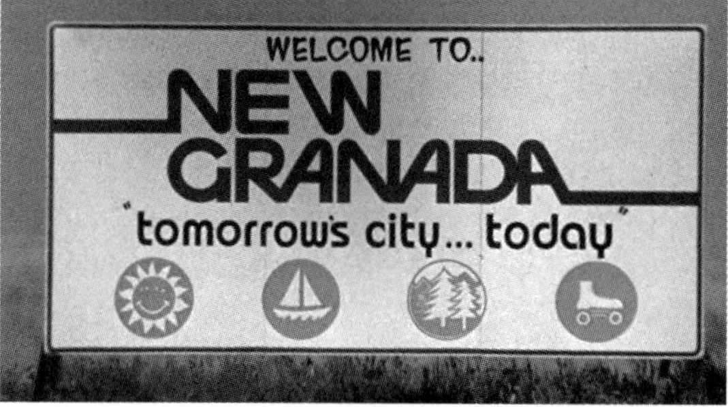

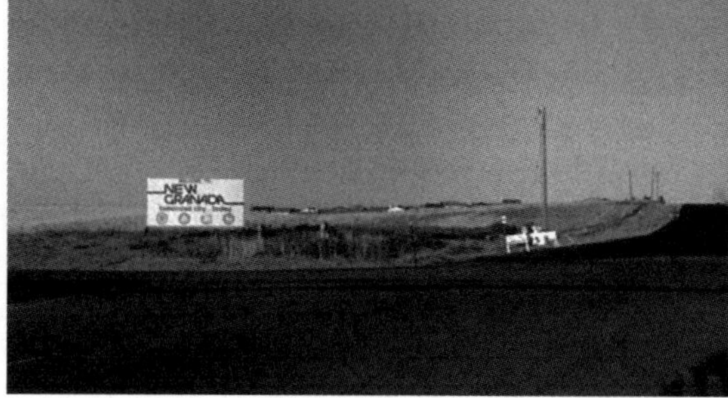

Figure 1. *Over the Edge* (1979), © Orion Pictures.

to structure the film as a whole. Carl (Michael Kramer) and friends retreat to the youth centre several times throughout the film in the face of a horde of hostile property owners and developers who are bolstered by a police force whose gratification involves the harassment and intimidation of these 'delinquents'. This youth centre, site of productive happiness, becomes the principal target of the malevolent Chief Doberman (Harry Northrup), who coerces the community into shutting it down. The teenagers are left to play amidst the ruins, forsaken, in unfinished condos and on vacant, rubble-strewn lots, trying to make the most of their containment within an at best dull, at worst virtually post-apocalyptic, suburban space. Their occasional 'crimes' are clearly envisioned by Kaplan as symptoms of an ennui for which the city-planners and -developers, the forces of capital that subordinate and ruthlessly reify the living environment into exchangeable 'lots', are entirely responsible. *Over the Edge*, indeed, deliberately critiques capital's construction and militarization of urban space as a means of control.

This creation of cadastral space in tandem with (and facilitating) police manipulation and repression becomes the central thematic in Kaplan's later masterpiece, *Unlawful Entry* (1992), the focal point of this chapter.

The genius of *Unlawful Entry* lies in its analysis of police repression as intertwined with the urban geography of Los Angeles itself – in its exploration and critique of Los Angeles as a city constructed in part to facilitate surveillance for the advantage of the state–corporate nexus. The film offers a critique of contemporary methods of police surveillance, à la Zygmunt Bauman and David Lyon's discussion in *Liquid Surveillance* (2013) and Paul Virilio's *La machine de vision/The Vision Machine* (1994 [1988]), displaying a profound suspicion of all forms of police surveillance, and, more so, the grid-like demarcation of cadastral space in Los Angeles that enables such diffuse and seamless surveillance. Los Angeles is envisioned by Kaplan as Mike Davis's 'fortress' from

City of Quartz (2006 [1990]: 221–63) – a constellation of walls and passages cordoning off space as a means to create, categorize, monitor and channel vectors of criminality. Kaplan's all-seeing camera becomes homologous with the sweeping, repressive motion of the surveillance (and assault) drones that would become globally notorious less than a decade after the film was made. Los Angeles, thus, is no longer envisioned as the electric sprawl of Jean Baudrillard's *Amérique/America* (1988 [1986]: 52–55), but, rather, as a carefully orchestrated arena enabling all-pervasive state surveillance.

In the context of a great deal of futuristic techno-babble regarding the contemporary urban aesthetics (and ethics) of Los Angeles – both apocalyptic and celebratory alike – *Unlawful Entry* serves as a reminder that, as David Harvey eloquently points out in *The Enigma of Capital* (2010), design in and of the city usually serves the interests of property developers (enforced by policing) above and beyond the interests of its inhabitants.

Unlawful Entry

The narrative of *Unlawful Entry* follows a mid-thirties couple, Karen Carr (Madeleine Stowe) and her property-developer husband Michael (Kurt Russell), who live in Los Angeles in one of the white-barricaded suburbs dissected by Mike Davis in *City of Quartz* (2006 [1990]: 151–219). Their house is broken into by an African American burglar in the opening scene, and in response to this break-in they develop a relationship – commercial and personal – with police officer Pete Davis (Ray Liotta). They contract him to install a new security system, and Michael hires him to plan security for a nightclub he is developing. When Officer Davis captures the suspect and beats him in front of Michael as part of a perverse male friendship ritual – a 'show' of brotherhood through violence, sickeningly recalling the racist history of LA and the LAPD (Davis 2006 [1990]: 267–322; Davis 1999 [1998]: 410–11) (and, of course, the Rodney King beating, occurring fifteen months before the film was released – 'Have you got a home video? Nowdays, you've gotta have a video,' a police officer jokes to Michael when he reports Officer Davis's harassment) – Michael decides it would be best to have nothing more to do with Davis. In response to Michael's (and eventually Karen's) rejection, Davis proceeds to stalk, harass, intimidate, illegally survey and physically attack the couple. This escalates into a life and death struggle in the final sequences of the film, with Karen and Michael killing Officer Davis.

The film is ostensibly in the mould of the suburban paranoia thrillers of the 1980s and early 1990s: *Fatal Attraction* (Lyne, 1987); *The Hider in the House* (Patrick, 1989); *The Hand that Rocks the Cradle* (Hanson, 1992). An evil outsider penetrates the sanctity of domestic space and is violently expurgated by the end of the film; the alien 'intruder', in the case of *Unlawful Entry*, just happens to be a cop.

However, from the opening sequence Kaplan explicitly ties this violence to urban design and 'ghettoization'. Crime and criminality are depicted as systemic products, the direct residue of a hostile, alienating urban experience that is necessarily facilitated by big

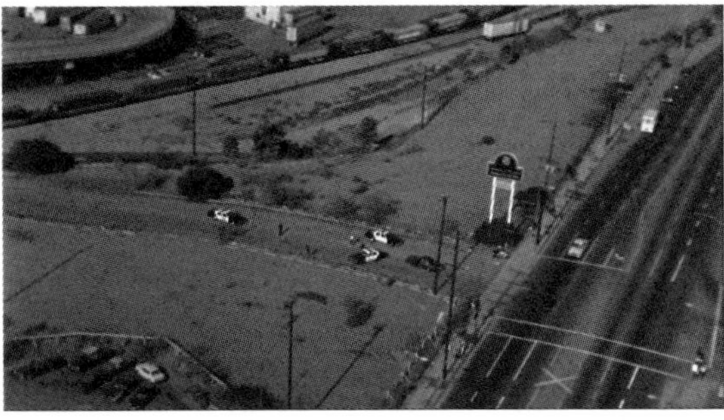
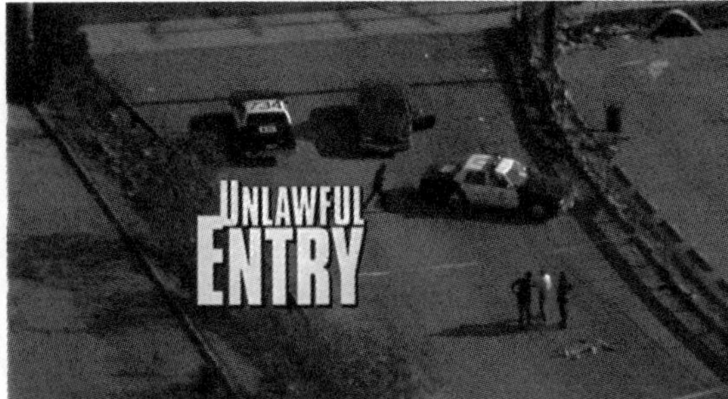

Figure 2. *Unlawful Entry* (1992), © Largo Entertainment and JVC.

capital and a repressive police force; Los Angeles is envisioned by Kaplan as a panoptic city designed to facilitate covert and overt police surveillance, repression and manipulation.

As the opening credits roll, the sound of a helicopter ushers in vision from above – presumably the point of view of one of the LAPD's infamous 'ghetto birds' – looking down upon a dead body. The corpse is surrounded by police, guns drawn; and police cars, lights flashing. The image is grey, washed out, the site some kind of abandoned concrete lot on the side of a freeway: Los Angeles as post-industrial wasteland. The sweeping, drone-like camera follows one of the police cars, accompanied by James Horner's melancholic, jazzy score, as it leaves the crime scene and accelerates down the freeway. The camera tracks across the river-made-concrete – a necessary landmark in every modern LA film – and up to a wide panorama of downtown, its skyscrapers obscured in a smoggy haze.

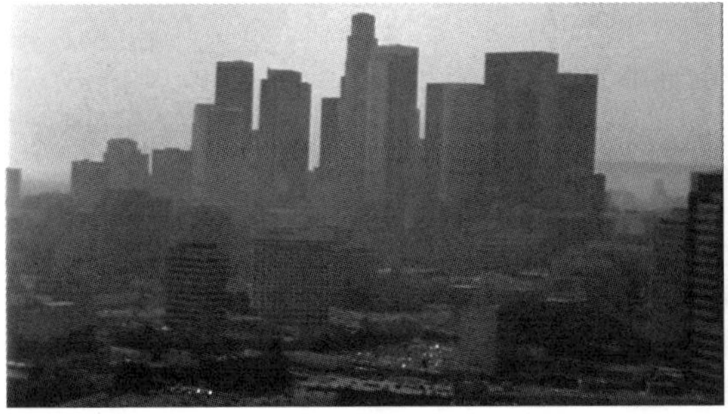
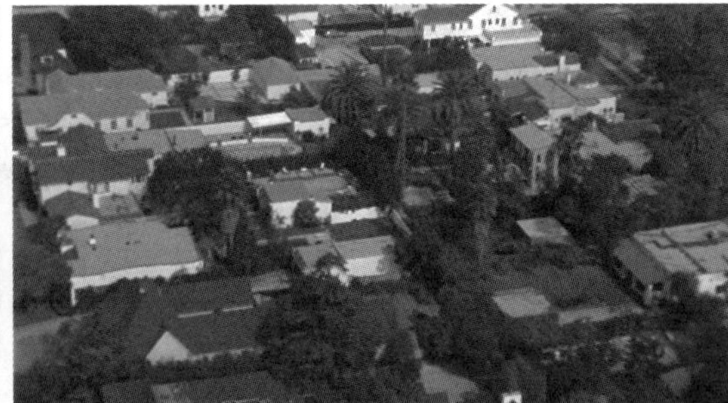

Figure 3. *Unlawful Entry* (1992), © Largo Entertainment and JVC.

The corpse of the opening image is directly linked to the urban at large, envisioned as a product of urban degradation – LA is imagined as a corpse of a city.

The film then cross-fades to a helicopter shot over one of the city's myriad suburbs. The bright blue of several pools – the pool, as a symbol of affluent middle-class suburbanity, becomes a critical topos as *Unlawful Entry* unfolds – breaks up the drab grey of the buildings crowding the rest of the image. A figure – a woman – is swimming laps in one of the pools, and there is something acutely voyeuristic at play as the camera homes in on this solitary swimmer, oblivious to this (the viewer's) eye in the sky.[1] Noises typically associated with the suburban seep into the soundtrack: birds, children playing, harmless chatter. This juxtaposition of the city skyline and the suburbs, in their sprawling and monotonous, grid-like arrangement, clearly invokes the discourse of many 1980s Reagan-era suburban-paranoia films, in which the urban is seen as a cesspool of crime in contrast with an immeasurably 'cleaner' suburbia.

The film cross-fades again to a sunwashed, street-level shot of a classic Los Angeles suburban home, stucco, Spanish and palm-tree bound, a product of the imaginary deftly analysed by Carey McWilliams in the 1940s in *Southern California: An Island on the Land* (2010 [1946]). The image fades into night – the streetlamp is now on, and light from a TV flickers in an upstairs window. To cap off this constellation of Brady-esque suburbanalia,

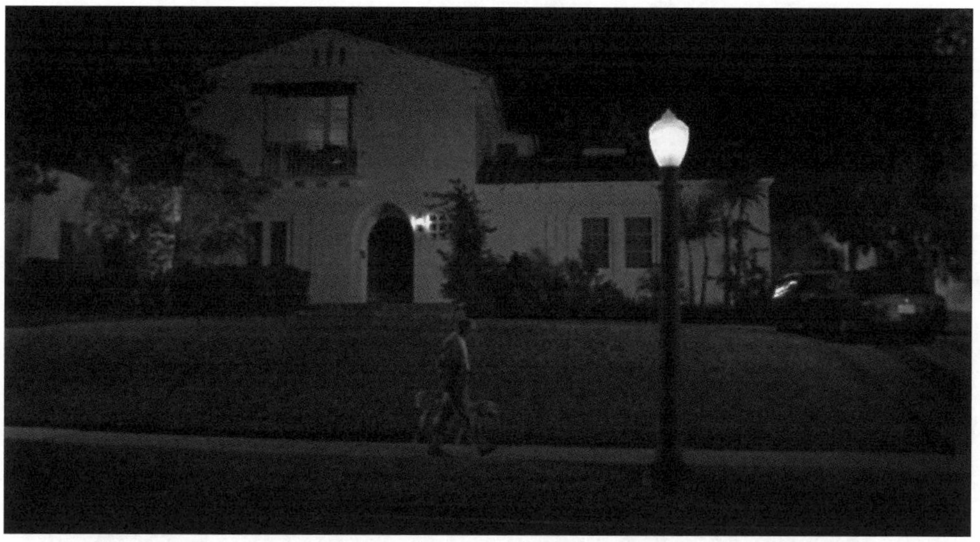

Figure 4. *Unlawful Entry* (1992), © Largo Entertainment and JVC.

a man walking a barking dog crosses the image, left to right. *This* is the LA suburb in all its abysmal glory: more banal and less 'old money' than the Chicago suburbs lampooned in *Risky Business* (Brickman, 1983) and *Ferris Bueller's Day Off* (Hughes, 1986), the antithesis of the New York neighbourhoods of Spike Lee and Woody Allen with their eclectic, electric mix of cultures.

The film cuts to a bedroom inside the house; playing on the television is a talk-show interview – a female subject is engaged in a discussion about her childhood, formerly private memories now public. Our attention is deliberately focused on *watching* by the homology between the opening police chopper and our own eye as cinematic spectator – between a paramilitarized brand of surveillance and our own scopophilic activity, recalling Virilio's argument in *Guerre et cinéma/War and Cinema* (1989 [1984]) regarding the symbiosis between military strategy and cinematic spectatorship – and then intensified by this seamless passage into the private domain of the bedroom: the chapel, so to speak, of domestic space. As though in complicity with this veiled critique of televisual (and surveillance) culture, the camera moves through the bedroom to rest on photos of our two stars, as yet unintroduced in the diegesis.

The camera then tracks, with undeniable eroticism, across a bare female leg, sticking out amidst rumpled sheets. It rests on the as-yet-unintroduced Karen Carr, asleep. There is a clanging noise off camera (the burglar) and her eyes open, coming into consciousness

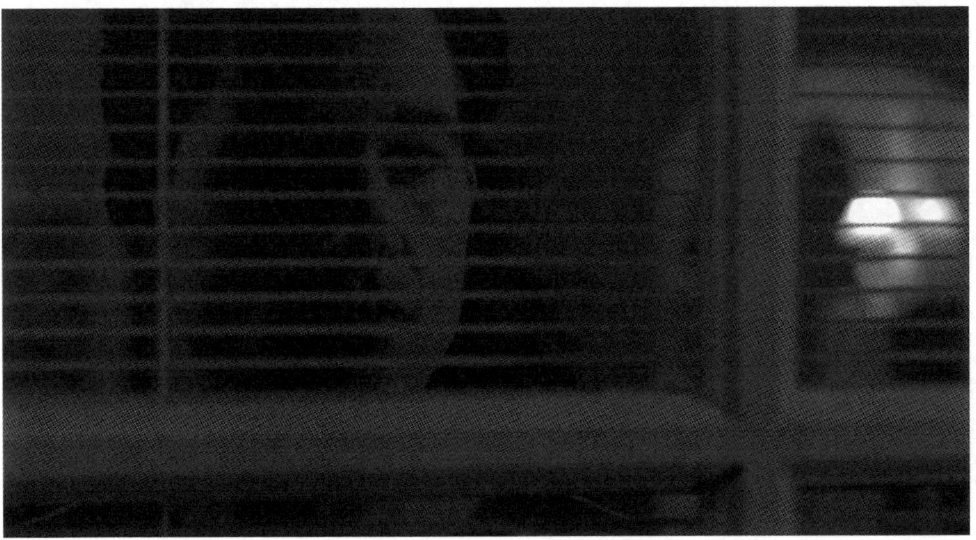

Figure 5. *Unlawful Entry* (1992), © Largo Entertainment and JVC.

within the frame of the narrative *in parallel with* the intrusion of the burglar, as though her recognition that an intrusion – an 'unlawful entry' – has taken place is equally directed at the viewer, at *our own* intrusion into her home.

She alerts husband, Michael, who heads off to investigate. He checks the myriad rooms of their house before pausing at the window and looking out at the street. As the camera cuts to the exterior, photographing his anxious eyes, blinds cutting across his face, it becomes exquisitely clear to the viewer that Michael is trapped within a self-made prison. He is the epitome, in this moment, of the paranoia – a paranoia that *imprisons* – of life in the surveillance age, of the white-suburban paranoia that classes the black and the urban as evil Other. The opening invasion sequence culminates, moments later, with this paranoia-made-true – the intruder attacks Michael, grabbing Karen as a hostage and holding one of their kitchen knives to her throat, before fleeing and leaving her in the pool, unharmed.

It is worth noting that the weapon, the knife, comes from the Carrs' house itself, given the connection Kaplan makes (and emphasizes as the film progresses) between suburban segregation, virtual gatedness, and urban degradation and deprivation. This crime is, if not created, then at least exacerbated, by the technologies and tools of the affluent. Furthermore, the scene immediately following this intrusion begins with an extreme close-up of a police car, its caption 'to serve and to protect' clearly legible in the upper-right corner of the frame. Given this ability 'to serve and protect' has already been called into question in the opening image of the film – police standing around a dead body – and given that the viewer's uneasiness is only amplified by the homology drawn between police surveillance and cinematic intrusion – it is only natural that this image should assume a particularly grim hue at this point, gesturing towards the savage violence against Karen and Michael to come, courtesy of the LAPD.

The imbrication of urban design and police repression

Thus, Kaplan's opening sequence draws the viewer's attention to the air-vision layout of LA, its horizontal design facilitating rampant police surveillance, presaging the 'droneism' that would come to full maturation in the twenty-first century,[2] and reflecting on the computerization and digitization of daily life so provocatively theorized by Baudrillard in *L'échange symbolique et la mort/Symbolic Exchange and Death* (1993 [1976]) and by McKenzie Wark in *Gamer Theory* (2007). Kaplan's presentation of the city's spatiality recalls David Harvey's critique of Hausmann's redevelopment of Paris in *Rebel Cities*: '[Hausmann] created an urban form where it was believed [...] sufficient levels of surveillance and military control were possible so as to ensure that revolutionary movements could easily be controlled by military power' (Harvey 2013: 16). It is worth recalling, similarly, Virilio's discussion of Blaise Cendrars's newspaper articles about Hollywood from the 1930s:

> Hollywood, the world capital of the cinema motor [is] a forbidden city in the state of California, a state under siege, patrolled by three police divisions responsible for mercilessly ousting undesirables: sick people or germ-carriers hoping to benefit from the temperate climate, and especially the unemployed, the single women, and the abandoned children who had come to stamp their feet and sink at the doors of vast studio factories, sealed off like fortresses, before finally being sent back to their state of origin or imprisoned in concentration camps in the middle of the desert. (Virilio 1995 [1993]: 77–78)

Kaplan presents a world of permanent surveillance and spectatorship that presages the Spectacle of Disintegration, the new social order postulated two decades later by McKenzie Wark in *The Spectacle of Disintegration* (2013) – a world defined through perpetual revelations of, and intrusions into, the private by the 'vision-machine', a world, indeed, where, as Wark writes, little sister and her friends have replaced (or work in tandem with) Big Brother: 'Big Brother is no longer watching you. In His place is little sister and her friends: endless pictures of models and other pretty things' (2013: 2).

Yet, at the level of *Unlawful Entry*'s diegesis itself, any kind of subversive strategy is fairly well masked for the first part of the film. A yuppie couple, in response to an invasion of Otherness, securitizes their manor assisted by the police force. The initial intruder is clearly racialized by both the Carrs and the Police: a black terror of the night who diabolically materialized in their sacred space.

From the 30-minute mark this radically changes, the film shifting away from an Othering discourse towards an examination of disciplinary power itself. Michael goes for a 'ride-along' with Officer Davis and his partner Roy (Roger E. Moseley), in which their chauvinism – they are overtly sexist, racist and classist – becomes starkly apparent; the night is capped off by Davis's 'gift' to Michael, his savage beating of the suspect. The 'criminal' is presented, now, as a destitute drug addict, rather than a figure of evil incarnate, a victim of socio-economic inequality and a product of failed social justice rather than an evil sylph of the night. Michael's initial attraction to Davis – as cop epitomizing the libidinal male power that Michael (as business yuppie) lacks – is held in stark antithesis to his repulsion at the revelation of the brutality that is the underside of Davis's male, fascist potency. Davis can protect Karen – and his 'protection' becomes tantamount to rape, as his masculinity – and by extension, the masculinity of the LAPD – becomes visible through and as a necessary precondition to racist and brutal violence. Henceforth, Officer Davis assumes increasingly menacing dimensions: stalking Karen and Michael, murdering his partner, and framing and imprisoning Michael so that he can 'have' his wife.

The film begins as a conventional middle-class paranoia film, with an explicit xenophobic element,[3] before tearing open this genre and laying bare its conventions and our expectations, in a trajectory paralleling the protagonists' awakening to the actual nature of 'law and order' in the city, epitomized, as it comes to be, in the figure of maniac cop Davis. By the end of the film, indeed, Michael and Karen have realized their (our) stark powerlessness before the 'door of the law', with philistine officers like Davis – more a norm than a deviation – replacing Kafka's gnomic gatekeeper. The myth of suburban isolation/invisibility is undone through the deployment, and then destruction, of racial anxieties (explicitly inscribed by Kaplan into the geography of Los Angeles).

One could argue, perhaps, that, rather than addressing issues of socio-economic injustice and the abuse of power on any systemic or structural level, the narrative of *Unlawful Entry* focuses on the psychopathology of Officer Davis himself. The film's denouement is thus de-politicized and becomes simply a matter of a masculine hero triumphing over, and excising, a masculine villain from the fabric of (an essentially good) society. This would, however, ignore the fundamental point of the film: as Davis's psychopathy is further revealed, the police force, and the law-and-order system in general, simultaneously appears increasingly repressive and menacing. The Carrs' realization of the character of Davis is paralleled by their disillusionment with the police force at large. Davis is one single psychopath – and yet is clearly cast by Kaplan as an extension of, rather than exception to, the police state; certainly, its most invasive ('unlawful') arm, but a limb of the same body in any case. The narrative is, indeed, increasingly punctuated by images of police cruisers, emerging from nowhere and sweeping around like drones,

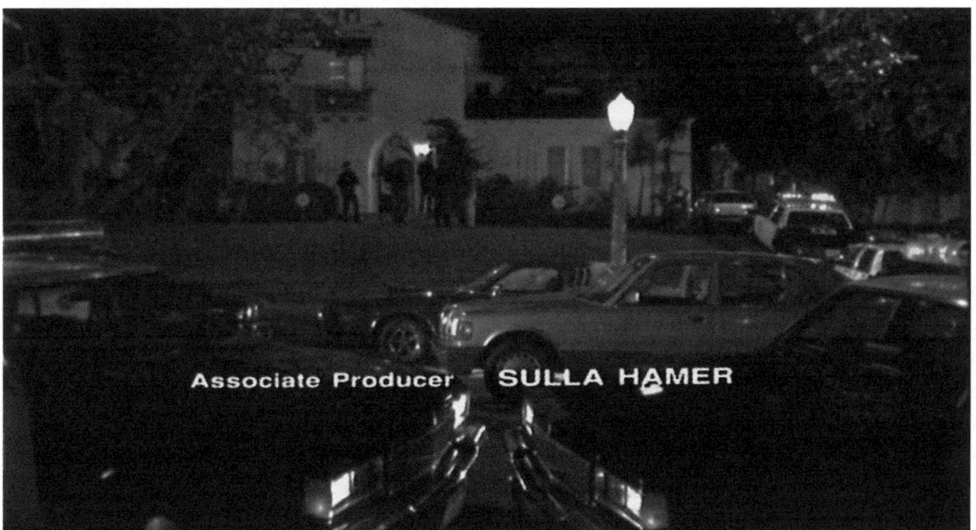

Figure 6. *Unlawful Entry* (1992), © Largo Entertainment and JVC.

driven by faceless officers, the components of a menacing 'Vision-Machine' (Virilio's 'perceptron') culminating in the closing sequence of the film, when every kind of police vehicle surrounds the Carrs' house: cruisers, helicopters and motorcycles.

This is decided overkill by a police force that strikes pre-emptively or too late. This final image is, furthermore, distinctly un-triumphant, belying the idea of the 'Hollywood happy ending' so frequently harped about in popular criticism (and in 'knowing' Hollywood fodder like Robert Altman's boorish *The Player* [1992] and Arthur Hiller's much worse *An Alan Smithee Film: Burn Hollywood Burn* [1997]).

Unlawful Entry is a critique of contemporary methods of surveillance, à la Virilio's *Vision Machine* and his discussions in *Stratégie de la déception/Strategy of Deception* (2000 [1999]) and *La vitesse de libération/Open Sky* (1997 [1995]). It displays a profound suspicion of all forms of police surveillance, and, more so, the grid-like distribution of cadastral space that enables such diffuse and seamless surveillance. The spatial design of the suburb, in Kaplan's film, is suffused with an irrepressible, incontrovertible panopticism. Domestic sanctity is premised, indeed, in the first place, on the brutal and repressive measures of the police apparatus. *Unlawful Entry* in fact consciously invokes this discourse in order to radically subvert it, highlighting – as monitoring the lines of suburban conformity, in the symmetry of the spatial (and psychological) arrangement of the suburban – a visionary disciplinarity that is as brutal as it is diffuse. The American suburban, Kaplan seems to be saying, is founded on a normalizing principle far more dangerous (and terrifying) than the criminal-urban of the traditional paranoiac thriller. This is a panopticism that is invasive, threatening, of substantial menace: the insidious potential of the police state – the 'accident' that reveals its substance – enabled through the literally 'square' design of the suburban environment that facilitates the smooth, drone-like vehiculation of the surveying apparatus. The violence of the film, furthermore, is clearly situated as the function of systemic social and spatial inequalities – rather than as the simple, readily dispensable problem of the psychopathological subjectivity of one individual – and this marks the key difference between *Unlawful Entry* and the other films of the suburban-paranoia-thriller subgenre.

Unlawful Entry, thus, radicalizes spaces at once generic, mythical and geographical through its critical negation and unveiling of ideological configurations of space around modalities of inclusion/exclusion. The film marks the re-grounding of hysterical 1980s suburban paranoia in a gritty contextual history and space – a history of the LAPD and LA: Rodney King, suburb-veillance and ghettoization, as well as economic phobia in the wake of the post-Japanese investment recession. It offers a reinterpretation of the relationship between the urban and suburban in Los Angeles in response to, in Marshall Berman's words, Reagan's 'theocratic police state' (1988 [1982]: 11), and its fragmentation and dehumanization of urban space – a critique of the colonization of the urban by the, as Hal Foster argues,[4] hyper-consumerist politics of the suburban. Berman, in *All That Is Solid Melts Into Air*, describes this 'new politics' of post-Fordist anti-urbanism thus:

This new order integrated the whole nation into a unified flow whose lifeblood was the automobile. It conceived of cities principally as obstructions to the flow of traffic, and as junkyards of substandard housing and decaying neighborhoods from which Americans should be given every chance to escape. (Berman 1988 [1982]: 307)

The developers and devotees of the expressway world presented it as the only possible modern world: to oppose them and their works was to oppose modernity itself, to fight history and progress, to be a Luddite, an escapist, afraid of life and adventure and change and growth. This strategy was effective because, in fact, the vast majority of modern men and women do not want to resist modernity: they feel its excitement and believe in its promise, even when they find themselves in its way. (Berman 1988 [1982]: 313)

The suburb is dead – long live the suburb! For twenty years following World War II, Berman proceeds to argue:

streets everywhere were at best passively abandoned and often (as in the Bronx) actively destroyed. Money and energy were rechanneled to the new highways and to the vast system of industrial parks, shopping centers and dormitory suburbs that the highways were opening up. (Berman 1988 [1982]: 317)

It is worth noting, furthermore, that by the end of *Unlawful Entry* the technology securing the Carrs' house, developed for them by Officer Davis, now-intruder, becomes their greatest enemy – trapping Karen in, and Michael out, thus realizing Berman's statement at the beginning of *All that Is Solid Melts Into Air*: 'it can be a creative adventure for modern men to build a palace, and yet a nightmare to have to live in it' (1988 [1982]: 7).

In this way, *Unlawful Entry* paints the 'scene' as a precursor to the LA riots; and, in the context of multinational corporate Hollywood, shows a unique solidarity with the rioters as reclaiming the city through appropriation of necessary goods of subsistence (Davis 1999 [1998]: 371–72, 375). The suburban kingdom that appeared to be so distinct from the 'urban jungle' is revealed as little more than at best a structural bubble keeping real conditions of exploitation from view, and at worst a structure supporting and enabling, through its rejection of the Other but also its dependence on and bolstering of the policing and surveillance industries (private *and* public in the film), the brutal physical, cultural and economic alienation and suppression of a racialized underclass. Kaplan deliberately attacks the city as source (as well as reflection) of the unequal distribution of wealth and power, à la David Harvey:

The results of [the] increasing polarization in the distribution of wealth and power are indelibly etched into the spatial forms of our cities, which increasingly become cities of fortified fragments, of gated communities and privatized public spaces kept under constant surveillance. (Harvey 2013: 15)

Conclusion: Los Angeles as vision-machine

Los Angeles is the locus, both origin and endpoint, of countless cultural myths, converging and diverging at different historical and aesthetic moments: Hollywood as reifying site of the American dream, the location for the apotheosis of the ordinary American into celebrity film star; and its inverse myth, LA as Nathanael West's vacuous and excessive hell, the LA of Easton Ellis's nihilistic fables, of Pynchon's picaresque nightmares, of Kramer's failed stardom in *Seinfeld* (David and Seinfeld, 1989–98), LA as accumulation machine in E. L. Katz's *Cheap Thrills* (2013). The South Central mythic casts LA (and the 'city' at large) as a breeding ground of paramilitary black and Latino gangs – *Colors* (Hopper, 1988), *The Shield* (Ryan, 2002–08), riots, looting and gangsta rap; its inverse myth revolves around suburban LA as paradise to urban LA's purgatory. Messianic LA offers another mythic constellation: L. Ron Hubbard, Satanism, cults, and the apocalypse encoded therein, so brilliantly depicted in Karyn Kusama's recent film *The Invitation* (2015). Historically, the most prominent myth has probably been Los Angeles as synecdoche of sunny SoCal – McWilliams's (2010 [1946]) 'island on the land', 1890s boosterism, the land of Steinbeck's 'grapes' pulling the Okies West, and Rusty James's horizon of dreams in *Rumble Fish* (Coppola, 1983); and, of course, *its* inverse has been perhaps even more generative: the corrupt LA-noir of Chandler, Ellroy, of *Chinatown* (Polanski, 1974) and *Who Framed Roger Rabbit* (Zemeckis, 1988).

Perhaps the most significant myth of the last thirty years in fact involves all of these and more – the myth of LA as pure 'mediation', LA as one of Marc Augé's (2008 [1992]) 'non-places': Fredric Jameson's LA; the LA of Michael Mann's *Heat* (1995); the postmodern, ahistorical Los Angeles so successfully debunked by Mike Davis in both *City of Quartz* (2006 [1999]) and *Ecology of Fear* (1999 [1998]). Los Angeles as vision-machine: the site of the perpetual quest for seeing and being-seen, as depicted in Dan Gilroy's *Nightcrawler* (2014); LA as defined through perpetual cycles of mediation and remediation.

Such representations of LA as media(ted) fantasy continue to proliferate, from *Crash*'s (Haggis, 2004) ham-fisted reification of racial and social politics to *This Is the End*'s (Goldberg and Rogen, 2013) LA of Armageddon-inducing excess. Rock band Motley Crue's career-long worship of LA-as-city-of-sin reaches its pinnacle with the literal hagiography of the damned, *Saints of Los Angeles* (2008); on the other end of the popular music spectrum, we find Lana Del Rey's fetish (via David Lynch) of LA as the site of dissolute-nostalgia in *Born to Die* (2012).

Unlawful Entry marks the reintroduction of sociopolitical noise into a space that continues to hide behind such mystiques of mediation – of a geo-historical sensibility rupturing the mediated myths and myths of mediation of the city, a kind of sensorial polemic against boosterism and techno-determinism. Kaplan's film attempts to refocus the viewer's attention on Los Angeles as a real, and not abstract, mediated, mythical – and therefore mystified – space. Revisiting *Unlawful Entry* – a film that attempts to lift this veil of excessive fetishization in order to reveal the social, political and urban relations that have created it and continue to sustain it – is critically important, if we are to look beyond, in Norman M. Klein's words, the 'promotional rhetoric' of these myriad mediations. 'Los Angeles is a city,' Klein writes in *The History of Forgetting*, 'that was imagined long before it was built. It was imagined to avoid city-wide bankruptcy in the 1890s, and has stayed on a knife-edge ever since, camouflaged by promotional rhetoric' (1997: 27).

And yet, perhaps, as Julian Murphet argues, 'The greatest difficulty in coming to terms with Los Angeles will always be not seeing it as such; not for a lack of representations of it, but because of their contradictory plenitude' (2001: 8). LA, through its unendingly mediated generation(s), becomes the urban epitome of Ernest Mandel's 'late capitalism', or Baudrillard, Berardi, et al.'s financial economy of reproduction without production, a capitalism that, to recall Berman, 'annihilates everything that it creates – physical environments, social institutions, metaphysical ideas, artistic visions, moral values – in order to create more, to go on endlessly creating the world anew' (1988 [1982]: 288). LA as city of the Spectacle, as site of the burgeoning of, in Virilio's words, the 'industrialization of perception'. Virilio thus summarizes Cendrars:

> Last century's oracles are silent, the trompe l'oeil journey ends at the Pacific; Hollywood with its studio factories is the terminus, the last stop where the next stage of the trip is already on the drawing board: the *industrialization of perception*, the ultimate coup d'etat. (Virilio 1995 [1993]: 79; original emphasis)

Uneven distribution of *space* undergirds this Society of the Spectacle – if the Spectacle is the mediation of social relations, as Guy Debord (1995 [1967]) argues, then, if we are to accept Edward Soja's (self-evident) argument in 'The Socio-Spatial Dialectic', it is also a mediation of spatial relations. Several LA works look at mediation via social relations – spectacle as social masquerade. The genius of Kaplan's film lies in its grounding of the Spectacle itself in spatial inequality, in the 'unevenly distributed' geography of LA.

But perhaps this 'grounding' of the Spectacle is simply another moment in its reproduction, harmonious with the Spectacle's own logic. It is pleasing to imagine that Kaplan's film marks some kind of messianic intervention into the logic of the mediated Spectacle (indeed, this whole chapter has been geared towards this idea), even if the logic of Hollywood, indice of LA, indice of a world under the domination of Virilio's 'turbocapitalism' (2012 [2010]: 76–78), is a logic of replication rather than creation, of networks rather than communities.

In any case, Hicks, the protagonist of Robert Stone's novel *Dog Soldiers*, summarizes his experience of LA in suitably mythical fashion: 'Fucking L.A., man – go out for a Sunday spin, you're a short hair from the dawn of creation' (1973: 164).

References

Altman, R. (1992), *The Player*, USA: Avenue Pictures and Spelling Entertainment.

Augé, M. (2008 [1992]), *Non-Lieux, introduction à une anthropologie de la surmodernité/ Non-Places: An Introduction to Supermodernity* (trans. J. Howe), London and New York: Verso.

Badham, J. (1983), *Blue Thunder*, USA: Columbia.

Baudrillard, J. (1988 [1986]), *Amérique/America* (trans. C. Turner), London and New York: Verso.

———— (1993 [1976]), *L'échange symbolique et la mort/Symbolic Exchange and Death* (trans. I. H. Grant), London: Sage.

Bauman, Z. and Lyon, D. (2013), *Liquid Surveillance*, Cambridge, UK and Malden: Polity.

Benjamin, M. (2013), *Drone Warfare: Killing By Remote Control*, London and New York: Verso.

Berardi, F. (2012), *The Uprising: On Poetry and Finance*, Los Angeles: Semiotext(e).

Berman, M. (1988 [1982]), *All That Is Solid Melts Into Air: The Experience of Modernity*, London: Penguin.

Boghosian, H. (2013), *Spying on Democracy: Government Surveillance, Corporate Power, and Public Resistance*, San Francisco: City Light Books.

Brickman, P. (1983), *Risky Business*, USA: Geffen.

Chamayou, G. (2015), *Drone Theory*, London: Penguin.

Coppola, F. F. (1983), *Rumble Fish*, USA: Hotweather and Zoetrope.

David, L. and Seinfeld, J. (1989–98), *Seinfeld*, USA: Castle Rock Entertainment.

Davis, M. (1999 [1998]), *Ecology of Fear: Los Angeles and the Imagination of Disaster*, New York: Vintage.

———— (2006 [1990]), *City of Quartz: Excavating the Future in Los Angeles*, London and New York: Verso.

Debord, G. (1995 [1967]), *La société du spectacle/The Society of the Spectacle* (trans. D. Nicholson-Smith), New York: Zone Books.

Ellis, B. E. (1998 [1985]), *Less Than Zero*, New York: Vintage.

Foster, H. (2002), *Design and Crime (and Other Diatribes)*, London and New York: Verso.

Gilroy, D. (2014), *Nightcrawler*, USA: Bold Films and Sierra/Affinity.

Goldberg, E. and Rogen, S. (2013), *This Is the End*, USA: Columbia.

Haggis, P. (2004), *Crash*, USA and Germany: Bob Yari, DEJ and Blackfriars Bridge Films.

Hanson, C. (1992), *The Hand That Rocks the Cradle*, USA: Hollywood Pictures.

Harvey, D. (2010), *The Enigma of Capital and the Crises of Capitalism*. Oxford: Oxford University Press.

———— (2013), *Rebel Cities: From the Right to the City to the Urban Revolution*, London and New York: Verso.

Hiller, A. (1997), *An Alan Smithee Film: Burn Hollywood Burn*, USA: Cinergi and Hollywood Pictures.

Hopper, D. (1988), *Colors*, USA: Orion Pictures.

Hughes, J. (1986), *Ferris Bueller's Day Off*, USA: Paramount.

Jameson, F. (1991), *Postmodernism, or, the Cultural Logic of Late Capitalism*, Durham: Duke University Press.

Kafka, F. (1979 [1915]), 'Vor dem Gesetz'/'Before the Law', *The Basic Kafka* (trans. W. Muir and E. Muir), New York: Pocket Books, pp. 174–81.

Kaplan, J. (1979), *Over the Edge*, USA: Orion Pictures.

——— (1992), *Unlawful Entry*, USA: Largo Entertainment and JVC.

Katz, E. L. (2013), *Cheap Thrills*, USA: Snowfort Pictures.

Klein, N. M. (1997), *The History of Forgetting: Los Angeles and the Erasure of Memory*, London and New York: Verso.

Kusama, K. (2015), *The Invitation*, USA: The Invitation and XYZ Films.

Lana Del Rey (2012), *Born to Die*, USA: Polydor.

Lefebvre, H. (2003 [1970]), *La révolution urbaine*/*The Urban Revolution* (trans. R. Bononno), Minneapolis and London: University of Minnesota Press.

Lyne, A. (1987), *Fatal Attraction*, USA: Paramount.

Mandel, E. (1978 [1972]), *Der Spätkapitalismus*/*Late Capitalism* (trans. J. de Bres), London and New York: Verso.

Mann, M. (1995), *Heat*, USA: Warner Bros.

Mattes, A. (2014), 'Action without regeneration: The deracination of the American action hero in Michael Mann's *Heat*', *Journal of Popular Film and Television*, 42: 4, pp. 186–94.

McLuhan, M. (2001 [1964]), *Understanding Media: The Extensions of Man*, London and New York: Routledge.

McWilliams, C. (2010 [1946]), *Southern California: An Island on the Land*, Salt Lake City: Gibbs Smith Publisher.

Motley Crue (2008), *Saints of Los Angeles*, USA: Eleven Seven Music.

Murphet, J. (2001), *Literature and Race in Los Angeles*, Cambridge, UK: Cambridge University Press.

Patrick, M. (1989), *The Hider in the House*, USA: Precision Films.

Polanski, R. (1974), *Chinatown*, USA: Paramount.

Ryan, S. (2002–08), *The Shield*, USA: Fox.

Soja, E. W. (1989), *Postmodern Geographies: The Reassertion of Space in Critical Social Theory*, London and New York: Verso.

Stone, R. (1973), *Dog Soldiers*, Boston and New York: Mariner Books.

Virilio, P. (1989 [1984]), *Guerre et cinéma*/*War and Cinema: The Logistics of Perception* (trans. P. Camiller), London and New York: Verso.

——— (1994 [1988]), *La machine de vision*/*The Vision Machine* (trans. J. Rose), London: BFI Publishing; Bloomington: Indiana University Press.

——— (1995 [1993]), *L'art du moteur*/*The Art of the Motor* (trans. J. Rose), Minneapolis and London: University of Minnesota Press.

————— (1997 [1995]), *La vitesse de libération/Open Sky* (trans. J. Rose), London and New York: Verso.

————— (2000 [1999]), *Stratégie de la déception/Strategy of Deception* (trans. C. Turner), London and New York: Verso.

————— (2012 [2010]), *Le grand accélérateur/The Great Accelerator* (trans. J. Rose), Cambridge, UK and Malden: Polity.

Wark, M. (2007), *Gamer Theory*, Cambridge, MA and London: Harvard University Press.

————— (2013), *The Spectacle of Disintegration*, London and New York: Verso.

West, N. (2006 [1939]), *The Day of the Locust*, London: Penguin.

Zemeckis, R. (1988), *Who Framed Roger Rabbit*, USA: Touchstone.

Notes

1. This recalls the sequence in John Badham's excellent critique of helicopter policing, *Blue Thunder* (1983), when our 'hero' policemen make lewd comments to one another as they hover around watching a naked woman doing yoga.
2. See Medea Benjamin's *Drone Warfare* (2013) and Heidi Boghosian's *Spying on Democracy* (2013) for recent histories of drone development. For a richer theoretical discussion of drones, see Virilio's *Strategy of Deception* (2000 [1999]) and *Open Sky* (1997 [1995]), or Grégoire Chamayou's *Drone Theory* (2015). *Blue Thunder* is probably the most sustained cinematic critique of helicopter policing.
3. See Davis's discussion in *Ecology of Fear*: 'the post-1980 boom in imagined aliens coincided with the increasing visibility of immigrants from Mexico, Central America, and East Asia in the daily life of the Los Angeles region. Like the Aryan survivalist novel, the fantasy of alien impregnation played off white fear and disorientation in the face of irreversible demographic change' (Davis 1999 [1998]: 341).
4. See Hal Foster's *Design and Crime (and Other Diatribes)* (2002).

Chapter 2

Blockbuster realism: Mapping Gotham in the *Dark Knight* films

Jarrad Cogle

Introduction

Marshall McLuhan's work commonly posits a situation emerging in the twentieth century, known as the 'global village' (1967 [1962]: 21; 1998 [1964]: 5). Here, the transnational and socially diverse nature of the world becomes increasingly visible within a western cultural context. For later theorists of postmodernity, this historical tendency presents a number of difficulties, both for the individual subject and textual material. In Fredric Jameson's work in particular, the struggle to position oneself within certain instances of postmodern architecture and contemporary urban space is conflated with a wider impossibility of understanding larger global networks. Jameson depicts certain postmodern examples of film, literature and visual art as symptomatic of these problems, seeing 'a new kind of flatness or depthlessness, a new kind of superficiality, perhaps the supreme formal feature of all the postmodernisms', as a reaction to this cultural situation (Jameson 1991: 9). Despite these regularly discussed attributes of postmodern space and textual material, narrative works concerned with exploring a notion of 'the city' persistently refer to certain tropes inherited from the nineteenth-century realist novel. In Christopher Nolan's *Dark Knight* series of Batman films – *Batman Begins* (2005), *The Dark Knight* (2008) and *The Dark Knight Rises* (2012) – for example, a fraught interaction occurs, whereby postmodern cultural material attempts to reconcile itself with rational, post-Enlightenment approaches to reality and aesthetics. For Nolan's *Dark Knight* films, this sense is exacerbated by a negotiation of recent trends in the genre of large-budget Hollywood action cinema. Over the last decade, films such as *Transformers* (Bay, 2007) have contributed to a highly fragmentary cinematic language, often called 'intensified continuity' or 'post-continuity' (Bordwell 2006: 121; Shaviro 2010: 123). Within this genre, films have also portrayed a wide variety of global spaces, in order to enlarge the scope of their narratives, as well as appeal to international audiences. This chapter will investigate the ways in which Nolan's *Dark Knight* franchise attempts to reconcile an ostensibly realist representation of the city with a larger global purview, within a generic form whose approach to the cognitive is increasingly disconnected.

Realism, postmodernity and Jameson's cognitive map

In *Bleak House* (Dickens 2003 [1853]), along with a number of other classical realist novels, the city takes on a number of formal characteristics: it appears as a self-contained entity which can be described in terms of its 'character'; an organizing device in which to frame the narrative; and a more complex series of interrelated social groups and districts which the text maps. Raymond Williams sees these notions of form, social mapping and characterization as being inherently combined in the London novels of Dickens: 'Dickens's ultimate vision of London [...] lies in the form of his novels: in their kind of narrative, in their type of characterization, in their genius for typification' (1973: 154). In tracing an ongoing Marxist interest in realism – one that extends from Marx up to Williams, Jameson and beyond – Julian Murphet claims,

> it would be fair to say that there remains an inescapable gravitational pull between a critical political economy geared towards a cognitive disambiguation of capitalism, and a literary aesthetic similarly invested in a pitiless anatomization of the bourgeois social terrain. (Murphet 2010: 53–54)

Georg Lukács stands as making a major contribution in this lineage, seeing realism as allowing for 'opposing social forces to be brought into human relationship with each other' through the representation of differing classes of characters in urban environments (Lukács 1962 [1947]: 36). For recent scholars interested in 'peripheral realisms', such as Jed Esty and Colleen Lye, Lukács is also 'best appreciated for having located a text's realism in its aspiration to totality, with "totality" defined not as something out there but as the demand to consider interrelations and interactions between disparate phenomena' (Esty and Lye 2012: 277).

For Fredric Jameson, the notions of totality and social interaction that Lukács attributes to the realist novel continue in the twentieth century within certain types of generic literature, particularly Raymond Chandler's canonical detective novels. For Jameson, the mapping ability of Chandler's detective Philip Marlowe becomes a new variant of the nineteenth-century novel's capacity to represent a social entirety:

> Los Angeles is already a kind of microcosm and forecast of the country as a whole: a new centreless city, in which the various classes have lost touch with each other [...] If the symbol of social coherence and comprehensibility was furnished by the nineteenth-century Parisian apartment house (dramatized in Zola's Pot Bouille) with its shop on the ground floor, its wealthy inhabitants on the second and third, petty bourgeoisie further up, and workers' rooms on top [...] then Los Angeles is the opposite, a spreading out horizontally, a flowing apart of the elements of the social structure [...]. Since there is no longer any privileged experience in which the whole of the social structure can be grasped, a figure must be invented who can be superimposed on the society as a whole, whose routine and life-pattern serve somehow to tie its separate and isolated parts together. (Jameson 1995 [1970]: 69)

Jameson expounds on this sense of urban representation in his major works on postmodernism, where he describes his process of cognitive mapping, drawing on the work of Kevin Lynch's *The Image of the City* (1960):

the alienated city is above all a space in which people are unable to map [...] either their own positions or the urban totality in which they find themselves. [...] Lynch's own work is limited by the deliberate restriction of his topic to the problems of the city as such; yet it becomes extraordinarily suggestive when projected outward onto [...] larger national and global spaces. (Jameson 1991: 51)

As discussed above, Jameson equates the dysfunctional perception of compartmentalized urban experience with a wider problem of understanding global relationships. Here, the subject remains unable to completely know or comprehend the multinational capitalist system. In *Postmodernism, or, the Cultural Logic of Late Capitalism* (1991), Jameson opens a space for an aesthetic project that might attempt to cognitively map some of these larger economic connections, but, at this stage of his career, he defers from seeing any cultural material as preforming this operation. Jameson's later essays, however, will occasionally see certain postmodern media working in this direction, often following realist tropes. *The Wire*'s (Simon 2002–08) extreme focus on Baltimore's social institutions, or Kim Stanley Robinson's utopian science fiction worlds, are two such examples for Jameson (2010; 2005: 393–416). It might be noted that these kinds of texts have also overtly referenced this older mode of literary realism, with *The Wire* in particular alluding to Dickens at certain moments.

The recent work on 'peripheral realisms' in postcolonial studies, has aimed to see certain contemporary fiction in a similar manner, using comparable Lukácsian frameworks to Jameson. Esty and Lye argue for 'the possible advantage of peripherality for thinking relationally across different kinds of subordinated positions on different scales' (2012: 272). Sharae Deckard, for example, seeks to see Roberto Bolaño's depiction of Ciudad Juarez in *2666* (2008 [2004]) as a cognitive mapping project of not just the Mexican border city, but also of wider global connections:

2666 can be understood as an [...] insurgent attempt to reformulate the realist world novel in order to overcome the reification of earlier modes of realism. [...] The novel's form is systemically world-historical, uniting a particular semi-periphery (Ciudad Juarez) and a particular historical conjuncture (late capitalism at the millennium) with a vast geopolitical scope. (Deckard 2012: 353)

In comparison, a more restrictive formal containment defines many of Jameson's examples, from Chandler's novels, to *The Wire*, to a variety of science fiction texts. The science fiction he discusses is limited by temporal barriers, whereby

the secession of the Utopian imagination from everyday empirical Being takes the form of a temporal emergence and a historical transition, and in which the break that simultaneously secures the radical difference of the new Utopian society makes it impossible to imagine. (Jameson 2005: 85–86)

Here, for Jameson, the progress from a contemporary society to a utopian one is only detectable in science fiction as a gap or absence. Meanwhile, Jameson sees the mapping of Los Angeles and Baltimore as worthwhile projects, but notes the insularity of their operations. In *The Wire*, for example, 'Baltimore is a complete world in itself; it is not a closed world but merely conveys the conviction that nothing exists outside of it' (Jameson 2010: 369).

Global cinema space in the era of multinational capitalism

Elsewhere, we can see a growing tendency in contemporary cultural material, where geographical and social space is increasingly depicted in global terms, but often in a dislocated or transitory manner. Recent action films specifically are prone to a disregard for coherent senses of space. Critics have commonly discussed Michael Bay's films in particular, in terms of an editing style that obfuscates viewer comprehension:

> Bay's visual presentation is so frantic and chaotic that one often can't tell which ship or characters are being shown, or where things are in relation to one another. [...] Much of the confusion, as well as the lack of dramatic rhythm or character development, results directly from Bay's cutting style, which resembles a machine gun stuck in the firing position for 2 1/2 hours. (McCarthy 1998: 37)

Bruce Isaacs, discussing *The Dark Knight* and other recent blockbusters, sees this kind of film language as a 'montage of astonishment, animated by a synthetic construction of frame composition, movement, diegetic and non-diegetic sound and genre signification: in short, synthetic gestures that seek an image "more than" the image of our perception' (2013: 13). While likenesses of Bay's editing style have become a standard element of many contemporary action blockbusters and have been commented on often, this chapter will be more interested in Isaacs's notion of 'generic signification'. Recent editing techniques have their own implications for visual or spatial coherence, but Bay's films also make rapid shifts in aesthetics in order to accommodate the multiplicity of genres they adopt. The *Transformers* franchise (Bay, 2007–2014), for example, commonly moves between science fiction, lowbrow comedy and action movie tropes from scene to scene. Bay's films often reference other examples of popular cinema within these shifts, with *Top Gun's* (Scott, 1986) fetishizing depiction of the US military and Steven Spielberg's sentimental tableaus being two prominent examples. Here, aesthetic coherence is disregarded in favour of cinematic intensities.

This sense of disparity in aesthetics impacts on representations of geographical space. In *Transformers*, visual tone shifts constantly when moving from scenes set in covert government bases, for example, to ones in idyllic suburban settings. This multiplicity of film aesthetics reinforces the notion that the locations are disconnected, or that they are unable to be mapped in relation to each other. Mark Bould also discusses a disjointed type of urban space in relation to the construction of *Transformers*'s Mission City. Bould notes how Mission City 'seems to be both twenty miles from the Hoover Dam and in California, with parts of a Los Angeles skyline and at least one building from Detroit' (2008: 165). Here, the numerous shooting sites, and the ways in which the films transition between different settings with little sense of space or locality, wilfully problematize any attempt at a cognitive map. This could be contrasted with the extreme spatial containment and visual coherence of previous examples of the genre, such as *Die Hard* (McTiernan, 1988). Adding to the notion of geographical incoherence is the increasing amount of international locations built into these narratives. *Transformers: Revenge of the Fallen* (Bay, 2009), for example, travels to Egypt and Shanghai, while *The Avengers* (Whedon, 2012) makes brief excursions to Calcutta, Russia and Stuttgart. Distance and temporality are rarely a concern as the films move between foreign environments and prominently display recognizable landmarks. The international reach of these films serves to enlarge the epic span of their narratives, but also contributes to an additional sense of spatial fragmentation, becoming symptomatic of McLuhan's 'global village'.

It should be noted that economic concerns are a major contributing factor in the development of these 'global' blockbusters, adding another nuance to depictions of global space. Hollywood films are increasingly conceived with worldwide markets in mind, and certain ambits in cinema studies have recently considered the exportation and transnational reach of North American culture industries. Paul Grainge's work on the *Lord of the Rings* (Jackson, 2001–2003) and *Harry Potter* (Columbus et al., 2001–2011) films discusses how:

> in a textual and industrial sense, both franchise examples lend themselves to discussion about the globalization of film. They ask questions about the nature of internationally exportable products and genres, about the mix of international finance, marketing and labour that underpin high budget studio movies, and about the commercial life of bankrolled blockbusters as they circulate and are consumed, as global brands. (Grainge 2008: 151–52)

Ongoing franchises, broad generic categorization, and attempts to appeal to transnational audiences are all factors that have become increasingly prevalent in recent action blockbusters. Toby Miller et al. (2009 [2005]: 10) describe a situation where 'the world market is crucial to the US. In 1998, the major US film studios increased their foreign rentals by one-fifth on 1997; the overseas box office of US$6.821 billion virtually equalled the domestic figure of US$6.877 billion'. In more recent years, these circumstances have only intensified, with Hollywood earning increasing amounts within Asian markets. John Berra has discussed the conditions in contemporary China, for example, where in 2011, the top-grossing film in the mainland market was *Transformers: Dark of the Moon*, taking US$170m. [...] This represented 18.8 per cent of the film's foreign sales and 12.9 per cent of its total sales, with China the second highest ticket-selling country after the US. (Berra 2013: 179–80)

In this context, a recent practice has begun to emerge whereby 'mid-to-big-budget films are finding ways to court Chinese government approval [with] scenes and moments and dialogue inserted entirely to ingratiate an American film with one specific market' (Murray, Robinson and Tobias 2013).

Gotham City's political landscape

In other ways, it is curious that these films are at the forefront of this globalizing development, given that they are commonly adapted from comic book properties whose heroes often have traditional homes: Superman resides in Metropolis, Spiderman in New York, and so on. These urban environments operate as formally limiting devices, whereby the destructive and fantastic action of the comic books is contained within a fictionalized city that has little sense of the larger world. Gotham City is one such example, with a diverse set of conventions appearing in the multitude of adaptations over Batman's lengthy history. The city appears as a major consideration for many famous Batman narratives, such as the influential graphic novels of Frank Miller, as well as Tim Burton's earlier film *Batman* (1989). Gotham is traditionally depicted as a dark and crime-ridden metropolis, but also has an official map and accepted set of landmarks that interpreters might reference. William Urrichio (2010: 121–23) describes these elements of Gotham in terms of a 'performative cartography', discussing the city's dense history explored within the comic titles, where narratives have dealt with its founding, its architectural history, and its place in events such as the American Civil War. Tied to these components is a notion of intertextuality, with Gotham traditionally being thought of as a fictionalized New York.

We can also ostensibly see Batman within a tradition of hardboiled detectives, of which Chandler's Marlowe is a paradigmatic example. Batman first appeared in the publication *Detective Comics*, the same year that Chandler's *The Big Sleep* (1939) was published. Batman's skills as a detective are often an element of the character's narratives, as is some of the social mapping that Jameson sees in this type of operation. Batman interacts with many different types of social institutions and criminals, while his alter ego Bruce Wayne moves amongst the business and upper class. Christopher Nolan's *Dark Knight* films reinforce the detective component and foreground Gotham as a city with a particular economic and social history, predominantly developed in *Batman Begins*. The films make significant characters out of police officers, politicians, lawyers, white-collar businessmen, criminals of varying social class, wards of the state, and so on. The perceived nature of the city by its citizens also stands as a dominant consideration within the films' plots, often having an influence on narrative events and characters' motivations. This conception of the city as a self-contained entity recalls nineteenth-century literary depictions of urban environments, and the films appeal to realism in other capacities. Nolan's commitment to shooting in film, to referencing neo-noir crime thrillers such as *Heat* (Mann, 1995), and to staging action sequences using practical effects, differentiates the series from generic counterparts such as *The Avengers*. Nolan's final Batman film, *The Dark Knight Rises*, even makes its own reference to Dickens, with the character Alfred quoting *A Tale of Two Cities* (1975 [1859]) in the denouement.

While Jameson sees the realist attention to social connection and historical content as being essential to meaningful Marxist engagement, the political valences of Nolan's films obscure these qualities in a number of ways. Interpreting the political aspect of the films has been a major component of their reception, both in mass media outlets and in academic work. Martin Fradley (2013: 15) sees this element of the film as deliberate, whereby '*The Dark Knight Rises* was presold not only as the event movie of 2012, but also as a heavily politicized talking point'. Articles published in mainstream media connected elements of the films with the Occupy movement, terrorism, surveillance and other contemporary concerns (Fradley 2013: 15–16). Interviewers have also often questioned Nolan about this aspect of his work, and the director has repeatedly avoided voicing his own politics or positioning the films in any particular manner. In one interview, he states, 'the films genuinely aren't intended to be political. You don't want to alienate people, you want to create a universal story' (Rolling Stone 2012). For Fradley, the films' murky politics are carefully constructed:

> *The Dark Knight Rises* deliberately concedes to the individual viewer the authority to decide what it means. One might find Bane a psychotic radical leftist whose muffled, incoherent proclamations and violent agenda provide a pro-hegemonic caricature of oppositional politics. Equally, the film deliberately grants Bane more than enough ingenuity, intelligence and pathos to allow a less conservative viewer to interpret him as a heroic martyr [...]. The political incoherence of *The Dark Knight Rises* is thus a commercial strategy, a marker of its status as a shrewdly constructed commodity. (Fradley 2013: 19–20)

Academics have also commonly read the film in symptomatic terms, often reasserting the neoliberal, conservative nature of the Batman character in general, with Slavoj Žižek's article, 'The People's Republic of Gotham' (2012), being one of the more prominent examples.

Žižek's essay delineates the contradictions of *The Dark Knight Rises*'s politics in particular. For example, Bruce Wayne's status as a billionaire orphan is used to inscribe a sense of social responsibility that the rich have to the poor within the films' plots. For Žižek, however, 'although viewers know Wayne is mega-rich, they often forget where his wealth comes from: arms manufacturing plus stock-market speculation' (2012).

Despite being a hugely profitable capitalist organization that develops an array of violent military technology, the family company is primarily depicted as working in the health sciences, conducting research into renewable energy, and being immensely charitable. The theme of social responsibility is introduced through the guilt Bruce Wayne feels in relation to his parents' deaths. Part of his hero's quest will be to live up to the tenacious humanitarianism and positive social influence of his father. Žižek sees the films dealing with the contradictions between capitalism and charity 'by resuscitating the archetypal Dickensian theme of a good capitalist who finances orphanages […] versus a bad, greedy capitalist' (2012). In each *Dark Knight* film, corrupt businessmen or authority figures will function in the plot as intermediaries, engaging in commerce with the more ideologically motivated villains, who in turn are constructed as the more dangerous threat to society. In *Batman Begins*, the mob boss Carmine Falcone and the corrupt psychologist Dr Crane, allow for Ra's al Ghul to infiltrate Gotham. In *The Dark Knight*, the Joker manipulates the relationship between Hong Kong businessman Lau and a variety of underground figures. These stereotypical characters remain underdeveloped, while the major antagonists are decidedly more nuanced. All the main villains articulate social ideologies that challenge the Wayne family's charitable capitalist model. In *Batman Begins*, the stated intent of Ra's al Ghul and his organization, the League of Shadows, to destroy Gotham, is framed within a philosophy that sees violent action as a way of bringing the moral corruption of the upper class into check. For Žižek, 'Ra's is thus not a simple embodiment of evil. He stands for the combination of virtue and terror, for egalitarian discipline fighting a corrupted empire' (2012). In *The Dark Knight*, the Joker's plans revolve around notions of chaos and anarchy, and he often aims to deconstruct the liberal ideology of Wayne and his upper-class counterparts, in order to demonstrate the more base instincts of society. It is in these moments that the films give their traditional plots of 'good versus bad' a certain amount of conceptual depth. Nonetheless, even if the various villains' manifestoes are charismatic and interested in social change, they are also ultimately depicted as misguided, violent and inevitably evil.

Still, Marxist theorists have seen the work of figures such as Balzac and Dickens in productive terms, even if the politics of their novels were less than complimentary. For the *Dark Knight* films' attempts at social mapping, however, the superhero genre presents a number of limitations. For example, a slippage inserts itself into the ideology of these films at a very early stage, in order for Bruce Wayne's development as a character to work amongst the thematic concerns for the economic and social. In *Batman Begins*, as the character Rachel Dawes lectures Wayne on his social responsibility to the fate of the city, the economic struggles of the destitute are attributed to mob boss Carmine Falcone. Dawes claims: 'this city is rotting […]. Falcone floods our streets with crime and drugs, preying on the desperate. […] Falcone may have not killed your parents Bruce, but he's destroying everything they stood for' (Nolan 2005). Here, despite the film's interest in social structure, the investigation of systemic corruption and economic history buckles: *Batman Begins* attributes the plight of the lower class to an archetypal gangster boss whom Batman will be able to dispense with, rather than a sense of a mode of production or superstructure. Even if, as Žižek suggests, Dickens's novels often ultimately reward virtuous, upper-middle-class figures, they do not have the added difficulty of seeing these characters' actions as solving the larger societal problems explored across their narratives.

Constructing the filmed city: Global relationships and cognitive gaps

The attempt to render the city as a functional space also has a problematic relationship with cinematic convention, creating another complication for reading the films in terms of a cognitive map. Most films cut liberally between environments, creating gaps in any mapping procedure. This is very different to the sense of Philip Marlowe, driving through Los Angeles and describing the act of crossing from one type of social area to another in *The Big Sleep*, for example. In certain moments, the *Dark Knight* films attempt this type of operation, such as in the scene described above featuring Rachel Dawes. Here, Dawes and Wayne drive from an inner-city environment dominated by office buildings into a subterranean area populated by the homeless (Figures 1–2). They then arrive at a bar where Falcone conducts business, linking the three locations visually. Elsewhere, aerial shots of the city display the poverty-stricken area called 'the Narrows' on the edge of a more affluent city skyline (Figure 3). This component of the film is undermined, however, by other factors. While the Nolan films are perhaps more highbrow in their adoption and utilization of generic signifiers, they often shift in a similar manner to Bay's films. *Batman Begins*, for example, adopts elements of film noir, supernatural horror and utopian science fiction in its running time. And, even if Nolan's films remain more aesthetically uniform than Bay's, there is still evidence of an exaggeration of reality, of Isaacs's 'montage of astonishment', in certain choices. *Batman Begins*, for example, utilizes an English country house built in the Victorian era for the filming of Wayne's residence. The size of the films' budgets and lengthy production schedules ensure a vast number of locations are employed for various settings and landmarks. In some instances, however, this leads to contradictory senses of the city's geography. The cutting between the noir environment of Gotham and Wayne Manor exacerbates the sense that the large estate is well outside the urban environment. This is particularly noticeable in the final scenes of *Batman Begins*, where wide shots display a vast, pastoral countryside in the background (Figure 4). The use of a British location amplifies the aristocratic nature of the Wayne family, and contributes to the films' occasional implementations of prestige drama aesthetics. These choices gesture towards the films' contemporaries in their construction of setting and genre, but prove incompatible with the effort to create a cohesive environment.

This notion of the city is further complicated by the manner in which it interacts with a larger sense of the global. The Nolan films make several excursions to both named locations, such as Florence and Hong Kong, or less specified settings, such as the Middle Eastern landscape and primitive prison of *The Dark Knight Rises*. In these moments,

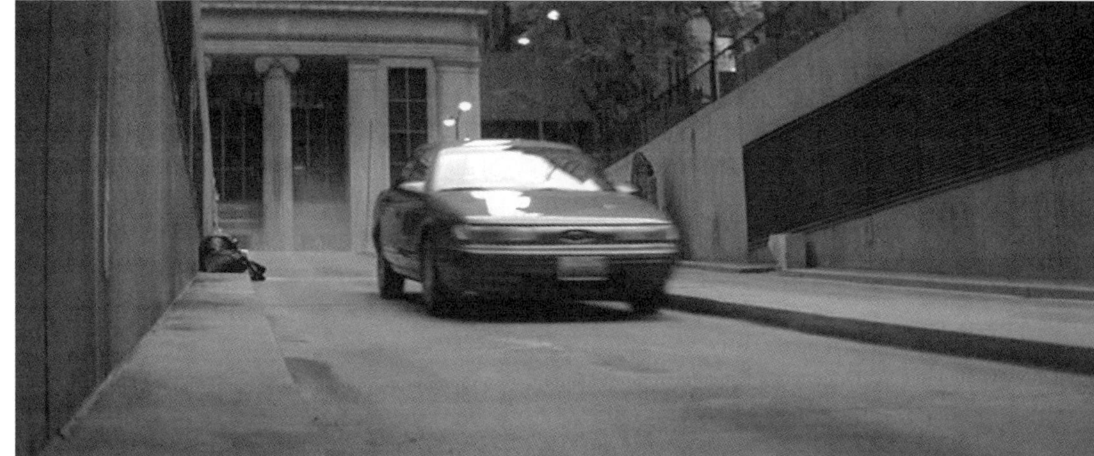

Figure 1. Bruce Wayne and Rachel Dawes driving from the urban surface to a subterranean area.

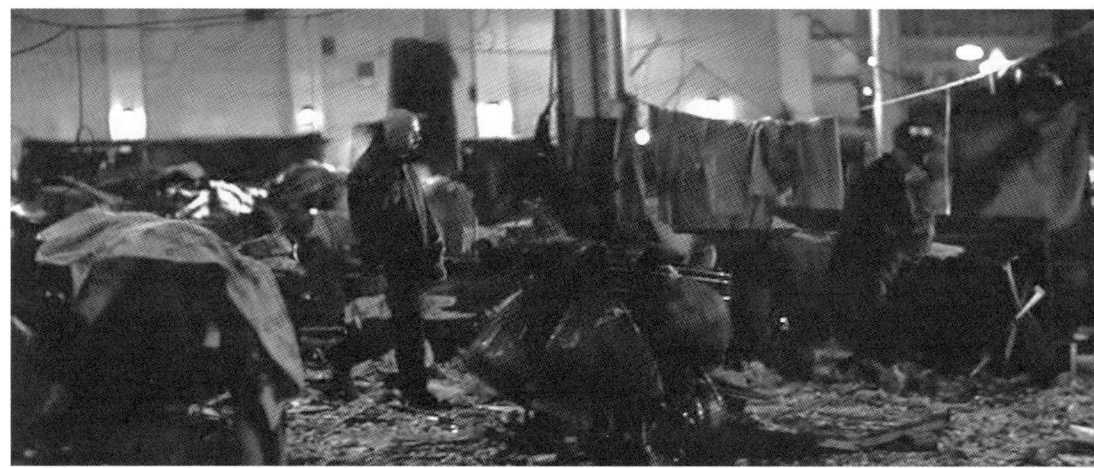

Figure 2. The subterranean environment.

the films again try to reconcile a notion of the realist city with the generic form of the global action blockbuster. *The Dark Knight*'s excursion to Hong Kong, for example, is a lengthy digression that doubles as a gleaming display of the city's architecture and bays. The sequence reads as a concession to similar international set pieces found in *The Dark Knight*'s generic counterparts, but also potentially adds another nuance to its mapping of

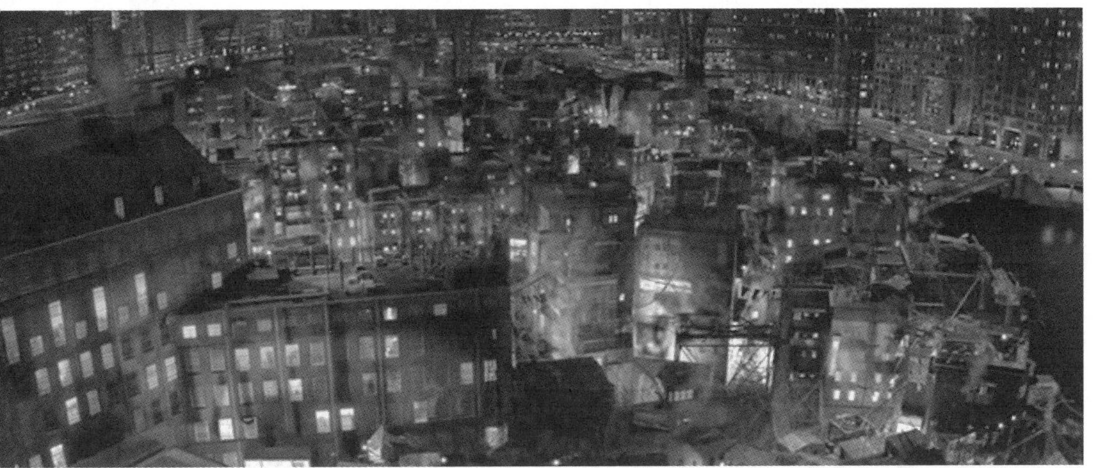

Figure 3. The Narrows, with a more opulent Gotham depicted in the background.

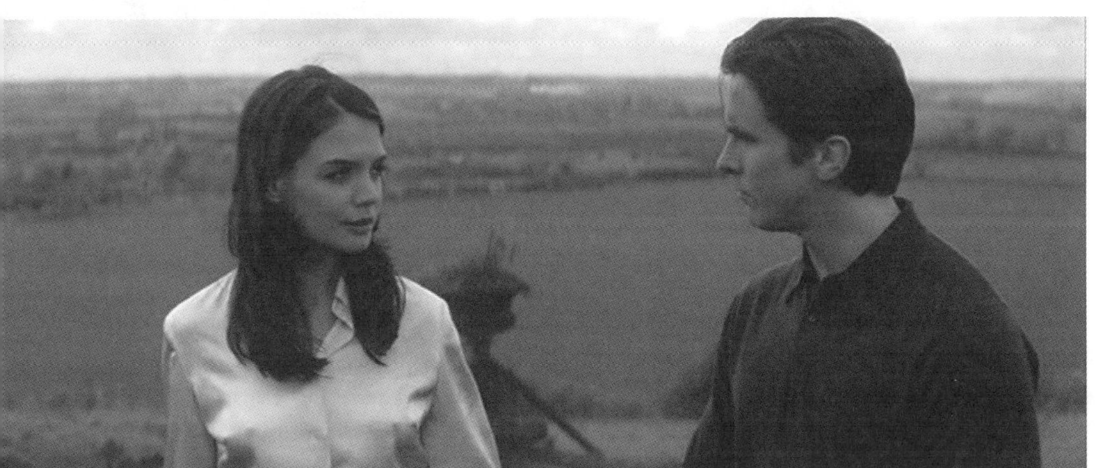

Figure 4. The pastoral landscape surrounding Wayne Manor.

Gotham. As with recent work on peripheral realisms, we can see these films as detailing a sense of worldwide economic relations and dependencies that are notably absent from the limiting aspects of localized detective or superhero stories.

This sense of global interconnectivity is only briefly engaged with, however, and the instability of this cinematic city (along with its geographical, social and historical

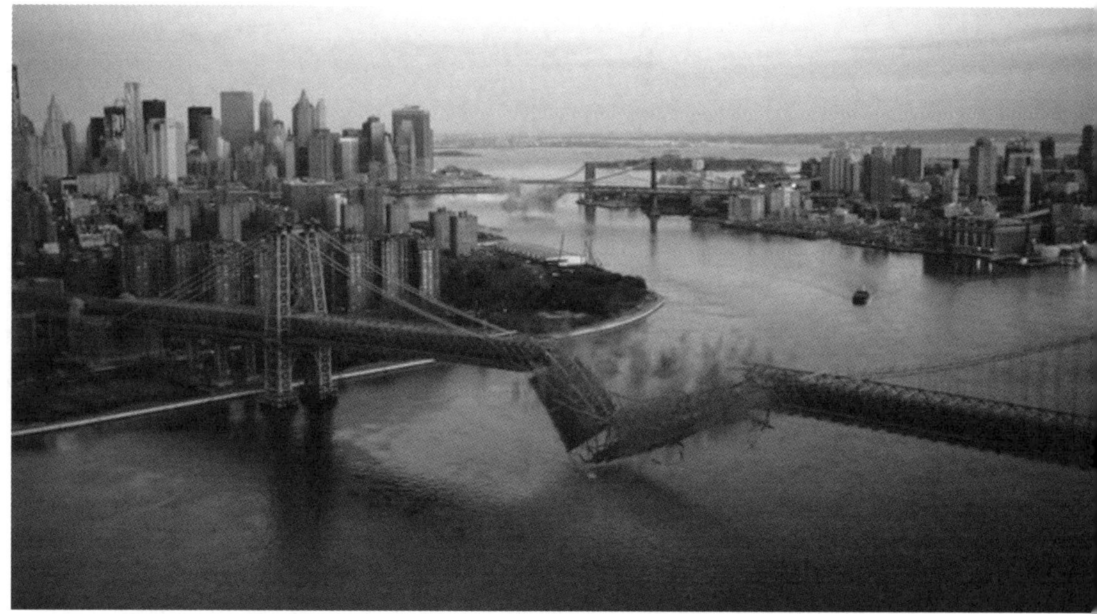

Figure 5. Bane destroys the bridges leading out of Gotham. The shots clearly depict the island of Manhattan.

components) comes to an apex in the final film. While *Batman Begins* asserts a sense of Gotham as Chicago, *The Dark Knight Rises* employs a multitude of locations, such as Pittsburgh, Newark and New York. In building to the film's climax though, the villain Bane destroys most of the bridges and tunnels leading in and out of Gotham, in order to hold the 'entire' city hostage (Figure 5). Here, Gotham transforms more overtly, effectively becoming the isolated island of Manhattan, and Bane claims that 'at the first sign of interference from the outside world or from those people attempting to flee' a huge bomb will be detonated (Nolan 2012). Nevertheless, Gotham remains a city with transnational reach and permeable borders. Wayne watches international newscasts about the situation from a prison ostensibly located somewhere in the Middle East. Government operatives infiltrate the city and Batman is also able to return to Gotham for the final action sequences to take place. This formal conceit, and the numerous penetrations of its supposed limitations, becomes symptomatic of the cinematic and conceptual difficulties the films find in asserting the city as a cohesive identity.

Conclusion

For Jameson (2010), *The Wire* and Chandler's novels offer necessary and convincing maps of the metropolitan environment. As he suggests, however, for a contemporary mapping project of the social totality it seems as if an interaction with the global nature of late capitalism is essential, in order to reach beyond the confines of a singular city and embrace a larger network of relationships. Nolan's films display ways in which this type of operation might be problematic on a number of levels: the attempt to map a large fictional city is fraught by cinematic convention, and the heavily ideological frameworks used to construct the social elements compromise their interconnectivity. The films' various excursions into international space offer the opportunity for a more thorough sense of global capitalism and its relationship to the modern metropolis, yet this component of the series can only intermittently be developed within the scope of the films. In these ways, the notions of historical and social totalities that Lukács and Jameson discuss, and their potential to be revealed in certain types of generic forms, are perpetually undermined in Nolan's films. Here, the formal qualities of cinematic space, the generic characteristics of the global blockbuster and the capitalist nature of its hero serially complicate every component that would seem to offer a potential for positive Marxist analysis. These films outline ways in which postmodern problems with *totalizing* have become obvious hurdles for contemporary cultural production that aims to map social groups, metropolitan areas or global capitalism, especially in a realist fashion. Despite the possibilities that these *Dark Knight* films surely denote, it remains to be seen whether a mainstream film, or indeed any type of contemporary cultural material, has the ability to properly interrogate these problems.

References

Anderson, A. (1998), *The Origins of Postmodernity*, London: Verso.

Bay, M. (2007), *Transformers*, USA: DreamWorks.

———— (2009), *Transformers: Revenge of the Fallen*, USA: DreamWorks.

———— (2011), *Transformers: Dark of the Moon*, USA: DreamWorks.

Berra, J. (2013), 'The SF cinema of Mainland China: Politics, production and market potential', *Science Fiction Film and Television*, 6: 2, pp. 177–201, http://muse.jhu.edu/journals/sff/summary/v006/6.2.berra.html. Accessed 10 May 2015.

Bolaño, R. (2008 [2004]), *2666*, London: Picador.

Bordwell, D. (2006), *The Way Hollywood Tells It: Story and Style in Modern Movies*, Berkeley: University of California Press.

Bould, M. (2008), '*Transformers* review', *Science Fiction Film and Television*, 1: 1, pp. 163–67, http://muse.jhu.edu/journals/sff/summary/v001/1.1.bould01.html. Accessed 23 February 2014.

Boumeester, M. (2011), 'Reconsidering cinematic mapping: Halfway between collected subjectivity and projected mapping', in F. Penz and A. Lu (eds), *Urban Cinematics: Understanding Urban Phenomena Through the Moving Image*, Bristol: Intellect, pp. 239–56.

Brooker, W. (2001), *Batman Unmasked: Analysing a Cultural Icon*, London: Bloomsbury.

—— —— (2012), *Hunting the Dark Knight: Twenty-first Century Batman*, London: I.B. Tauris.

Burton, T. (1989), *Batman*, USA: Warner Bros.

Chandler, R. (2008 [1939]), *The Big Sleep*, New York: Penguin.

Coonan, C. (2014), 'China film import quota will open up in 2017, says top local producer', *Hollywood Reporter*, http://www.hollywoodreporter.com/news/china-film-import-quota-increase-696708. Accessed 25 May 2015.

Deckard, S. (2012), 'Peripheral realism, millennial capitalism and Roberto Bolaño's 2666', *Modern Language Quarterly*, 73: 3, pp. 351–72, http://mlq.dukejournals.org.ezproxy2.library.usyd.edu.au/content/73/3/351.short. Accessed 12 May 2015.

Dickens, C. (1975 [1859]), *A Tale of Two Cities*, London: Macdonald.

—— —— (2003 [1853]), *Bleak House*, London: Penguin.

Esty, J. and Lye, C. (2012), 'Peripheral realisms now', *Modern Language Quarterly*, 73: 3, pp. 269–88, http://mlq.dukejournals.org.ezproxy1.library.usyd.edu.au/content/73/3/269. Accessed 12 May 2015.

Fradley, M. (2013), 'What do you believe in? Film scholarship and the cultural politics of the *Dark Knight* franchise', *Film Quarterly*, 66: 3, pp. 15–27, http://www.jstor.org/stable/10.1525/fq.2013.66.3.15. Accessed 30 March 2015.

Grainge, P. (2008), *Brand Hollywood: Selling Entertainment in a Global Media Age*, New York: Routledge.

Hassler-Forest, D. (2012), *Capitalist Superheroes: Caped Crusaders in the Neoliberal Age*, Winchester, UK: Zero Books.

Hutcheon, L. (1998), *A Poetics of Postmodernism: History, Theory, Fiction*, New York: Routledge.

Isaacs, B. (2013), *The Orientation of Future Cinema: Technology, Aesthetics, Spectacle*, London: Bloomsbury.

Jameson, F. (1991) *Postmodernism, or, the Cultural Logic of Late Capitalism*, Durham: Duke University Press.

—— —— (1995 [1970]), 'On Raymond Chandler', in J. K. Van Dover (ed.), *The Critical Response to Raymond Chandler*, London: Greenwood.

—— —— (2005), *Archaeologies of the Future: The Desire Called Utopia and Other Science Fictions*, London: Verso.

—— —— (2010), 'Realism and Utopia in *The Wire*', *Criticism*, 52: 3–4, pp. 359–72, http://muse.jhu.edu/journals/criticism/v052/52.3-4.jameson.html. Accessed 5 December 2014.

Lukács, G. (1962 [1947]), *The Historical Novel* (trans. H. Mitchell and S. Mitchell), London: Merlin.

Lynch, K. (1996 [1960]), *The Image of the City*, Cambridge, MA: MIT Press.

Mann, M. (1995), *Heat*, USA: Warner Bros.

McCarthy, T. (1998), 'Armageddon', *Variety*, 371: 8, p. 37, http://go.galegroup.com/ps/i. do?id=GALE%7CA20925484&v=2.1&u=usyd&it=r&p=EAIM&sw=w&asid= 4df0345bf6b927b615a4fbf3ac684fe5. Accessed 25 May 2015.

McLuhan, M. (1967 [1962]), *The Gutenberg Galaxy: The Making of Typographic Man*, London: Routledge.

——— (1998 [1964]), *Understanding Media: The Extensions of Man*, London: Routledge.

Mendelson, S. (2013), '*Pacific Rim* and more domestic "flops" that became global hits', *Forbes*, http://www.forbes.com/sites/scottmendelson/2013/09/02/pacific-rim-and-more-domestic-flops-that-became-global-hits/. Accessed 25 May 2015.

Miller, T., Govil, N., McMurria, J., Maxwell, R. and Wang, T. (2009 [2005]), *Global Hollywood 2*, London: Palgrave Macmillan.

Murphet, J. (2010), '*The Wire* and realism', *Sydney Studies in English*, 36, pp. 52–76, http://openjournals.library.usyd.edu.au/index.php/SSE/article/view/4742. Accessed 12 May 2015.

Murray, N., Robinson T. and Tobias, S. (2013), 'How Asia is reshaping American film', *The Dissolve*, http://thedissolve.com/features/the-conversation/296-how-asia-is-reshaping-american-film/. Accessed 25 May 2015.

Nolan, C. (2005), *Batman Begins*, USA: Warner Bros.

——— (2008), *The Dark Knight*, USA: Warner Bros.

——— (2012), *The Dark Knight Rises*, USA: Warner Bros.

Rolling Stone (2012), 'Christopher Nolan: *Dark Knight Rises* isn't political', *Rolling Stone*, http://www.rollingstone.com/movies/news/christopher-nolan-dark-knight-rises-isn-t-political-20120720. Accessed 25 May 2015.

Scott, T. (1986), *Top Gun*, USA: Paramount Pictures.

Shaviro, S. (2010), *Post-Cinematic Affect*, Winchester, UK: O Books.

Simon, D. (2002–08), *The Wire*, USA: Home Box Office.

Uricchio, W. (2010), 'The Batman's Gotham City™: Story, ideology, performance', in J. Ahrens and A. Meteling (eds), *Comics and the City: Urban Space in Print, Picture and Sequence*, New York: Continuum.

Whedon, J. (2012), *The Avengers*, USA: Paramount Pictures.

Williams, R. (1973), *The Country and the City*, London: Chatto and Windus.

Žižek, S. (2012), 'The People's Republic of Gotham', *New Statesman*, http://www.newstatesman.com/culture/culture/2012/08/slavoj-žižek-politics-batman. Accessed 25 May 2015.

Chapter 3

(Re-)Framing urbanity: Contestation, the moving image and the right to the city

Joern W. Langhorst

Introduction

Throughout history, contestation has been one of the main conditions of urbanity. Urban space, and its patterns, configuration and inhabitation have developed as location of, framework for, catalyst for, and response to various conflicts and their negotiation. The underlying causes of urban conflict comprise social, economic, ethnic, ecological, spatial and political issues – often overlaid on and compounding each other, and further fuelled by density and an often more than critical mass of people and capital. One could assume that therefore urban conditions often have a catalytic effect on conflicts latent in a society or culture and become manifest first and foremost in cities. Consequently, urban form in general can be read as a result of the ongoing negotiation of these conflicts, and the palimpsest that we tend to call 'big city', 'urban agglomeration' or 'metropolis', with its visible and hidden layers, is but a series of battlefields (Marot 2003). Conversely, as film co-evolved as a medium with the spatio-political realities of twentieth-century cities, its representations of urban realities can shed light on contemporary conditions and interpretations of urbanity. Further, film can operate as one of the few modes in which disenfranchised and marginalized individuals and communities can actually attain a degree of representation, and subvert the capitalist-hegemonic agendas and interests that shaped the urban form and conditions that marginalize them, enabling them to develop, represent and enact much more inclusive and socially and environmentally just visions and versions of the city.

Film and city: A contested co-evolution

The evolution of technologies that made the twentieth-century city possible have also made possible the modern motion picture. MacDonald (2001) suggests that the developments of the modern city and the cinema have been not only simultaneous but interlocked, and that the city has been central to two very different strands of film history: first, as an environment for melodrama in Hollywood's mainstream (from Harold Lloyd's comedies to film noir). Second, 'the modern city has been a frequent subject of film identified with and often claimed by two traditions of independent cinema: documentary film and avant-garde film' (MacDonald 2001: 149). Uricchio (1988) argues that:

The motion picture evolved during a period of tremendous urbanization. Its development, survival and spread was, to a great extent, a function of this growth. From the outset, there was a natural interaction between the rapid developments of urban life and the medium capable of observing and commenting upon it. (Uricchio 1988: 17)

To early film-makers, the city displayed the key characteristics of modernity – the increasing speed and standardization of time; the rise of consumerism and the movement of capital; the emphasis on spectatorship, distraction and entertainment; a focus on technology, expediency and mobility; and concerns with overstimulation and ephemerality. The city paved the way for the cinema. Through the capturing of images and editing, there is a sense of motion through space. In the context of modernist film-making, the city street became the laboratory, recording the passage of time so significant to the modernist sensibility, and the opportunity to eschew constructed sets for the 'reality' of city life. Accordingly, Siegfried Kracauer and Walter Benjamin associated the photographer with the wandering *flâneur*. Vidler (1993: 55–56) quotes Sergei Eisenstein's celebration of montage as collision and in a comparison of architecture as cinematic montage, reformulating architecture as 'frozen music', and argues that in modelling how we move through space, 'architecture is film's predecessor'. Indeed, 'Modernity can best be understood as inherently cinematic [...] and cannot be conceived outside the context of the city' (Charney and Schwartz 1995: 2). Classic films, such as *Berlin: Symphonie einer grossstadt/Berlin: Symphony of a Great City* (Ruttmann, 1927), a film arranged to simulate the events of a single day; *The Man with a Movie Camera* (Vertov, 1929); and *Rien que les heures/Nothing but the Hours* (Cavalcanti, 1926), canonize the urban experience in a particular way, exploring and exploiting film's ability to render the vibrant chaos and intersecting patterns of simultaneous movement and action that characterized the modern city, not dissimilar to cubism's deconstruction of linear and hierarchical space on canvas.

Ruttmann, who wanted to honour Berlin as the quintessential modern European metropolis, uses the symphony structure as analogous to the structure of city life. Equivalent to the relation between musician and orchestra:

in the city the individual contributions of millions of people are subsumed within the metropolis' mega-partite movement through the day, a movement that reveals several predictable highs and lows, culminating in a symbolic fireworks that celebrate the conclusion of the metropolis' productive daily and weekly cycle. (MacDonald 2001: 152)

Weihsmann writes:

The cinema is certainly an exemplary product of urban modernity, but it is also a producer of urban culture and civilization [...] From its beginning, film has been linked with the metropolis and the motion picture medium has featured the cityscape frequently and prominently [...] the city was the primary subject matter of early avant-garde cinematography in the mid-1920s. A new genre was born: 'city film', or, better, 'city symphonies'. (Weihsmann 1997: 9–10)

The camera was initially seen as a recorder of fact and scientific reality, Weihsmann further notes: 'Thus the realm of cinematography was of documentary value, and "reality" became a synonym of "actuality"' (Weihsmann 1997: 9). The emergence of editing techniques, in particular the cinematic montage, which, much like collage, allowed cinematographers to deconstruct and reassemble footage, subverting or emphasizing its original spatio-temporal order, quickly became the only language that was able to represent how the city was perceived. Referencing Kevin Lynch's idea of 'imageability', Weihsmann suggests that:

> architectural form relates to the form of film as one text to another, in terms of a structure composed of so many patterns, or rather fragments of structure or language, organized in time through space. Film becomes analogous to the modern perception of the city, continuous sequences of space frames perceived through time [...] a silent witness of reality [...] depicting the hidden yet omnipresent and commonplace character of everyday existence in public places. (Weihsmann 1997: 9)

With a growing awareness of urban realities hidden underneath the modernist-utopian master narrative, a second theme about cities began to emerge during this same period: the city as nightmare.

Based on the tenet that cultures reflect and construct the social reality of the modern era, 'a number of forms of expression and modes of critical analysis arose to make sense of the dramatic and rapidly changing social reality in the city' (Stout 1999: 153). In narrative film, the city emerged as a place with human affections: evil, sinister and alienating (achieved primarily by the use of shadow and light) in 1920s and 1930s film noir. This portrayal of the sinister city was lost with the introduction of colour, until more recent films such as *Blade Runner* (Scott, 1982) and *Batman* (Burton, 1989) successfully resurrected it, introducing the postmodern, apocalyptic vision of the 'neo-noirs', such as *The Man Who Wasn't There* (Coen Brothers, 2001); Christopher Nolan's *Following* (1998) and *Memento* (2000); and culminating in more recent 'post-apocalyptic' films, such as *28 Days Later* (Boyle, 2002) and *I Am Legend* (Lawrence, 2007). The presence of urban space, with its different appearances of order and disorder, carries a large part of the narrative expression, and cultural ideas about moral values, social hierarchy and the role of the individual in society. The city's role in film noir clearly transcends that of mere 'setting' – it acts as both symbol and main character in Helphand's (1986) sense.

Early film theoretician Bela Balazs contends that:

> The screen provides us with more and more examples of machinery and factory work as the menacing examples of a smoke-blackened destiny. We see the machine acquire a face in film, its movement transformed into a terrifying expressiveness. We have seen more than once how the neutral 'terrain' of a factory becomes a grim 'landscape', a landscape both alive and lethal. (Balazs 2011 [1924/30]: 54)

This applies very much to the appearance of the city in film noir. His argument that landscape in the cinema can be read like a human face for its mood and is never neutral suggests that film is a modern art that can most authentically address the horrors of industrialization and urbanization.

This shift coincides with the racial tensions, decay and neglect that in mainstream media became increasingly synonymous with the American industrial city before and after World War II.

Beauregard writes:

> The postwar traumas of the large cities thereby travelled beyond the actual sites of deterioration and neglect. By doing so, they exacerbated the ambivalence toward cities that Americans have embraced for over half a century. In turn, postwar decline fused urban ambivalence to widespread anxieties about racial relations, prosperity, national identity, upward mobility, and personal safety. The city became the discursive site for society's contradictions, and anxiety emerged as the discourse's dominant quality. (Beauregard 2003: VIII)

This understanding of the city as a contested terrain, a location of discourse and a localized discourse itself, marks a distinct shift from the city as monolithic-modernist master narrative, emphasizing the rational and utopian, and articulating what Habermas calls the 'project of Enlightenment', to the postmodern city as a 'heterogeneous, diachronous, polyvocal, and uneven' construct (Krause and Petro 2003: 2).

If 'time, fragmentation, decentralization, militarization and surveillance are among the most important attributes of the postmodern city' (AlSayyad 2006: 17), then it is clearly visible in contemporary narrative film, such as Fernando Meirelles's *City of God* (2002) and Anthony Minghella's *Breaking and Entering* (2006), as well as in Spike Lee's documentaries on post-Katrina New Orleans, *When the Levees Broke* (2006) and *If God Is Willing and da Creek Don't Rise* (2010). All of these films engage postcolonial[1] cities that are both battleground and active agent. Consequently, these films with their 'gritty' appearance of urban reality and particular modes of camera-work and editing contrast with the sleek, dynamic and 'cool' rendering of the city as a backdrop in mainstream movies, TV shows and TV ads that reference, visualize and ultimately stabilize the current neoliberal-hegemonic culture and its narratives.

Film as empowerment

Spike Lee reappropriated the 'city symphony' to construct a counter-hegemonic narrative in *Do the Right Thing* (1989), showing one day in the life of people on one city block. While in Vertov's and Ruttmann's films individuality is subsumed within the machine of the city (MacDonald 2001: 172), Alberto Cavalcanti's *Nothing but the Hours* introduces a set of individuals through which the workings of the city and their consequences are rendered. Spike Lee goes much further, forming a dialectical opposite to *Berlin: Symphony of a Great City*: 'Individuality is virtually irrepressible, people find ways of distinguishing themselves, often by directly confronting those around them' (MacDonald 2001: 173). Lee's city is not constructed by the suppression of individual personality into a 'harmony', but through the 'friendly or hostile interactions of particular citizens' (MacDonald 2001: 173). This clearly replaces the notion of 'overarching harmony' (with all its hegemonic connotations) with a much more 'polyphonic' understanding: conflict is thus rendered as intrinsic and central to city life.

Do the Right Thing goes further in critiquing and supporting the very notions of a multicultural democracy – MacDonald (2001: 173) calls it a 'democratic polemic'. Lee's setting, one block in the Bedford-Stuyvesant section of Brooklyn, can be seen as representative of the city as a whole. Its citizens in their African American 'ghettos' are typically presented as stereotypes and usually marginalized by the media in general, and both mainstream and independent cinema. Lee demonstrates that in the very variety of these marginalized citizens lies the 'energy of democracy' (MacDonald 2001: 173). The film ends in the violent destruction of an Italian pizzeria. While Cavalcanti's *Nothing but the Hours* shows crime as not only 'an inevitable dimension of city life, but one of the things that renders city life exciting and romantic', 'Lee suggests that, while violence is inevitable in the racist version of capitalist democracy, it is anything but romantic' (MacDonald 2001: 174).

Do the Right Thing truly forms a counter-narrative, deconstructing the city and rendering urban conflict not only as intrinsic, but *integral*. And while history (and the build form of cities) is usually written by the victorious and the powers that be, cinema has the ability of giving a voice to those marginalized and disenfranchised; to infuse the reading of urban form and occupation with another layer critical to understanding its history and current condition. This renders a 'thick' reading (Marot 2003), necessary to understand and engage issues of uneven urban development, social and environmental justice, capital hegemony and the right to the city (see e.g. Lefebvre 1968 and Smith 1984).

This is nowhere clearer than in Spike Lee's documentary *When the Levees Broke*, and its successor *If God Is Willing and da Creek Don't Rise*. *When the Levees Broke* presents the untold stories and history of the Lower 9th Ward and its citizens in New Orleans, the systematic discrimination and ignorance towards it and its ultimate exploitation. This tale appears too familiar – any postcolonial study of Third and Fourth World countries would render comparable narratives and insights, but to see it unfold in a First World

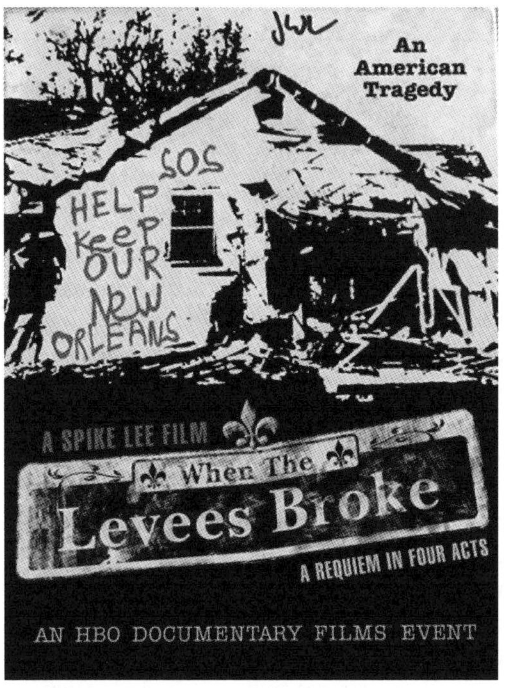

Figure 1. *When the Levees Broke* (2006), © 40 Acres & a Mule Productions.

nation is disturbing. It is not the destruction of Katrina that is truly disturbing[2] – it is the underlying dysfunctionalities and injustices of the political, cultural and economic systems that were revealed in the aftermath. Lee succeeds in not only mercilessly exposing those and their perpetrators, but in telling a story of the traditions of defiance, resilience and resistance that created the Lower 9th Ward as both place and community. For the first time, a mainstream audience across the United States was exposed to this powerful counter-narrative – showing that the Lower 9th Ward is not merely a disposable – or developable – piece of land below sea level, and its citizenry not something that could be displaced without conflict or consequence.

The predominant narrative that rendered the Lower 9th Ward and other low-lying areas as 'green space' or 'park' provided a seemingly unarguable conclusion, driven by topographic 'facts'. The ignorance of cultural, social, economic and historic conditions and processes with the goal of remaking the city in a different (neoliberal and whitewashed) image is indeed typical of the ruthless ways the processes of capital accumulation and hegemonic power are played out. This battle is played out not just within the physical reality of the city itself, but it is in fact fought on the maps and plan drawings, the simulacra deployed by globalized capital interests and hegemonic elites for centuries (Harley 1999; Cosgrove 1998; Rose 2007; Langhorst 2012).

Using representational tools – the well-established forms of projection drawing – planners and designers reduce a 'place' to a 'site', reducing it to a condition of static receptivity, making it 'real' and meaningful only through what is supposed to happen there in the future. These renderings tend to emphasize the 'spectacle' (Debord 1967) of built form, software-assisted animated fly-throughs or equally 'hyperreal' (Baudrillard 1981; Langhorst 2013) drawings that resemble a cinematic utopia where only certain people have a place – and those tend to be markedly different from current residents. These images preclude the conceptualization and realization of 'more complex adaptive human–environment interactions' (Krog 1981: 375). This conscious erasure of history and meaning is indeed one of the most incisive and consequential acts of disempowering a community and place – it is ultimately the act of determining the scope and content of any discourse on the future of a place. It in fact imposes a narrative on the past and future of a place and its community – a narrative that has more to do with the devices and desires of the hegemonic than the actualities of the history (and future) of that particular place as experienced by its community. 'The right to narrative', Homi Bhabha (2003) argues, is 'to tell stories that create the web of history, and change the direction of its flow'. The power of changing the flow of history – in other words, the future, the description of a 'preferred situation' – has been usurped by the powers that be, and the ability of a community to imagine its own future by narrating (and thus understanding) its own past and present is severely compromised. Representing the narrative of place and community as experienced by its members through traditional projection drawings appears impossible – chiefly because the representational traditions in marginalized cultures are often radically different (e.g. traditions of oral history), and because the representational media have been compromised and controlled by the hegemonic interests. It could be argued that marginalized cultures developed narrative traditions that relied less on the continuous existence of artefacts in response to the latent or acute threats, to patterns of displacement that required them to be mobile, and frequently resulted in the loss of material possessions (see e.g. Deleuze and Guattari 1986).

Film then has at least the potential to be one of the few modes in which disenfranchised and marginalized individuals and communities can actually attain a degree of representation, a 'voice', in the very processes that marginalize them – aided by the availability and easily attained mastery of a technology that was in the realm of privilege a decade ago. An excellent example of this is Tia Lessin and Carl Deal's *Trouble the Water* (2009), a documentary made by two Lower 9th Ward residents about their experiences during and after hurricane Katrina.

Often relying on personifying the consequences of processes that are considered 'anonymous' – such as globalization, capital accumulation by dispossession (Harvey 2004), urban renewal, border security, etc. – such films facilitate an understanding of not just the process itself, but its fallout. Ultimately, they disallow the audience to pretend that there are no real consequences and that the processes as such are automatic, inevitable, beyond their (or anybody's) control, and hence nobody can be held accountable.

Between battlefield and dreamscape: Rights to the city, or, contesting dystopia and utopia

Henri Lefebvre's (1968; 1991) concepts of the 'production of space' and of the 'right to the city' have been both influential and problematic in the discourses on spatial, social and environmental justice and the way cities and 'the urban' are socially produced and reproduced, developed and redeveloped. Lefebvre proposes 'appropriation' and 'participation' as fundamental aspects of this right, counteracting the dominant neoliberal modes of economic and political restructuring of cities and their attendant exclusionary practices. Purcell (2002) suggests that:

> The right to the city offers an approach that at once is exciting and disconcerting. It is exciting because it offers a radical alternative that directly challenges and rethinks the current structure of both capitalism and liberal-democratic citizenship. It is disconcerting because we cannot know what kind of a city these new urban politics will produce. They could play out as a truly democratic challenge to marginalization and oppression, but they could also work to reinscribe new forms of domination. (Purcell 2002: 99)

Spike Lee's work operates within this context. The way he portrays the event and aftermath of hurricane Katrina, and daily life in a neighbourhood, is in marked contrast to the resurgence of the genre of the 'post-apocalyptic' in narrative cinema.[3] Many 'post-apocalyptic' movies tend to only allude to the catastrophic event, but still render the day-to-day lives of their protagonists as a version of an epic battle, as a 'spectacle' in Debord's (1967) sense, making it impossible for an audience to relate the events on the screen to their own lives. Spike Lee's lens is a different one – he ultimately focuses on the day-to-day experience, the lives of 'ordinary people', and the many ways in which their mundane actions imprint the places they inhabit. He implicitly constructs an argument that prioritizes and opposes the appropriation and participation of ordinary people through their everyday actions against the forces and agendas of neoliberal politics and economics. DeCerteau, in his essay 'Walking in the City' (1984), explores this very dialectic, counter-positioning the everyday 'user' of urban space, who participates through many acts of 'everyday practice', such as walking, and the 'voyeur', the person in a privileged position who 'looks down' on the city and does not participate in acts that truly generate meaning.

Mainstream cinematic representations of 'city' and 'the urban' foreground its quality as a spectacle and prioritize the hidden forces and processes that 'made' the urban condition – whether dystopian or utopian. The actual, human authorship is camouflaged,

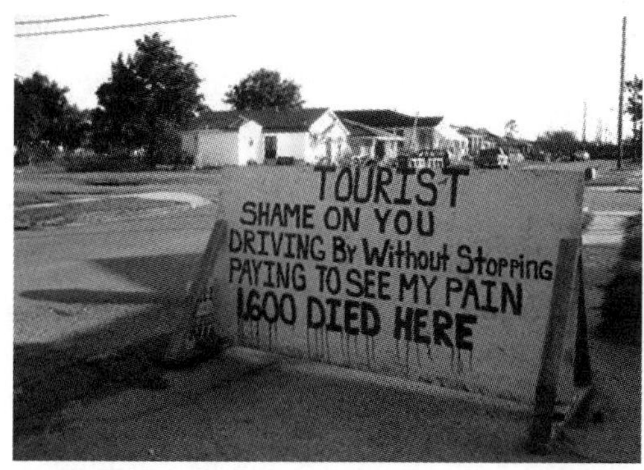

Figure 2. 'Tourist – Shame on You.' Posted by residents in the Lower 9th Ward, January 2006 (Photo: Author).

'naturalized' (Spirn 1997; Langhorst 2013), and removed from any individual responsibility or criticism, appearing as a natural disaster, non-human organism or result of a large-scale war. What makes Lee's films so compelling is that he humanizes both the catastrophic event and the actions and reactions of residents, and thus makes possible a participatory and open discourse on the event itself, and on how to respond to it. The conversations about how to 'remake' a devastated place then become contextualized in a much wider, deeper and more critical understanding of the multiple histories and narratives. The resultant constructions of that place form a powerful alternative to the hegemonic master-narratives of urban renewal and resilience. In turn, this makes the inhabitants and their day-to-day actions as much (or, in DeCerteau's sense – more of) an author than the depersonalized processes of globalization and capital accumulation.

While the instigators and processes of urban 'renewal' or 'revitalization' make implicit assumptions about the validity and viability of the past and current state of a neighbourhood, they also relegate it to the 'setting' for a film for which they are writing the script. As stated above, a place rich in history and meaning is reduced to a 'site', the location of a future *mise-*

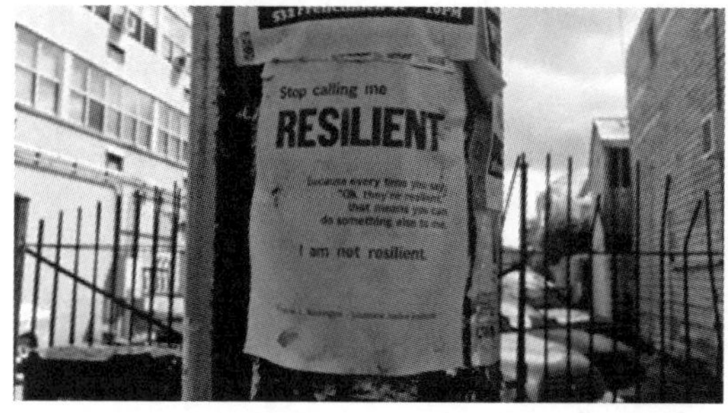

Figure 3. 'Stop Calling Me Resilient.' Poster in New Orleans, (originally blogged at http://candychang. com/resilient/ and reposted at https://www.opendem-ocracy.net/print/78842). Acccessed 6 February 2014.

en-scène that will supersede and erase all that happened before, negating both appropriation and participation for the people that inhabit that location, effectively excluding them from their 'right to the city' and the place they shaped. David Harvey (2004) describes this process as 'accumulation by dispossession'. Spike Lee's emphasis on the residents' participation in the past, current and future making and remaking of their neighbourhoods also changes and expands the role of place and city in his films – it moves from being a subject, symbol and setting to becoming a character, an entity with its own agency. This understanding has the potential to activate the discourse on the future of places, neighbourhoods and cities by exploring them not just as passive entities, the results of cultural production, but as active agents in the complex processes of making and remaking cities and urbanity. This foregrounds the reciprocally constitutive relationship between a place and its inhabitants. The city then becomes much more the battlefield upon which conflicts are acted out.

The city as character

If the spatial and cultural form of 'city' is a result, however dynamic and ephemeral, of how the aforementioned conflicts and differentials play themselves out spatially and socially, how they 'take place', then film is uniquely suited to understand and analyse these processes.

Film as a medium is at least three-dimensional – it adds the dimension of time to the two-dimensional screen, creating a more and more perfect illusion of a four-dimensional – real – space. Parts of actual experience can be provided by film, such as movement, activity, temporal and spatial change. The medium can even create more than perfect illusions of place, it is able to go beyond and change the temporal and spatial context of reality, thus creating a 'heightened reality'. Its 'unique and specific possibilities can be defined as dynamization of space and, accordingly, spatialization of time' (Panofsky 1967 [1934/36]: 18); it is 'free of the limits of time and space' (Vertov 1984 [1924]: 15–17). Cinematic place (and its constituting processes and conditions) can then be interpreted as 'subject', 'setting', 'character' and 'symbol' (Helphand 1986).

These constructs of cinematic place enhance and make visible processes and phenomena otherwise hidden. Vertov's and Ruttmann's use of camera angles, time-lapse photography, overlay and split-screen edits emphasize the choreography of movement and change typical of the urban condition. There are a great number of films that aestheticize the urban conflicts in different ways and to different ends, but all succeed in creating the illusion of 'place', and revealing the cultural and social interactions that make those places.

The 'ghetto', the 'hood' or the dystopian urban ruins, left over after some catastrophe that is mostly alluded to, but barely ever explained, often functions as 'supporting actor' – or, in Helphand's sense, as character. They are much more than just the setting in which the urban conflict plays itself out – they are an integral part of it, whether as studio pastiches or as real locations.[4] In different ways all of these films represent the connection between the 'place' and the 'action' portrayed within the frame. Every single one of them is reflective and revelatory of the critical discourses outside of the cinematic frame, around the time of the inception and shooting of the footage.

Conclusion

The study of city in film, and of film in and of the city, as outlined here in snapshots of a complex history, illustrates how the study of the interrelation of landscape and film might form the basis of an analysis of a different kind – one that foregrounds the development of city over time, understood as ongoing interaction between place and people. Abbas (2003: 144) suggests that 'the practices of the cinema constitute a kind of empirical evidence for an understanding of urban space but also that such evidence is not necessarily evident and only emerges through visual-spatial critique'.

The change in the ways urban conflicts and their 'places' are represented in cinema is not only a portrait of their actual qualities, properties and conditions, but also indicative of different perspectives, readings, attitudes and interpretations. Thus, it can be analysed to understand the relationship between society and the processes it employs to resolve conflicts – or not – and their manifestation in places (see also Hopkins 1994).

Looking at how the manners in which urban conflicts are negotiated and the urban condition is represented and present inside and outside of the cinematic frame, invites the question to what degree the cinematic frame allows for a projection back onto the frames and conditions of actual urban situations and conflicts,[5] and its agency in changing them. On the back of Baudrillard's (1991; see also Best and Kellner 1999) concept of 'hyperreality' one could suggest that the close interrelation and co-evolution of cinema and city and its mutual influences might create a situation within which the city mediates film as much as film mediates the city.

A more thorough exploration of this mutual mediation, the question of 'authorship' of urban conditions and processes, and the agencies of urban form and cinema, seems promising, in particular in regards to independent cinema. The question of representation and empowerment (who/what/how/to what end) seems to be particularly interesting. If nothing else, it might involve people and interests that are usually excluded from the decision-making processes about urban form.

References

Abbas, A. (2003), 'Cinema, the city, and the cinematic', in L. Krause and P. Petro (eds), *Global Cities: Cinema, Architecture, and Urbanism in a Digital Age*, New Brunswick, NJ: Rutgers University Press, pp. 142–56.

AlSayyad, N. (2006), 'From postmodern condition to cinematic city', in N. AlSayyad (ed.), *Urbanism: A History of the Modern from Reel to Real*, New York: Routledge, pp. 123–47.

Balazs, B. (2011 [1924/30]), *Bela Balazs' Early Film Theory: Visible Man and the Spirit of Film* (trans. R. Livingstone), London: Berghann Books.

Baudrillard, J. (1981), *Simulacres et Simulation*, Paris: Éditions Galilée.

Beauregard, R. A. (2003), *Voices of Decline: The Postwar Fate of U.S. Cities*, New York: Routledge.

Best, S. and Kellner, D. (1999), 'Debord and the postmodern turn: New stages of the spectacle', *Substance #90*, pp. 129–56.

Bhabha, H. K. (2003), 'On Writing Rights', in M. Gibney (ed.), *Globalizing Rights*, Oxford: Oxford University Press, pp 162–82.

Boyle, D. (2002), *28 Days Later*, UK: DNA Films.

Burton, T. (1989), *Batman*, USA: Warner Bros.

Cavalcanti, A. (1926), *Rien que les heures*, France.

Certeau, M., De (1984), 'Walking in the City', in M. DeCerteau (ed.), *The Practice of Everyday Life*, Berkeley: University of California Press, pp. 91–110.

Charney, L. and Schwartz, V. R. (eds) (1995), *Cinema and the Invention of Modern Life*, Berkeley: University of California Press.

Coen, J.and E. (2001), *The Man Who Wasn't There*, USA: Good Machine.

Cosgrove, D. (1998), *Social Formation and Symbolic Landscape*, Madison: University of Wisconsin Press.

Debord, G. (1967), *La Société du spectacle*, Paris: Editions Buchet-Chastel.

Deleuze, G. and Guattari, F. (1986), *Nomadology and the War Machine*, New York: Semiotext(e).

Harley, J. B. (1999), 'Maps, knowledge, power', in D. Cosgrove (ed.), *Mappings*, London: Reaktion Books, pp. 279–312.

Harvey, D. (2004), 'The 'new' imperialism: Accumulation by dispossession', *Socialist Register*, 40, pp. 63–87.

Helphand, K. (1986), 'Landscape films', *Landscape Journal*, 5: 1, pp. 1–8.

Hopkins, J. (1994), 'A mapping of cinematic places: Icons, ideology, and the power of misrepresentation', in S. Aitken and L. E. Zonn (eds), *Place, Power, Situation, and Spectacle: A Geography of Film*, Lanham: Rowman & Littlefield, pp. 47–63.

Krause, L. and Petro, P. (eds) (2003), *Global Cities: Cinema, Architecture, and Urbanism in a Digital Age*, New Brunswick, NJ: Rutgers University Press.

Krog, S. (1981), 'Is it art?', *Landscape Architecture*, 71: 3, pp. 273–376.

Langhorst, J. (2012), 'Recovering place: On the agency of post-disaster landscapes', *Landscape Review*, Special Issue 'Post-Disaster Landscapes', 14: 2, pp. 48–74.

———— (2013), 'Rendering the unseen: The pragmatics, aesthetics and ethics of place representation', *Representation: Journal of the Design Communication Association*, 2013–14, pp. 54–61.

Lawrence, F. (2007), *I Am Legend*, USA: Warner Bros.

Lee, S. (1989), *Do the Right Thing*, USA: Forty Acres & A Mule.

—————— (2006), *When the Levees Broke*.

—————— (2010), *If God Is Willing and da Creek Don't Rise*, USA: 40 Acres & a Mule.

Lefebvre, H. (1968), *Le droit à la ville/The Right to the City*, Paris: Anthropos.

—————— (1991), *The Production of Space*, Oxford: Blackwell.

Lessin. T. and C. Deal (2009), *Trouble the Water*, USA: Elsewhere Films.

Luke, T. W. (1989), *Screens of Power: Ideology, Domination and Resistance in Informational Society*, Chicago: University of Illinois Press.

MacDonald, S. (2001), *The Garden in the Machine: A Field Guide to Places about Film*, Berkeley: University of California Press.

Marot, S. (2003), *Sub-urbanism and the Art of Memory*, London: AA Productions.

Meirelles, F. (2002), *City of God*, Brazil: O2 Filmes.

Minghella, A. (2006), *Breaking and Entering*, UK: Miramax.

Nolan, C. (1998), *Following*, UK: Next Wave Films.

—————— (2000), *Memento*, USA: Newmarket Capital Group.

Panofsky, E. (1967 [1934/36]), 'Style and medium in the motion pictures', in D. Talbot (ed.), *Film: An Anthology*, Berkeley: University of California Press, pp. 15–32.

Purcell, M. (2002), 'Excavating Lefebvre: The right to the city and its urban politics of the inhabitant', *GeoJournal*, Special Issue 'Social Transformation, Citizenship, and the Right to the City', 58: 2/3, pp. 99–108.

Rose, G. (2007), *Visual Methodologies: An Introduction to the Interpretation of Visual Materials*, London: Sage.

Ruttman, H. (1927), *Berlin: Symphonie einer Grossstadt (Berlin: Symphony of a Great City)*.

Scott, R. (1982), *Blade Runner*, USA: Warner Bros.

Smith, N. (1984), *Uneven Development: Nature, Capital and the Production of Space*, Oxford: Blackwell.

Spirn, A. (1997), 'The authority of nature', in J. Wolschke-Bulmahn (ed.), *Nature and Ideology: Natural Garden Design in the 21st Century*, Washington DC: Dumbarton Oaks, pp. 249–61.

Stout, F. (1999), 'Visions of a new reality: The city and the emergence of the modern visual culture', in R. T. LeGates and F. Stout (eds), *The City Reader*, New York: Routledge, pp. 150–53.

Uricchio, W. (1988), 'The city reviewed: Berlin's film image on the occasion of its 750th Anniversary', *Film and History*, 18: 1, pp. 16–24.

Vertov, D. (1929), *The Man with a Movie Camera*, Soviet Union: VUFKU.

—————— (1984 [1924]), *Kino-Eye: The Writings of Dziga Vertov*, Berkeley: University of California Press.

Vidler, A. (1993), 'The explosion of space: Architecture and the filmic imaginary', *Assemblage*, 21, pp. 44–59.

Weihsmann, H. (1997), 'The city in twilight: Charting the genre of the 'City Film' 1900–1930', in F. Penz and M. Thomas (eds), *Cinema and Architecture: Melies, Mallet-Stevens, Multimedia*, London: British Film Institute, pp. 8–27.

Notes

1. I argue that, while cities like New Orleans and Detroit are not *located* in a classical colonial/postcolonial setting, they are *situated* in and shaped by the processes and discourses of postcoloniality. See Langhorst 2012.
2. The author has been closely involved in the recovery of the Lower 9th Ward from Autumn 2005 onwards.
3. See e.g. *28 Days Later, I Am Legend, The Road* (Hillcoat, 2009) and *The Book of Eli* (Hughes Brothers, 2010).
4. As in *Training Day* (Fuqua, 2001), or Robert Altman's *Short Cuts* (1993), which provides a stunning cross-section and sociocultural topography of Los Angeles, or the settings of Fernando Meireilles's films, *City of God* and *The Constant Gardener* (2005), both filmed in actual informal settlements, the latter in Kibera, outside of Nairobi, and considered to be the largest slum in the world.
5. In a very literal way, the increasing presence of 'urban screens', as in Times Square in New York, or Piccadilly Circus in London, suggest to explore their potential to 'reflect' or 'project' back and their agency in affecting the reading of and interaction with the urban situation in their immediate and larger contexts. See Luke 1989.

Chapter 4

Architects of *Playtime*: Cities as social media in the work of Jacques Tati

Lisa Landrum

Introduction

It has become commonplace to consider cities as heavily mediated environments, where mediated is taken to imply an intervening realm of digital imagery and information, influencing the way we perceive and interact with all things and all people, most everywhere and all the time. The expression 'mass media' – popularized by Marshall McLuhan to designate the whole gamut of electronic and environmental devices through which, like it or not, 'everybody becomes involved' (McLuhan 1964: 349) – is still apt for describing the pervasive reach of digital mediation in the twenty-first century. But does 'digital' best describe the kind of mediation fundamental to cities? Digital mediation may be increasingly omnipresent, but is this of primary importance when considering configurations of urban settings for human affairs? Might the pervasiveness of digital mediation, and the associated fragmentation of experience that McLuhan predicted, be obscuring other modes of mediation that have always been and may long remain fundamental to viable cities? In his book *Ambient Commons* (2013), Malcolm McCullough approaches such questions. Regarding media-saturated cities with equal fascination and concern, McCullough advocates balancing absorption in mediating technologies with quieter 'unmediated' perceptions (2013: 292–93). Yet, is there such a thing as 'unmediated' perception? Philosophers have long argued that there is no immediate, bare or direct perception, since human experience is always already mediated by intervening agencies, such as language, history, memory, social relations, situational contingencies, corporeal capacities, cultural presuppositions and personal inquisitiveness. Pitting 'unmediated' against 'mediated' experience could, thus, hardly advance our understanding of urban phenomena involving myriad kinds and degrees of interaction.

This chapter argues for a fundamental shift in thinking about mediation, especially with respect to cities. The aim is to restore to mediation its most common senses, including social, situational and interpretive senses, which the act of mediating still entails in spite of present preoccupations with hi-tech media. One could approach this topic philologically, by attending to the roots of 'media'. Literary critic John Guillory has recently accomplished this by tracing 'the path by which this ancient word for 'middle' [*medius*] came to serve as the collective noun for our most advanced communication technologies' (2010: 321). Alternatively, one could interrogate built examples, unpacking, as David Leatherbarrow has done in *Uncommon Ground*, the 'mediating function of architectural edges' (2000: 198). This chapter, though informed by these studies, examines different evidence: namely, the mediating interplay of citizens and city as represented in Jacques Tati's 1967 film *Playtime*. Exemplary for its portrayal of human interactions with – and against – their fabricated milieu, *Playtime* is also relevant because its production commenced in the same year that Marshall McLuhan published *Understanding Media* (1964); which is to say, just when media and mediation were felt to pose problems for understanding. Although the mention of McLuhan is said to have drawn blank stares from the comedic mime turned film-maker (Rosenbaum 1995 [1983]: 165), theories of McLuhan do resonate with the theatrics of Tati, since both expose tacit but meaningful reciprocities between people and environments. Previous architectural studies of Tati's *Playtime* have emphasized the film's comic critique of modernity, and its lead character's productive state of distraction.[1] This chapter focuses on the film's largely non-verbal exchanges, seeking to recover and reinterpret some of the most basic ways in which mediation manifests in cities.

Conceived as a satire of post-war urbanization, *Playtime* depicts the city of Paris bereft of distinctive historic architecture (save for fleeting reflections) and besieged by generic infrastructural and mechanical devices, including glass curtain-walls, modular partitions, escalators, elevators, automatic doors, turnstiles, air-conditioning systems, parking meters, public intercoms and personal televisions. These devices were incorporated into an extensive purpose-built set, dubbed Tativille, which ultimately (and infamously) bankrupted the director (Bellos 1999: 241–50). Together with these now normative mechanized urban elements, *Playtime* showcases more ridiculous devices intended to mock consumer fascination with novel gadgetry: battery-powered brooms with headlights; eyeglasses with hinged lenses (for applying mascara); and cigarette-dispensing table lamps. If Tati were making *Playtime* today, he would no doubt extend his satire to smartphones, Google-glasses, drones, airport security scanners, etc. However, *Playtime* not only satirizes mediating gadgetry, it also dramatizes – through meticulous choreography – other mediating agencies embodied in social situations and interpretive individuals. Although Tati's Paris appears radically transformed by innovative gadgets, it is these other embodied and interpretive modes of mediation that are more efficacious in bringing about restorative civic change. So, setting gadgets aside, the mediating agents to consider first are the film's human intermediaries.

Human intermediaries: Hulot as serendipitous architect and tacit guide

Playtime features a double storyline involving groups and individuals making their respective way through a foreign city with the help and hindrance of others. The film begins by following a group of American tourists as they arrive at Orly Airport and are then corralled – methodically – through an ultra-modern Paris on a one-day stopover during an organized tour of Europe. Alongside these tourists, *Playtime* follows an individual Frenchman, Monsieur Hulot (played by Jacques Tati), as he, too, arrives in Paris and

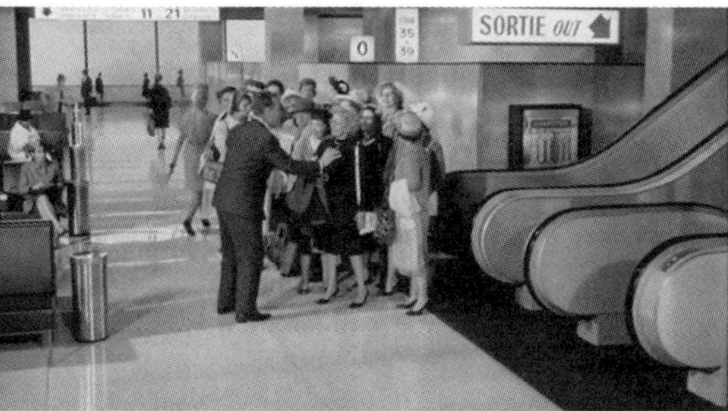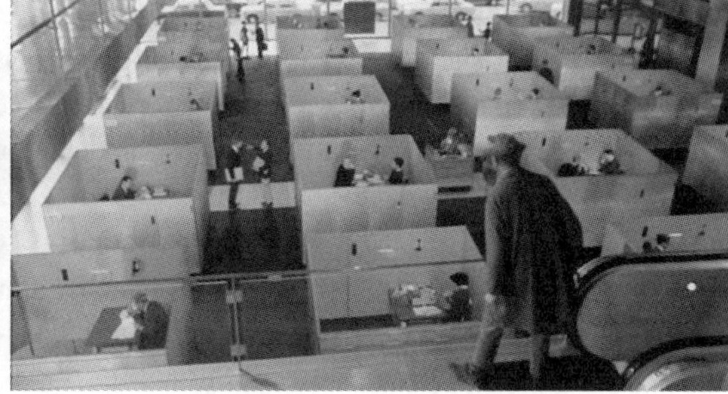

Figure 1. Tour guides directing American tourists (left); Hulot leading audiences as he pursues Gifford (right). *Playtime* (1967), Public Media Home Vision.

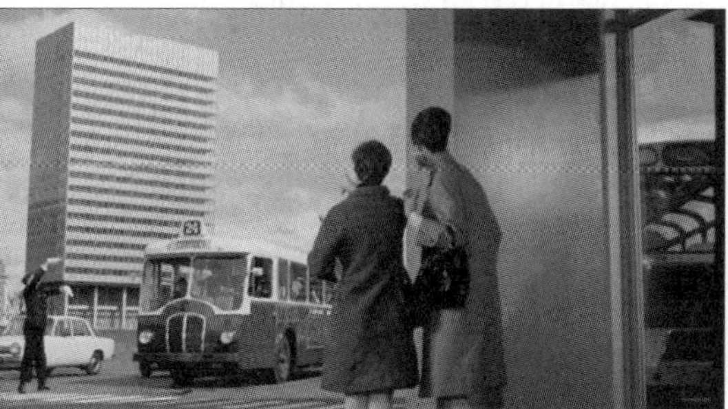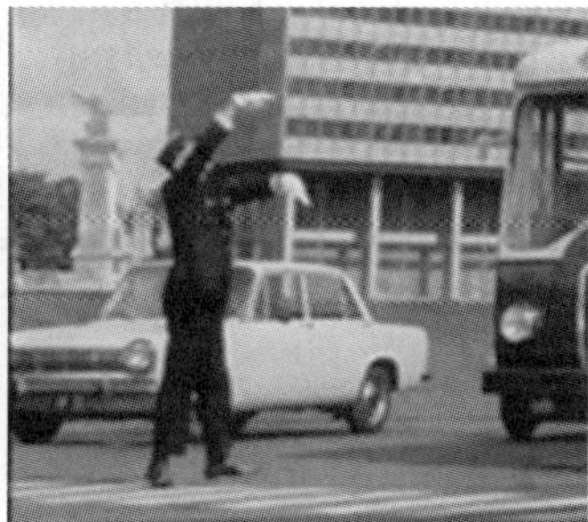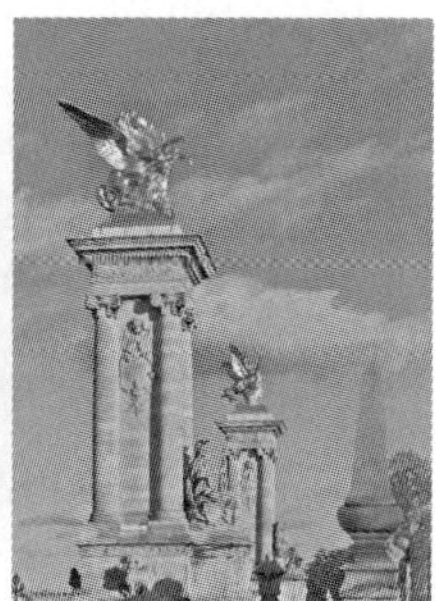

Figure 2. Pont Alexandre III, full screen (left); detail (centre); Left Bank pillars of Pont Alexandre III, © CNP Collection/Alamy Stock Photo, 2011.

engages the city in a more socially entangled way. Whereas the tourists obediently follow a prescriptive itinerary, experiencing the city via the mediating directives of official guides, Hulot accepts directions from strangers and, more ambivalently, searches and drifts, taking filmic audiences along with him wherever he goes. Unlike the tourists, whose every move is efficiently managed while on their way to do nothing of particular importance, Hulot strives to meet Gifford, a busy executive, but a barrage of modern conveniences impede his pursuit. This double storyline – which culminates with all characters revelling in the same nightclub – introduces two distinct sets of intermediaries: tour guides, on the one hand; and Hulot, together with Hulot-like strangers, on the other. Whereas the tour guides operate more in the foreground – controlling mass movement and directing group attention to predetermined sights, enforcing a closed narrative – Hulot, and other

Hulot-like characters, act in the margins, diverting and dispersing attention in ways that open-up multiple associations and potentialities.

In one scene, these intermediaries converge to elucidate the city's layered history. In this scene, an American tourist points towards a generic office tower and mistakenly observes, 'From what the book says, that should be *le Pont Alexandre Trois* [the Bridge of Alexander the Third]. I'm sure it is!' Her confidence in the guidebook, in spite of what we recognize as an obvious incongruity, establishes the ironic humour of this scene. However, if we look askew, away from the misidentified office building and towards a whistle-blowing traffic cop (played by Tati), we discover in the background two ornamental pillars of the famous bridge completed for the opening of the 1900 World's Fair, easily identified by their allegorical sculptures of the taming of Pegasus. Although this monument to a previous century's technological aspirations may be accurately marked in the guidebook, in being almost completely obscured by the modern office tower (and unknown to the tourist), it is only recognized with the diverting assistance of a Hulot-like guide: a marginal intermediary whose mediating gestures – as framed by Tati – are more directive of interpretive attention than vehicular traffic.

Whereas the instrumental tactics of the film's tour guides derive from efficiency-driven attitudes of techno-bureaucratic society, the mediating agencies of Hulot stem from an anonymous architect whose peculiar gait and fallible behaviour had greatly impressed Tati (Gilliatt 1973: 40).[2] This performative affinity between Tati, Hulot and architects is of central importance to *Playtime*, not only because Tati counted architects among his closest artistic collaborators and considered architecture the star of his film,[3] but also because a fallible architect character is featured in the culminating nightclub scene. In the Royal Garden restaurant, a nervous architect (with a roll of drawings under his arm) emerges from behind a curtain on opening night, just as the guests begin to arrive. While the nightclub fills with boisterous patrons and musicians, the situation gradually slips into chaos, as the club becomes afflicted by accumulating technical and design malfunctions, which the architect records in a punch list. Towards the end of this long scene, the title 'architect' is taken away from the ineffectual character and transferred to Hulot. The circumstances are both comical and revealing. Having intervened to help a woman obtain a golden apple lodged beyond her reach in an ornamental screen, Hulot inadvertently brings down the ceiling. His well-meaning gesture has the accidental effect of stripping away elitist pretentions cheaply built into the classy club, while alluding to mythopoetic narratives involving apples of discord and the demise of Edenic gardens. More pertinent to *Playtime*, this unexpected transformation of decor initiates a corresponding transformation in decorum, gradually turning the formal club into a more informal bistro. Recognizing this liberating transformation, an elated tourist snatches the drawings away from the architect of the Royal Garden, saying, 'You're fired!' He then awards these drawings to Hulot, announcing, 'He's the new architect.' This symbolic transfer recognizes Hulot as an alternative agent of architectural transformation, one who initiates a loosening of the rigid social order built into the club. While the official architect strives to bring the environment into conformity with his drawings, becoming increasingly frustrated with deviations and malfunctions, Hulot simply responds to basic existential desires of the people. Two further points must be made about Hulot's mediating actions as a serendipitous architect: he is completely caught up in the midst of situations, while remaining strangely aloof from them; and the circumstances in which he meddles are not of his own devising – he is wholly involved, to be sure, but the scope of transformation is beyond him.

Throughout *Playtime*, Hulot and a variety of Hulot-like intermediaries act alongside (and somewhat against) more officially sanctioned guides to palpably influence perceptions of situations in and beyond the film's narrative. But perceptions of the city, as a complex work of mediation, are also guided by Tati's carefully mediated approach to cinema.

Multi-mediation: Tati's polychronic approach to cinematic media

Tati used what were in the 1960s the most advanced technologies in cinematic media, including wide-screen formatting, colour-film processing and surround sound. However, he used these new media in ways that, ironically, recovered and reinterpreted more basic and enduring modes of mediation.

Wide-screen formatting: Broad awareness and focused attention

Tati shot *Playtime* with the newly available 70mm film, enabling a projected aspect ratio much wider than 35mm film had previously allowed. Audiences loved this new media for its immersive effects, since the wider screen enveloped viewers in expansive landscapes and exciting spectacles, like those featured in *The Sound of Music* (Wise, 1965) and *Lawrence of Arabia* (Lean, 1962). Compared to these films, the wide scenes of *Playtime* appear empty and unremarkable, for Tati used the extra-ordinary breadth of frame to capture ordinary situations (like waiting in public spaces), and to heighten awareness of 'infra-ordinary' details latent in such situations.[4] As Tati himself explained in a 1964 interview, 'What I like in wide-screen film are not cavalcades, gunfights, crowd scenes and so on, what I find extraordinary is that the device allows the viewer to have a fuller appreciation of a mere pin dropping in a large empty room' (Bellos 1999: 259). In other words, Tati appropriated wide-screen formatting for attending to narrowly focused details within an expanded field of awareness, viewing peculiarities of phenomenal events and human practices against broader cultural milieus. This new media helped make inconspicuous aspects of everyday experience more legible by contrast and, so, more available for comic appreciation and critical interpretation.

Aside from using 70mm film to re-frame quotidian content, Tati explored this new medium's compositional possibilities. But instead of rapid jump cuts, daring camera movements and dramatic close-ups, as explored by early film greats such as Sergei Eisenstein,

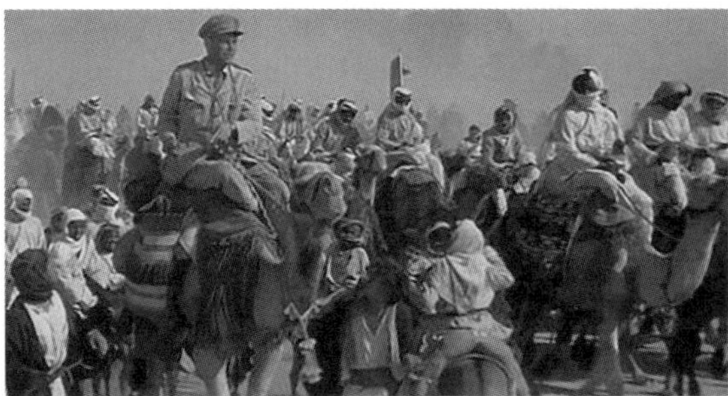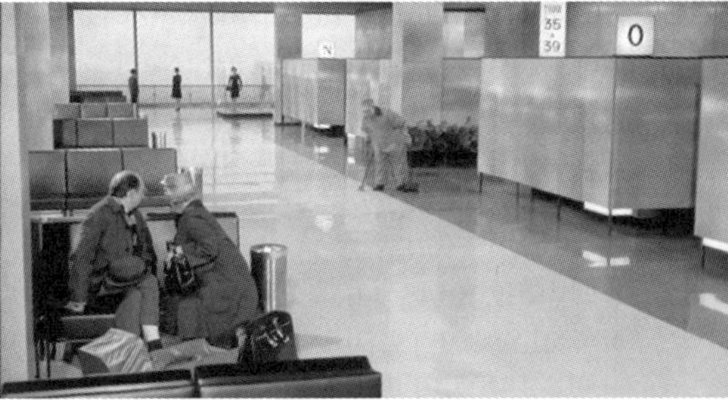

Figure 3. An extraordinary cavalcade in *Lawrence of Arabia* (left); an infra-ordinary situation of waiting in *Playtime* (right). *Lawrence of Arabia* (1962), © ; Columbia Trista. *Playtime* (1967), ©. Public Media Home Vision.

Orson Welles and Carl Dreyer, Tati preferred fixed-position filming and long-shot tableaux. These basic formats enabled Tati to present actors fully – from head to toe – milling about their milieu on the screen much as they would appear to one another when moving about the city, or to an audience when performing on the stage of a theatre. Tati thus treated the wider screen as a generous window onto social reality, a kind of urban proscenium, which spectators could imaginatively reconstruct for themselves upon leaving the cinema. Tati's compositional strategy was also unique in that he did not cluster activity in the centre of the screen, but instead distributed small events around the periphery. With so many simultaneous events happening in the margins and background, it is impossible to follow all that transpires in a single viewing. One must return for repeated viewings, or pause the film to scan the motionless screen (as we have the luxury of doing now). Such unhurried modes of visual inspection and retrospection are more appropriate to photography and painting. Indeed, Tati drew inspiration from photography, notably Robert Doisneau's 1962 composite photo-collage *La maison des locataires/A Home for Tenants* (Ede and Goudet 2002: 143). He also frequently compared himself to a painter, and 'quite consciously used the screen as if it were canvas, over which the eye could roam' (Bellos 1999: 261). Fruitful comparisons have been made between certain scenes of Tati and those of Raoul Dufy and Pieter Bruegel, whose paintings Tati may have encountered while apprenticing in his father's framing shop (Ede and Goudet 2002: 137–42). Such comparisons are helpful not simply because they posit the screen as canvas and film-maker as painter, but because they reveal the special way of seeing that Tati cultivated in his audiences. Spectators of *Playtime* were invited to become not thrill-seekers but patient observers, gradually discovering for themselves surprisingly layered and humorous associations in slowly disclosed but

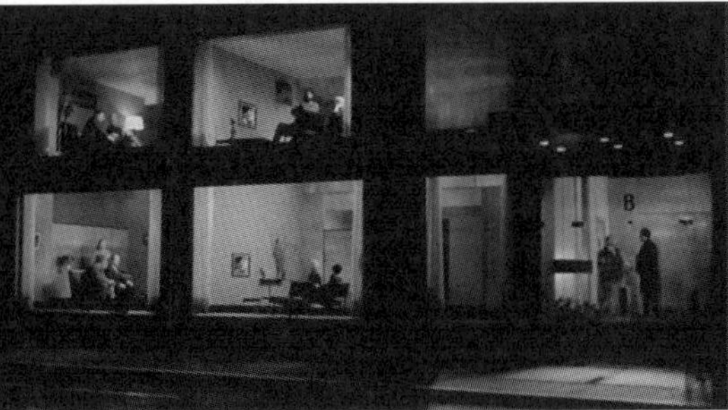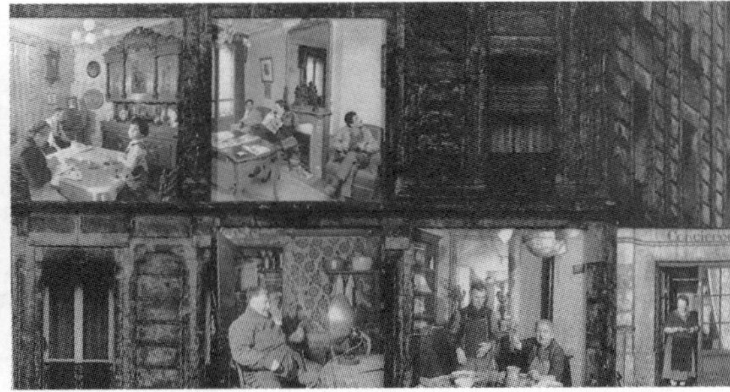

ʒure 4. Picture windows of Schneider's apartment building in *Playtime* (left), and in Robert Doisneau's *La maison des ataires/A Home for Tenants* (1962) (detail, right). *Playtime* (1967), © Public Media Home Vision.

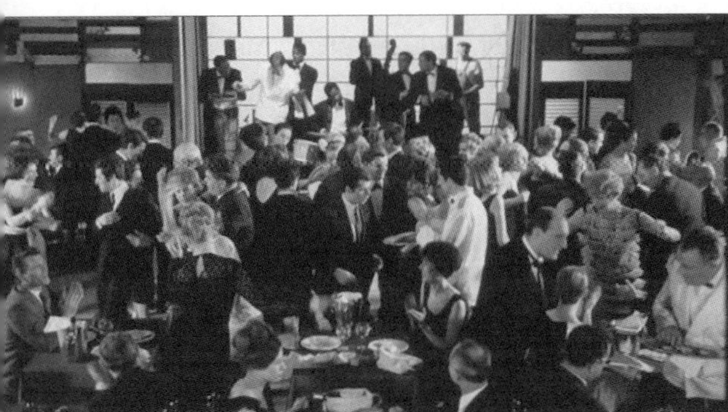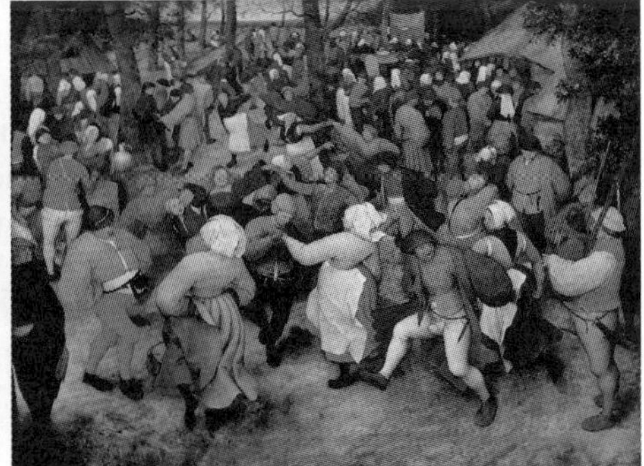

ʒure 5. *Playtime*'s nightclub scene (left); Pieter Bruegel the Elder, *La danse de la mariée en plein air* (1566), Detroit Institute Arts (right). *Playtime* (1967), © Public Media Home Vision.

eventful juxtapositions. As Tati remarked, my work 'demands an entirely different form of attention on the part of the spectator' (1968: 15). Though some moviegoers were baffled, bored and even resentful of *Playtime*'s slow disclosures, Tati was convinced that their openness and prosaic multivalence activated the spectators' poetic and social imagination, allowing them to find and construct their own story.

Tati embraced wide-screen media in ways that negotiated older mediums, including painting, photography and stage performance, as well as the fundamental mediating agency of interpretive observation. What, then, is recovered and revealed through his use of colour film?

Colour film: Polychromatic meaning amid monochromatic tones

Early colour films, like *On the Town* (Donen and Kelly, 1949), were saturated with colour, showing-off what the new media could do with flamboyant costumes and decor. Such films have been characterized as 'medium-driven' (Bellos 1999: 111). *Playtime* takes a subtler approach. Though shot in Technicolor, *Playtime* appears nearly monochromatic, as if shot in black and white. Where colour is featured, it is used selectively to endow particular agents and aspects of the setting with heightened legibility and significance. For instance, most of the anonymous people in *Playtime* are clad, like their milieu, in varied tones of black, blue and cool metallic grey. Against this uniform ground, Hulot sports warm grey, together with tan shoes and striped socks. The Hulot lookalikes typically wear overcoats of beige. The flustered architect is dressed in brown tweed. This close coordination of colour and pattern visually reinforces the interdependence of dress and decor, while subtly distinguishing the architect-like figures whose actions serve to adjust perceptions of that interdependence.

Aside from using colour medium in nuanced ways that build on prior understandings of tonal and textural contrast inherent to black-and-white film, Tati used colour symbolically to reveal narrative and allegorical meaning. Green, for instance, performs as a telling gauge of changing social atmospheres. Near the beginning of *Playtime*, isolated office workers appear lethargic, quarantined within pale-green walls of identical office cubicles. Later, a stifling green neon light poisons the social dynamic in a drugstore, highlighting the sickly stance of customers and the unhealthy adjacency of food and pharmaceuticals. At narrative transitions in the film, dark-green city buses rumble by, recalling the rhythmic pulses of a greater social body. In the nightclub scene, an emerald

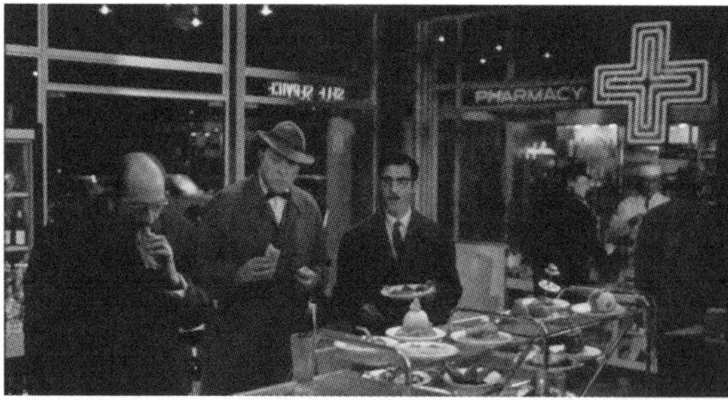

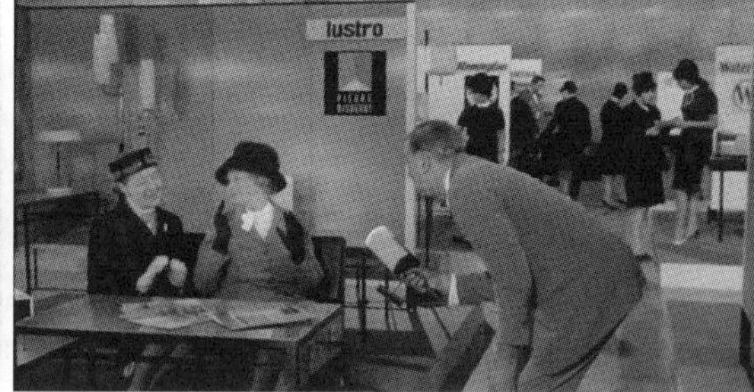

Figure 6. A stifling green light in the pharmacy (left); a delightful red glow at the exposition (right). *Playtime* (1967), © Public Media Home Vision.

green dress identifies Barbara, the only tourist who, like Hulot, regards her surroundings with curiosity. By her wine-drinking, piano-playing and modestly flirtatious behaviour, Barbara – in her sparkling green dress – embodies a desirable and liberating kind of social interaction that is lacking in those pale-green office cubicles. Finally, in a closing exchange, Hulot (somewhat smitten) offers Barbara – via a Hulot-like intermediary – a farewell gift wrapped in a similar sparkling green.

It is equally rewarding to observe Tati's selective use of red. At the start of *Playtime*, red is associated almost exclusively with flagrant emblems of the modern city: automobiles (an Avis car-rental sign); controlled movement (exit and no-entry signs); electronically mediated communication (intercom and telephone lights); and corporate authority (lapel pins of executives). However, amid these dominant signs of modernity, one also finds crimson reminders of life's more sensual pleasures: flowers and flowered hats (tokens of ephemeral beauty and the absent natural landscape); a decorated gift (offered in an absurdly decorous exchange); a jelly dessert (made unappetizingly brown by that ill-placed green light in the drugstore); a flattering glow (eliciting joy at the International Expo); and a red-handled screw-driver (a telltale attribute of the elusive artisans working behind every scene). After the revolutionary events in the nightclub, with its devilishly malfunctioning red neon arrow, red is taken back for the people, being re-associated with common props of everyday life: cigarettes, daily news, morning coffee and goods for exchange in the market. In the closing scene, when the tour of Paris ends in a traffic-jammed roundabout experienced as a cosmopoetic carousel ride, red helium-filled balloons rise amid a proliferation of colourful automobiles, cranes, concrete-mixing trucks, fuel stations, decorated curtain walls, civic monuments and children of every age.

With this selective distribution of colour over the duration of the film, Tati gradually reveals the festive potential latent in the generic city. Reactivating comedy's most archaic function of positive civic renewal, *Playtime* ends with a new beginning, allegorized as colourful vitality emerging from muted grey.

Surround sound: Polysemic languages of silence and gesture

Together with wide-screen formatting and Technicolor, Tati used the newest acoustic media: five-track stereophonic sound. All the same, *Playtime* is permeated by silence. Like the monochromatic set, silence establishes a neutral ground from which meaningful sounds emerge, such as bodily contact with the built environment (especially footsteps), and incongruous sounds having comically symbolic effect, like a rooster's crow at dawn in the midst of the city (Borden 2000; 2002). Tati and his technicians laboured for months creating postproduction sound effects, many of which ironically foreground the background noise of a modern city: the clamour of traffic outside; the hum of fluorescent lights, together with buzzes and blips of mechanical equipment, within. As for dialogue, we hear only isolated snippets of speech amid largely unintelligible murmurs of conversation. As David Bellos puts it (in a rather McLuhanesque way), 'What we hear is not speech as such, but the sound of speech being made' (1999: 124). Nevertheless, *Playtime* is full of articulate discourse, since actors communicate constantly through body language. The film's relative silence allows these significant actions to resound.

With corporeal skills gained from his formative career as a mime performer, Tati directed *Playtime* as an expertly choreographed ballet. Tati even cast a professional ballet dancer to perform a perfect prosaic leap from a delivery truck during a split-second scene in the traffic-jammed roundabout (Bellos 1999: 279). Most of his actors, however, were non-professionals, since he preferred teaching ordinary people to mime themselves. In being meticulously crafted by Tati, every gesture, no matter how banal or brief, was made to speak with the eloquence of mime. This ancient dramatic medium underlies the gestures of *Playtime*'s modern intermediaries, including those of the white-gloved cop directing traffic; the white-gloved guides directing tourists; a white-gloved clerk directing businessmen; and a white-collared receptionist directing phone calls. Mime is also active in the suggestive transformation of social movements. Whereas, at the start of the film, employees travel like vectors, conforming to orthogonal architecture, towards the end, individuals stagger, swagger and stroll, moved more by their own desires and in complex harmony with dynamic social and metaphysical situations. Tati frequently commented on *Playtime*'s intentional transformation of human movement: from straight lines and right angles, to going round in circles (Rosenbaum 1973). Broadly speaking, as adherence to the imposed modern grid loosens, self-expression, collective festivity, regenerative rhythms and cosmic cycles thrive.

On a more detailed level, these movements of social life reveal the important mediating role of embodied routines and habits of inhabitation. Throughout the film, non-verbal cultural practices are satirized and celebrated, but there are two scenes in which such practices become the riveting focus of attention. One occurs when Hulot encounters an old friend across the street. Although Hulot sees the man, he does not recognize him. Even when the friend calls out, 'The army, remember?' Hulot draws a blank. It is only after the friend re-enacts a bit of a military drill that Hulot recalls their bond. This embodied routine remains for Hulot the catalyst of their friendship, the trigger for memory, and the target of attention. Another early scene sets two contrasting manners of waiting in vivid relief. As Hulot waits for Gifford in a vacuous glass-walled room, he roams around with casual inspection: walking cautiously over the tractionless floor; studying the sparse progressive furniture; watching with contentment life in the city, all the while being watched by straight-faced executives whose menacing portraits dominate the space. Then, while Hulot is engrossed with his synthetic seat cushion, an American businessman is escorted into the room. Self-absorbed and comfortably alien to his situation, this man accepts at once the seat he is directed to. Taking no interest in the typical waiting situation, the busy man commences a cacophony of habitual gestures, performed with the accompaniment of various gadgets pulled from his pockets and zippered case. He consults his wristwatch, clips a fingernail, stretches his neck, clears

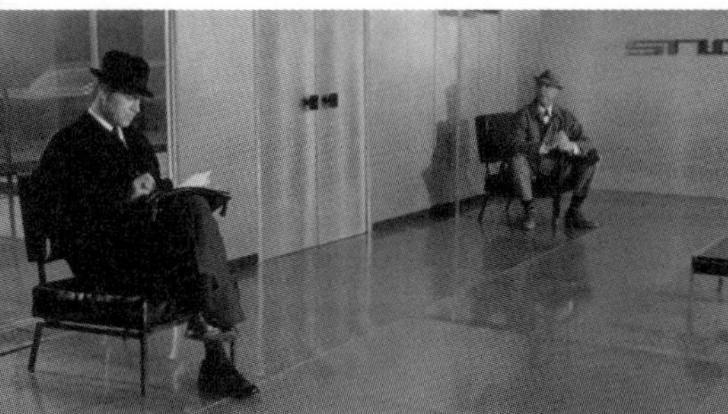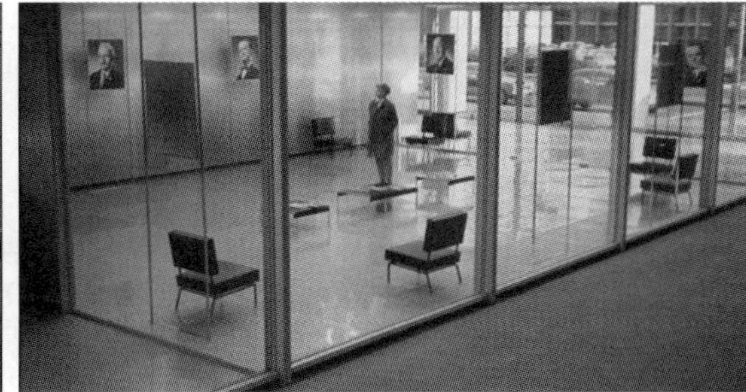

Figure 7. Two situations of waiting: with an American businessman (left); with Hulot (right). *Playtime* (1967), © Public Media Home Vision.

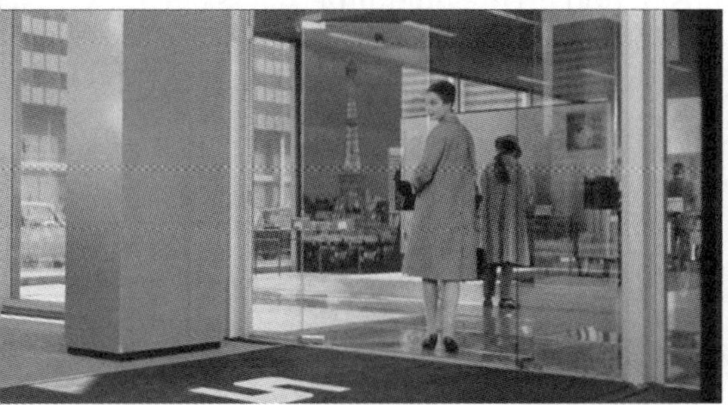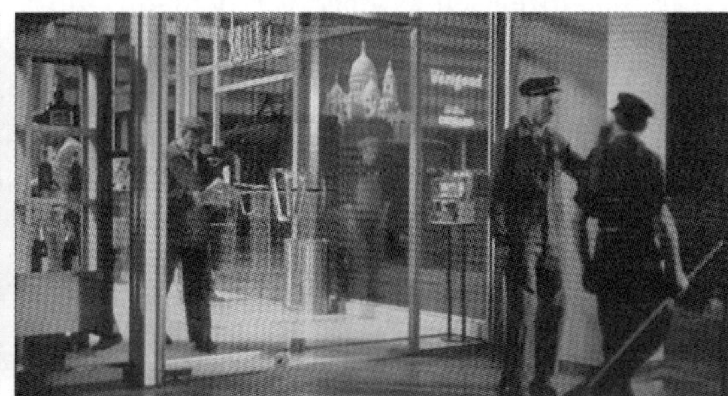

Figure 8. Mediating thresholds at the International Expo (left), and the Drugstore (right). *Playtime* (1967), © Public Media Home Vision.

his nose, smacks his lips, retrieves a form, signs his name, ingests a mint, and inhales antihistamine, all the while brushing and adjusting his pristine attire. His movements are executed with mechanical precision and punctuated with percussive taps, sniffs, pops and zips. While this man noisily fidgets, Hulot (our tacit guide) watches in reflective silence, inviting audiences, likewise, to observe the situated practices of everyday life with comparable interpretive intensity.

More as a witness than a judge, Hulot testifies in profound silence to the 'speechless speaking' embodied in patterns of life pulsing in and around the waiting room. Such non-verbal scenes of *Playtime* should not be reduced to either Tati's suppression of language or Hulot's loss for words. Rather, to paraphrase philosopher Hans Georg Gadamer, there is more to say about such life events than speech will allow (Kidder 2013: 27).

In each instance of multi-mediation described above, Tati made use of the most advanced cinematic media while involving strategies learned through prior mediums and more basic modes of interpretive engagement – a common strategy in media arts, much discussed by McLuhan (1964: 193). In other words, Tati was driven by a hybrid enthusiasm: both for new media, and for what these media reactivate and reveal about human practices and situations. Somewhat like Hulot, and other Hulot-like intermediaries, *Playtime*'s novel media (70mm film, Technicolor and surround sound) impart their influence while withdrawing from prominence, providing novel cinematic experiences that simultaneously renew manifold engagement with everyday reality.

Mediating thresholds: Where everyone becomes involved

In conjunction with human intermediaries and artistic media, *Playtime* features architecture itself as an active mediator. Most conspicuously, the ubiquitous glass surfaces of *Playtime* perform in media-reflexive ways, presenting fleeting images of an elusive Paris to characters in the film, much as the cinematic screen presents flickering images of city life to spectators. Yet, media reflexivity is not the only message. Along with acting like a cinematic (or digital) screen, the glass surfaces of *Playtime* also directly invite and enable human exchange by performing socially mediating roles in the midst of use. Those grand Parisian monuments appear on moving glass doors not arbitrarily, but at specific transitional moments in the narrative, just when these doors are being used for common activities: going in and coming out; receiving and discharging guests; and serving as a shared site of face-to-face exchange. Moreover, on these ordinary occasions, the reflected cultural landmarks conjure a specific variety of correspondences, comically and critically expanding on prosaic activities underway. The Eiffel Tower, an elegant civic expression of nineteenth-century technology, is glimpsed as Barbara enters an International Exposition promoting trivial twentieth-century gadgetry. The Arc de Triomphe, a monument to Napoleon's foreign exploits, appears as a hotel concierge opens the door for arriving sightseers, welcoming the onslaught of neocolonial tourism. Having conquered the sites, these weary tourists (commodified *spolia* in hand) march through the triumphant archway on their way to king-size beds. A moment later, the Obelisk at Place de la Concorde appears in the same hotel windows as a different group of tourists depart for the nightclub. This obelisk, a 'gift' from Egypt erected at a site linked to the violent aftermath of the French Revolution, would seem to point not only to its own dynastic origins and the fall of the French monarchy, but also to future turmoil at the exotic Royal Garden. Finally, the Basilica de Sacré-Coeur in Montmartre, a long-thriving site of sacred and artistic confluence, is reflected in the doorway of the Drugstore as a deliveryman engages in friendly chatter with a street-sweeper during their morning routines.

Beyond providing postcard-like reflections of celebrated monuments at salient moments, these dynamically mediated thresholds spark reflection on society's technological, political and cultural practices. By shifting attention – to and fro – between the mundane routines of Tativille and the monumental works of Paris, these thresholds fuse present and past, typical and exemplary, ephemeral and permanent. Performing what Gadamer called 'twofold mediation', each encounter gathers focused attention, while redirecting attention 'to the greater whole of the life context which it accompanies' (1993 [1975]: 108). Insightful reflections emerge both in the midst of use, being 'elicited from the flux of manifold reality' (Gadamer 1986: 129), and in the midst of comparative thought, arising from dialogical and reciprocal awareness. These architectural thresholds of *Playtime*, thus, open up space and time for serious hermeneutic 'play'. This liberating yet grounded form of interpretive interplay is a mediating activity crucial to understanding our complex participation in civic life.

Whereas glass surfaces on some occasions readily facilitate social exchange, others in the film problematize and hinder human interaction: as when a stranger on the street seeks the favour of a doorman to light his cigarette, but is obstructed by intervening glass; or when Hulot strives to meet Gifford face-to-face, but is misled by reflections. Such disruptions turn modern architecture's promise of transparency and fluid interconnectivity into instances of discontinuity and disorientation. But these scenes are equally important for reinforcing the importance of architectural thresholds as interactive sites where the medium of social exchange becomes accessible for interpretation. Throughout *Playtime*, the experience of the city becomes most intensely mediated at thresholds: at windows, doorways, vestibules, landings, security checkpoints, commercial checkout counters; and other middle spaces between buildings, between office partitions, between insides and outsides, even between cars. Hulot's entrance into the film from the socially entangled back door of a public bus, and his farewell gift exchange with Barbara (via a Hulot-like intermediary) at the front door

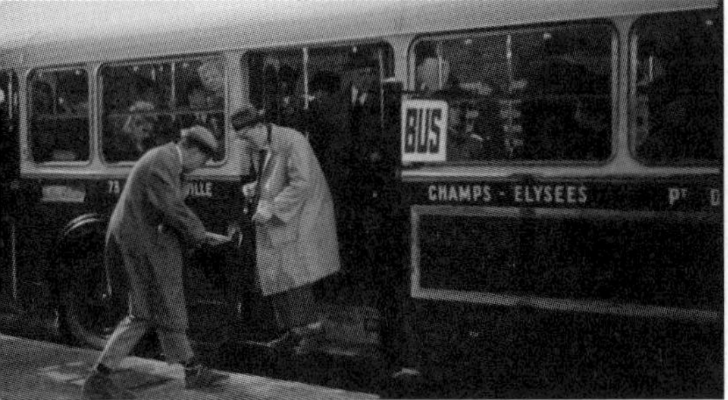

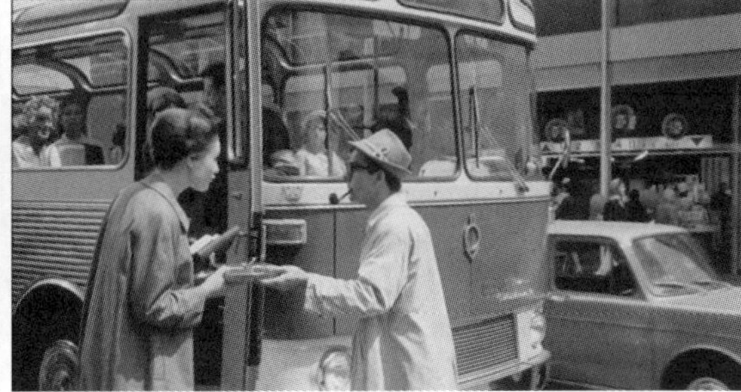

Figure 9. Hulot's socially-entangled entry (left), and exit (right) from the film. *Playtime* (1967), © Public Media Home Vision.

of a departing tour bus, establishes mediating thresholds as a primary paradigm of the film's double plot. Its tragicomic climax happens at the main entrance to the nightclub. While disagreeing over whether to stay or leave, Hulot (who wishes to go) and his old army friend (turned nightclub doorman) inadvertently shatter the glass door. However, although the glass pane is gone, the socially mediating threshold remains active, being embodied in the decorous gestures of Hulot, the miming doorman and the people themselves. Bearing these examples in mind, we may conclude as follows: if we are to consider *Playtime*'s doors and windows as 'media' reflexive, and the film in general as contributing to our understanding of mediated cities, then we must include the social entanglements and interpretive exchanges enacted across these thresholds as fundamental modes of mediation.

Conclusion: Enabling interplay

When asked about his critical stance toward modern architecture, Tati typically shifted attention to his more important underlying motive. In a 1981 interview, he offered this telling response, '*Je ne suis pas architecte, je suis là pour defender les locataires* [I am not an architect, I am here to defend the inhabitants]' (Sichère 1985: 86). Tati frequently qualified his role as 'defending' the people (Gilliatt 1973: 39), acting as an 'arbiter' or 'attorney of the human being' (Tati 1977: 03:20–30). This chapter has similarly attempted to defend the mediating agencies of interpretive individuals and social situations, together with advocating for a richly layered approach to artistic media grounded in ethical concerns. This is not to say that media is the only message, nor that the kinds of basic and performative media valued here preclude or invalidate digital media. Rather, the argument is that by loosening our fixation on mediating gadgets, we can more fully engage the subtle but enabling interplay of underlying social, situational and interpretive agencies that make us, and our cities, human. In this synthetic way we might – with an active imagination and proper sense of humour – sustain those most efficacious modes of mediation that can help us construct viable cities, pursue mutual understanding, and sustain our shared capacity for delight.

References

Bellos, D. (1993), *Georges Perec: A Life in Words*, Boston: D.R. Godine.
———— (1999), *Jacques Tati: His Life and Art*, London: Harvill Press.
Borden, I. (2000), 'Material sounds: Jacques Tati and modern architecture', *Architectural Design*, 70: 1, pp. 26–32.
———— (2002), 'Architecture's *Playtime*: The pleasures of city modernism in the films of Jacques Tati', in N. Leach (ed.), *The Hieroglyphics of Space: Reading and Experiencing the Modern Metropolis*, London: Routledge, pp. 217–35.

Cairns, G. (2013), '*Playtime*: A commentary on the art of the Situationists, the philosophy of Henri Lefebvre and the architecture of the modern movement', in G. Cairns (ed.), *The Architecture of the Screen: Essays in Cinematographic Space*, Chicago and Bristol: Intellect, pp. 97–107.

Ede, F. and Goudet, S. (2002), *Playtime*, Paris: Cahiers du Cinéma.

Gadamer, H. (1986), 'The play of art' (trans. N. Walker), in R. Bernasconi (ed.), *The Relevance of the Beautiful and Other Essays*, Cambridge: Cambridge University Press, pp. 123–30.

——— ——— (1993 [1975]), 'Play as the clue to ontological explanation', *Truth and Method: Second Revised Edition* (trans. J. Weinsheimer and D. G. Marshall), New York: Continuum, pp. 101–10.

Gilliatt, P. (1973), 'Profiles: Playing', *The New Yorker*, 27 January, pp. 35–49.

——— ——— (1976), *Jacques Tati*, London: Woburn Press.

Guillory, J. (2010), 'Genesis of the media concept', *Critical Inquiry*, 36: 2, pp. 321–62.

Hilliker, L. (2002), 'In the modernist mirror: Jacques Tati and the Parisian landscape', *The French Review*, 76: 2, pp. 318–29.

Kahn, A. (1992), 'Playtime with architects', *Design Book Review*, 24, Spring, pp. 22–29.

Leatherbarrow, D. (2000), *Uncommon Ground: Architecture, Technology and Topography*, Cambridge, MA: MIT Press.

McCullough, M. (2013), *Ambient Commons: Attention in the Age of Embodied Information*, Cambridge, MA: MIT Press.

McLuhan, M. (1964), *Understanding Media: The Extensions of Man*, New York: McGraw-Hill.

Ockman, J. (2000), 'Architecture in a mode of distraction: Eight takes on Jacques Tati's *Playtime*', in M. Lamster (ed.), *Architecture and Film*, New York: Princeton Architectural Press, pp. 171–96.

Penz, F. (1997), 'Architecture in the films of Jacques Tati', in F. Penz and M. Thomas (eds), *Cinema and Architecture: Méliès, Mallet-Stevens, Multimedia*, London: British Film Institute, pp. 62–69.

Perec, G. (1999), *Species of Spaces and Other Pieces* (trans. and ed. John Sturrock), London: Penguin.

Rosenbaum, J. (1973), 'Tati's democracy', *Film Comment*, 9, May–June, pp. 36–41.

——— ——— (1995 [1983]), 'The death of Hulot', *Placing Movies: The Practice of Film Criticism*, Berkeley: University of California Press, pp. 163–79.

Sichère, M. (1985), 'Jacques Tati, "Où est l'architecte?"', *Monuments Historiques*, 137, Feb-Mar, pp. 85–90.

Tati, J. (1968), 'Le champ large: Entretien avec Jacques Tati par Jean-André Fieschi et Jean Narboni', *Cahiers du Cinéma*, 199, March, pp. 8–21.

——— ——— (1977), 'Jacques Tati Interview from 1977' [Interview by Derek Malcolm, Savoy Hotel, London – Online video], http://www.theseventhart.org/dailies/2013/09/26/jacques-tati-interview-from-1977/. Accessed 26 May 2015.

Thompson, K. (1979), '*Playtime:* Comedy on the edge of perception', *Wide Angle*, 3: 2, pp. 18–25.

Notes

1. Kahn (1992); Penz (1997); Ockman (2000); Borden (2000; 2002); Hilliker (2002); and Cairns (2013).
2. Tati retold this anecdote about modelling the Hulot character on an architect in several interviews, including a public discussion with Albert Johnson following the American premier of *Playtime* at the 1972 San Francisco International Film Festival. This interview is included on the Criterion Collection 2006 DVD Edition of *Playtime*.
3. Tati's architect collaborators included Raymond Laroche, who designed the elegant street lamps at Orly Airport, which Tati featured in the opening and closing scenes of *Playtime* (Ede and Goudet 2002: 38); Eugène Roman, who designed and built Tativille; and Jacques Lagrange, who produced numerous design models, sketches and collages for each of Tati's films (Bellos 1999: 206–07, 265).
4. *L'infra-ordinaire* is a neologism penned by George Perec in 'Approaches de quoi', first published in *Cause Commune* (February, 1973), republished in *Species of Spaces* (1999: 209–10). It is unlikely that Tati read Perec, but Perec did watch the films of Tati (Bellos 1993: 168).

Chapter 5

Film and the urban nightmare: Pier Vittorio Aureli's
city-archipelagos as urbanities woven from media images
in Pete Travis's *Dredd* and Christopher Nolan's
The Dark Knight Rises

Maciej Stasiowski

Introduction

In his book, *The Possibility of an Absolute Architecture* (2011), Pier Vittorio Aureli outlines architecture and urbanism as opposing forces that shape the plan of the city. While architecture, in his study, generally denotes single, site-specific interventions, the process of urbanization is understood after Ildefons Cerdà's initial use of the term, as an 'over-expanding and all-encompassing apparatus that is the basis of modern forms of governance' (Aureli 2011: X). This distinction is crucial to Aureli's argument hailing architectural forms – which he analyses through the example of the architectural, while also somewhat utopian projects by Oswald Mathias Ungers, Étienne-Louis Boullée and Giovanni Battista Piranesi – as those which delineate, regulate, direct or break the flows of urbanization.

The processes themselves, in reality – even though mainly described in terms of velocity and dynamics – occur rather slowly, and are subjugated to a changing dynamic in their urban models. In her article published in the *System City* issue of *Architectural Design* (2013), Marina Lathouri outlines the ways in which urban expansion has been mapped through the ages, noting that:

> reflection on the city was historically situated in a space of economic and administrative relations, and not solely on the basis of the symbolic relationship between a geometrical figure and the territory. Yet in the 19th century the city came to be thought of as an open and dynamic system, its planning essentially linked to patterns of distribution of land and population as forms of spatial organization. (Lathouri 2013: 34)

The dynamic quality of this model calls for a time-based medium that would adequately represent its behaviour, while also discussing it on the grounds of utopian proposals for cities or city-scale architectures, like Piranesi's 'Campo Marzio dell'antica Roma' – a speculative *vedute*, characterized by a critical rhetoric toward excavated buildings and ruins, and exuberant, collaged form that reveals a utopian 'hinge' in the sense of a reinterpretation of the Roman antiquity. At an intersection of this pictorial practice and the tradition of utopian literature, twentieth-century cinematic representations of urbanism and architecture came to undertake the role of graphical forays into new speculative territories. With the proliferation of recent futuristic and superhero epics, which are prone to formulaic visions of dystopian societies, box office hits seem like an ideal place to conduct this debate.

Mainstream cinema governs itself by rules of narrative progression and condensation. Descriptive, contemplative shots are mostly reserved for arthouse films and documentaries. Still, each plot has to unfold in a concrete setting, which most frequently refers to a specific aesthetic in urban/architectural history, even when under the guise of the fantastic. Furthermore, the evolution of a cinematic language over more than one hundred years has come to develop surrogate ways to depict amorphous concepts and entities. Cinema came to favour, due to production constraints (financial, technical, temporal), the synecdoche – representing whole through part – which allows one to depict whole cities by showing only a cluster of buildings. This substitution allows not only for an encapsulation of the material, but simultaneously invokes iconic, media-circulated images to stand in for an urban/architectural issue that would otherwise have had to be discussed at a greater length by means of numerous examples. Let's call upon a scene from *Brazil* (Gilliam, 1985), in which Sam Lowry's character enters into the Ministry of Information. The building's unrivalled grandeur and geometric rigidity evokes both Albert Speer's architecture of the Third Reich, and its French revolutionary predecessor – the designs of Étienne-Louis Boullée. Onyx tiles only add up to the palette of subliminal terror transmitted through set design. Here, iconicity acts as an intertextual reference, although it could also be read at a more basic, even subliminal level – through associative connotations with the colour black. Still, the image quoted appears as a sort of intrusion, isolated (while also detached from the differentiated types of architecture we see in *Brazil*), seemingly belonging somewhere in between the viewer's overinterpretation[1] of the filmic text and a digression, adding mood through interior design to a scene which otherwise would not have been so appealing. It is reminiscent of one aspect of Aureli's book, which interprets many building projects as micro-manifestos of a city – the sort of architecture that ought to be extrapolated into urban form.

Method and analysis

Monument-images

Discussing iconic images as if they were stand-alone architectural constructions within a 'sea' of the film's narrative, forwards an argument that these forms of visual intertextuality do not only programme our bias towards certain problems of an urban and architectural nature (as depicted and incorporated into the plot, and thus being a part of the director's/ scriptwriter's critical commentary), but that they also function as forms of televised, or at least media-circulated, collective memory. This occurs not because of their archival or documentary nature – as in the case of a direct quotation from film archives, showing the demolition of Pruitt-Igoe or the destruction of Mostar bridge – but because of the tension they create within the structure of the film. In this we refer to both the context of the narrative and the general image of the fictitious city (Gotham, Megacity One), that the scenes and sequences build up to.

In *Cinema 1: The Movement-image* (1986), Gilles Deleuze presented a classical-Hollywood model of cinema (along with European pre-modernist films), as far from being a sequence of static images brought to life by the movement of the film strip through a projector (Deleuze 1986: 56–70). Instead, he coined the term 'movement-image', in order to view the portions of projected film reel as 'immobile sections of movement', to be thought of as freeze-framed actions rather than successions of still lives (Deleuze 1986: 9–11). These sections are highly charged with the sensory-motor quality of the real-life events they refer to (and which they reanimate within the logic of the film's plot). For Aureli (2011), the fragmentary architectures of Piranesi and Boullée acted as break points, regulating the flow and distribution of urban fabric (therefore the overall structure, on the scale of the city, gained an archipelago metaphor – a conglomerate of architectural islands upon the sea of urbanism). Key scenes revealing urban fragments and architecture-filled frames – as portrayed in cinema – create an image of the city in a manner similar to Aureli's, although through cinematography and montage.

Still, the transformations which a 'city system' undergoes are far too amorphous to grasp. The issue, whether we ourselves construct an image of the city as a topography of urban mesh or as a juxtaposition of monumental architectures, has been addressed throughout and ever since Kevin Lynch's book *The Image of the City* (Lynch 1960: 40, 46–49). With cinema – and its present focus on terrorism and other threats to the twenty-first century metropolis – the discussion re-emerges. In fact, both case studies presented here act upon a synecdoche of the city, rendering it an archipelago – an iconic remembrance surrounded by a contemporary sprawl of urbanity. Will urban decay or 'urbicide' obliterate their distinctive image? As films remain the biggest suppliers of iconography that goes beyond a merely archival function, their voice might just now become relevant. They interlock fragmentary memories of the déjà vu and capture a dynamic outline of conflicts unravelling at the heart of urbanism.

Mapping the field of cinematic narratives set in a modern *polis* (or its future rendition), this chapter aims to show how cinematic images (taken from two blockbusters of 2012 – Travis's *Dredd* and Nolan's *The Dark Knight Rises*) carry a load of historical references and contextualized meanings despite being hidden in 'discreet packaging' that does not disrupt the plot's flow. Nevertheless, it is made obvious when interpreting the film text against a background of architectural/urban history (as conveyed through iconic televised images).

Film overview

In both *Dredd* and *The Dark Knight Rises*, which coincidently are comic book adaptations, the metropolis plays a crucial part. Both highlight the problems of rampant urbanism, overpopulation and possible independence/separateness of city-states through portrayals of urban turmoil. From the standpoint of a rhetorical device, this creates an opportunity in the plot for an examination of the failings that a present-day metropolis is subjected to. In order to emphasize these crises, *Dredd* and *The Dark Knight Rises* support their argumentation that such visual references relate prominently to specific episodes in the history of urban form. They are brought up in the text in order to contrast two distinct portraits of the 'burning city', the first (*Dredd*) being condensed into the form of a vertical structure of a block of flats, or rather, a megastructure; while the second (*The Dark Knight Rises*) prefers a horizontal arrangement of its plot's hotspots, within an enclosed fragment of the city.

In the films, we are looking at two imaginary agglomerations modelled after nightmarish versions of the biggest American cities. Gotham City, even in its comic book form, was made to resemble the morbid renderings of Hugh Ferriss (2005), which presented fantastical, exaggerated views of New York and Chicago. Ferriss metamorphosed early-twentieth-century skyscrapers into stalagmite towers growing out of the night's empty streets. All were shown at a low angle making the building's form even more perpendicular, while dark tones and a greyish palette communicate their gigantic scale. Gotham, in Nolan's third installment of the Batman series, is less grim than in Ferris's originals, while still depicted in cold tones reminding one of Manhattan in mid-winter. In turn, the second cinematic attempt at John Wagner's *Judge Dredd* franchise (1977–), supplies us with the scorched-earth look of a post-World War III urban mesh of tower blocks, labyrinthine underpasses, and vast plots of land resembling forsaken battlefields. Megacity One is an overpopulated city. Instead of being terminated, war shifted from air raids and mass operations to conflicts in the neighbourhood; now battles rage among residents of megablocks, among them is Peach Trees – the one we, the viewers, will be made to behold. In an attempt to materialize visionary projects of the 1960s – the megastructures of Yona Friedman's 'Spatial City',[2] Paolo Soleri's arcologies,[3] or the Metabolists' cubic hotels – *Dredd*'s set design team distilled those proposals to large blocks of compacted (or rather, overpacked), vertically organized self-sufficient cities. Travis's film operates upon this city-in-miniature, in spatial and political terms, as the distribution of governmental hierarchy is by definition top-down. We watch the mobsters taking control of Peach Trees megablock and settling on the rooftop, where all CCTV monitors and steering systems are situated, while citizens taken hostage are made to crowd together on the ground levels.

There is a slight difference in pacing in these two filmic texts. While the conflict driving the narrative in *Dredd* is introduced in the opening scenes, *The Dark Knight Rises* gradually builds up towards the second part of the movie in which the villain (Bane) carries out his terroristic revolution – taking it to the streets – while Gotham's protagonists (Batman and the police forces) are literally trapped in the sewers. With such radical overturning of hierarchy, the film's plot proceeds along the lines of 'carnivalization'. Mikhail Bakhtin's term describes the rationale behind most festivities, involving a temporal suspension of prevailing law and order, and an inversion of its symbols (Bakhtin 1999: 122). Before *The Dark Knight Rises*'s plot moves on to 'Lent' and restoration, cinematography will supply the viewer with a wealth of visual associations and media-circulated images which refer to historical events probably chosen due to their high levels of violence; they are comprised of spectacular and drastic footage bearing iconic significance. Neither of the films recreate the events of September 11 directly, although they display similar gravitas. By this strategy, both films present the city as yet another – or maybe the most important – hostage.

Gotham détourned

Probably the most interesting part of Christopher Nolan's film occurs around seventy minutes into the movie, when the banished and disgraced Batman/Bruce Wayne disappears below ground, expelled to a Moorish bottom-of-the-well prison. At the same time, Bane's plan of seizing and severing the city-island from the mainland meets no obstacles on the way to its execution. However, the sequence showing stages of the plan being carried out presents the viewer with hardly more than discontinuous fragments. We watch large trucks cruising the streets, masked villains hurrying about, Bane grinning. We are unable to grasp the plan's totality in the course of its unfolding, at least not until we are to witness its 'inauguration ceremony' held at a hijacked football stadium. Then and there, Bane sets off the explosives, isolating Gotham from the hinterland metropolis, turning it – like Manhattan – into a nearly desolate island. To raise the stakes even higher, Tom Hardy's character gives the city an ultimatum – a deadline synchronized with the nuclear reactor's core meltdown time; the same reactor that is hidden somewhere in the back of a moving vehicle, one among many, constantly circling the (already shrunken) city. It is a game of cups with two empty trucks and a ticking time bomb in the third. Unless the mechanism of this complicated plot is dismantled, the city remains an urban-game with an impossible set of rules.

Despite all attractions described above, the carnivalization of Gotham also has a downside. New, self-proclaimed authorities impose their rule through subverting architectural symbols of former power, starting from the stadium, which – in this situation – stands in for the central square, while the municipal hall becomes its own medieval caricature, a kangaroo court. Limits of the city, too, are rendered grimly literal, functioning as execution grounds that mark the end of existence for the former authorities accused of treason, doing it with the expanse of a frozen river ready to crack under a convicts' feet. Wealthier citizens' houses are being looted and prisons emptied, thus ex-criminals roam the streets. Martial law has been imposed. There is hardly any traffic. The city is like a limb amputated from the arteries that would normally pump blood into the transportation system. Due to Bane's threat of bomb detonation with the first person who tries to escape, Gotham automatically becomes a 'gunpoint situation' for the military surrounding this islet city. Even though army forces besiege it, they are not able to do anything else but helplessly behold the spectacle. That is the very definition of a 'situation'.

Along with other members of the Situationist International, Guy Debord frequently criticized the changes made during the Haussmannization of Paris, which, in his opinion, had destroyed the 'old town' by broadening the boulevards, eradicating important monuments and transforming the collective imaginary of the city. As many of the changes made were strategic to preventing any future revolution from happening, Debord, himself a revolutionist, sought to proclaim a need for the individual and radical reappropriation of city space; a plan to be executed by means of intuitive drifting ('psychogeography') and responsiveness to affective vistas (Sadler 1999: 76–95). The Situationists were trying to invent an alternate tactic of experiencing the city as well as developing a critical look at the commercialism of contemporary life, generally through the appropriation and overturning of the iconography of capitalist culture, in an act called détournement, or 'the assimilation, reuse and redirection of images and objects' (Spiller 2007: 44). This hijacking of symbols, taking them out of context and putting together in new arrangements, was expected to create collage-like structures of inhomogeneous elements. The juxtaposition was there – as in the case of cinema – to create tension. In *The Dark Knight Rises*, we can see a détournement in the act of reappropriating the sports facility. Bane's troops do not only cause the football pitch to collapse and reveal levels of concrete-slabs underneath; they take the game away from the assembled audience and introduce their own 'game' into the streets of Gotham. Even the antagonist's exposé sounds more like the announcement of a set of rules rather than an official welcome. The irony goes even further, as, in place of blowing the referee's whistle, a sudden noise sounds the execution of the first hostage.

Simultaneously, yet in the background, a second détournement is in progress, as the images of a captive city start to sabotage the assumed unity of the film's narrative – the homogeneity of the Dark Knight's world (Sadler 1999: 17). We can identify this as commentary, made more explicit by those scenes and sequences which do not propel the plot forwards. They connect all the drastic events depicted in the film with images and footage originating from mass media and broadcasting history. In the case of *The Dark Knight Rises'* 'reign of terror' portion of the movie, we can rediscover its source in the footage transmitted by CNN as coverage of the Iraq War (2003–11), and the London bombings of 2005 – events that would still be vivid in the minds of a 2012 film audience. However, some shots date back even further, like the crane view of an empty street covered in snow, complete with a tank patrol. It could have been taken out of the archives containing footage reels showing the first days after the introduction of Martial Law in Poland, back in December of 1981. The same can be said of the troops stationed at the city's perimeter, and how they are depicted, because similar scenes date back to the Serbian siege of Sarajevo (1992–96) – a time when television viewers were fed with an overload of drastic imagery, as CNN and the BBC constantly reported on the state of a deteriorating city, far in the Balkans – a slow death that the Western audience was forced to watch.

Each of these (historical) event-images brings a superfluous contextual span of a greater breadth, and might be treated as an additional lens to calibrate the perspective through which we focus our view upon the city. Bane's order to sever the connection with the mainland, in a spectacular scene depicting the destruction of bridges, adds another level to the argument (Siege of Mostar). Moreover, this televisual iconoclasm brings back a memory of crisis with each of the 'event-images' recalled; a breaking point, when the city – a prevailing modern form of mass habitation – had become an entrapment, making citizens vulnerable to terroristic acts and topographical dead ends in an urban war. The role of 'media-digested' images is all the more important, for they preserve actual memories, relevant to both the cinematic and non-cinematic metropolis.

Dredd the hof

In *Dredd*, the city becomes even more concentrated, engulfed and cornered. The film itself relies heavily on fragmented and partial perspectives of hard-cut actions, in order to create a compelling mental picture of the metropolis in a state of crisis. In Pete Travis' film, objectives are set straight – two protagonists were sent to pacify a building full of criminals. Slo-Mo is the drug that acts as a MacGuffin,[4] mainly to introduce a substitute currency in the Peach Trees block, which becomes overrun by the Ma-Ma gang. Judges are called in and trapped by the drug cartel, right after their arrival at the crime scene. Ma-Ma, its leader, 'hijacks' the tower block, sealing it shut from the outside world. In consequence, this vertical city turns into something that resembles a closed thermodynamic system in which all former activities instantly die down. Surprisingly, entropy seems to operate here in reverse, as the two Judges standing against a platoon of criminals cool down the overheated mob setup.

The block takes the shape of a gargantuan social-housing project executed in the form of a high-rise, or to be more precise, a 'hof', if one refers to the 1920s Red Vienna-period[5] superblocks, nicknamed *Des Volkswohnungspalasts* (workers' palaces), 'whose spatial and programmatic principle was based on monumental interior courtyard reminiscent of the monastic typology of the cloister' (Aureli 2011: 201). The cloister is not necessarily a misleading comparison, for the inhabitants of Peach Trees are ordered straightaway to stay in their 'cells', while the Judges-made-criminals trudge like righteous monks through this crime-infested place. The residents were ordered by Ma-Ma not to coalesce with law enforcers. Unable to seek any help from them, the enclosed city turns desolate in the worst *High Noon* (Zinnemann, 1952) kind of way. The *Dredd* version of a hof structure is therefore an exemplary type of monolithic, self-sustaining architecture against its own good.

Each superblock was equipped with basic community services such as a clinic, library, laundry, gym, restaurant, and kindergarten. These facilities were designed to provide the superblock with both self-sufficiency and monumental character that was intended to convey the political image of these complexes through the use of their collective spaces. (Aureli 2011: 201)

Most of these spaces are clearly visible in the first shots revealing the interior courtyard and ground-level streets inside Peach Trees. This system ceases to function without the daily flow of commodities, supplies and services. As in Nolan's film, there is the prospect of a China syndrome but without any specified 'meltdown' time. In Peach Trees, events unfold according to a typical time-bomb disarmament scenario. The system corrodes because of two forces acting at the same time. First is the isolation – lack of support and maintenance, disconnectedness from the outside world; as it is sealed off, there is neither a chance for makeshift aid nor for overriding supervision. Second is the criminal element, which causes disorder and mayhem, unrest in the community and overall dysfunctionality. From all this comes a mechanical destruction of the building from within, which in *Dredd* occurs mainly due to use of heavy artillery.

There is also a third factor at work; one concerning the issue of size. In an observation made by Rem Koolhaas in his *S, M, L, XL* (Koolhaas, Mau and Werlemann, 1995), the architecture of 'bigness' is defined as that which cannot be controlled by a single architect, and comes into being as a sprouting of a multiplicity derived from basic geometrical forms.

> The architecture of bigness artificially reconstructs the city just as the city is under the assault of urbanization. 'Bigness' refers to the scale of gigantic architecture forms – not those developed horizontally, as in the case of megastructures or suburban sprawl, the two primary oppositions for the American postwar city, but rather those that develop vertically as finite architectural forms. (Aureli 2011: 218–19)

In this way, Koolhaas (through his research undertaken with The Office of Metropolitan Architecture OMA) and Aureli demonstrate that 'bigness' is the kind of architecture that tends to get out of control. Its scale diminishes the significance of its inhabitants. Thus, the inhabitants of Peach Trees are forced to submit and take sides in the conflict, which becomes a showcase of attitudes towards the new authority as well as to the former one as represented by the now-'outlawed' Judges; when read contextually, these are in fact representatives of 'architects' versus superintendents. On one side, the Judges enforce commitment through Dredd's propaganda of 'harsh justice'. On the other, Ma-Ma, through the radio node, promises, threatens and voices her grudge against the indifference of the Megacity One's government, underlying her motivation for this blackmail and the residents' current situation. Analogically to the web of relations in *The Dark Knight Rises*, social politics of the small-scale city model are mapped out spatially (top-down governance), as well as encrypted into architectural interiors. In between outbursts of gunfire and violence, that frequently take place in *Dredd*, we witness scene-setting shots of deserted corridors, empty staircases and devastated hallways sprayed all over with graffiti. There are broken light bulbs, scattered debris, walls covered with visible cracks, floors infested with litter and garbage. Deterioration arrived here much sooner than the final havoc.

Similar scenes can be found in Chad Friedrichs' documentary *The Pruitt-Igoe Myth* (2011). Here, they are compiled from archival footage. We see settings very much like those in *Dredd*, which are marked by signs of wreckage. The director's aim was to come up with answers to questions about the downfall of the housing complex. The 'catastrophe' of Minoru Yamasaki's project, epitomized by its subsequent tearing down, was hailed by Charles Jencks as the end of modernism in architecture (Laurence 2014: 9–10). For a little more than two decades it was the modernist ideal of standardized living. Friedrichs points out several interlocking reasons, one of them being advancing de-urbanization in the 1960s, the so-called 'white flight'; segregation; rising crime rates; deteriorating conditions; lack of police protection; and an isolationism policy caused by frequent reports of patrol cars or fire trucks being attacked on arrival at Pruitt-Igoe. 'It was too big, too unmonitored. Criminals could get in and get out', says one of the former inhabitants. Or, as Koolhaas writes: 'if Bigness transforms architecture, its accumulation generates a new kind of city. [...] Bigness no longer needs the city; it competes with the city; it represents the city; it pre-empts the city; or better still, it *is* the city' (Koolhaas, Mau and Werlemann 1995: 514–15, original emphasis).

Even before any images of the structure's demolition were circulated via mass media, TV viewers would connect the sight of broken windows, out-of-order elevators and dried blood splattered upon the concrete, in connection with the name Pruitt-Igoe. Switching from black-and-white footage to CGI-enhanced colour, old blood in *Dredd* becomes replaced with fresh blood. Bullet-ridden walls are offered by the film as extra. Also, the hypothesis about the downfall of the complex matches the argument in the script. We could easily view the protagonist, (Judge) Dredd, as the executioner in command of the renovation project. Unlike temporary alliances with criminals, the one carried out by force strongly opposes isolationism and consent for deterioration due to criminal activity. In Dredd's hof, Pruitt-Igoe will likely not happen.

One interesting aspect of the film's rhetoric is that – contrary to J. G. Ballard's *High-rise* (2005 [1975]) – the structure is not condemned as pathological from its inception (at least, any reading of the architecture as pathological is not deemed as the chief perpetrator). 'Bigness' in *Dredd* becomes gargantuan due to the lack of proper maintenance, as well as of 'proper spirit' that would unify the community. It also suffers because of desolation. One of the general flaws in Pruitt-Igoe was negligence to fostering a sense of community for those resettled there. Blacks were separated from whites and strict rules were imposed on families applying, thus barring many people from occupying the complex. As Friedrichs' documentary recounts, in many families, the fathers had to stay unlawfully, or hide away from the social welfare representatives, as the apartments were granted mainly to single mother families (Kitchen and Schneider 2002: 128–30). Anguish, anger and avoidance did the rest to propel it on the road to ruin. Still, we have stock footage and (with *Dredd*) a fictional double to remind us of this.

Conclusion

As these case studies illustrate, rich media images are part of a wider cultural context, remotely detached from the plot, and serve as entry points for criticism and commentary on the state of the city form. They inject additional content from beyond the plotline – namely, scenes and sequences that could be subjected to a historicized, architecturally iconographic double-reading as film texts constructing urbanism through synecdoche, that usually come to depict cities in extremis, debased by natural or man-made disasters. Frequently, this dynamic is caused by the inner frictions of the system itself. In *Dredd* and *The Dark Knight Rises*, one could point to a clash between the drives of independence and self-sufficiency, the emergence of present-day versions of the Greek polis and the anxiety of isolation, encapsulated in acts of modern warfare: the siege, terrorism, hijacking. When discussing contemporary cities, conflicts (although of a lesser calibre) foster complex organization patterns.

Writing about Deleuze and Guattari's abstract machines, Manuel De Landa (2000) characterized them as generators of either horizontal (meshwork) or vertical (hierarchies) forms/structures, showing that 'contemporary studies in nonlinear urban dynamics teach us, that, in many cases, frictions (delays, bottlenecks, conflict, uneven distribution of resources) play a crucial role in generating self-organization' (De Landa 2000: 41). Aureli's archipelago model follows this juxtaposition of urban meshwork, whose flow is 'regulated' by buildings – architectural interventions solving city problems on the cellular level. If we translate his polemic on cinematic cities as composed of contextualized images (frames), and subsequently map this city as a dynamic urban system then architecture would serve as a break point to two issues. First, the flows of cinematic representations of the city (or rather, the amorphous urbanism, as in films we can only see fragmented and reassembled parts); and second, the very flow of narrative. Be they mediatized memories of the decline of the Pruitt-Igoe development or of Sarajevo under Serbian siege recorded on film, cinematic images of the city incorporate a critical view upon present tensions as well as the memory of its past conflicts.

Given that these films show urbanism that is inscribed over time with both events altering the contemporary landscape and visual representations of the city's history, they can testify for the way in which we (re)view our cities. One could only try to imagine its real-life counterpart, e.g. complementing Michael Arad and Peter Walker's 'Reflecting Absence' project at Ground Zero – the North and South Pools materializing the absent foundations of the World Trade Center towers – with a film projection set against it, constantly replaying footage of the buildings' disappearance in pillars of black smoke. The image of the city that derives from cinematic portrayals literally becomes a city seen as a 'patchwork' of images. Those images are of dual origin due to the fact that with increasing frequency films blend profilmic settings with CG visuals, and both 'discreetly' bring in outside contraband references to the final image we perceive on-screen. If the 'iconic architectural moments' in *The Dark Knight Rises* and *Dredd* were meant to document the real-life metropolises, they might just as easily have been culled from film and television archives. Instead, as they came into being as semi-digital collages operating on the level of parts representing a whole, they elevate the discussion to a universal level, broadening the context in a way that would include the trauma embedded in urban form[6] buried underneath the postcard skylines of today's cities. In the context of narrative 'flows' and descriptive/visual 'break points', we are introduced to another area of speculative research focusing on the artificial landscapes that surround us, which inscribe the image with collective memory. At the end of the day, cinema supplies us with enough relevant data to serve as a reservoir of 'memory-images', standing witness to forces of urban change. This standpoint emphasizes memory as constitutive tissue for urban forms; it is a view that can be regarded as an attempt to apply the historical perspectives of Aldo Rossi's *L'architettura della città/Architecture of the City* (1982 [1966]) or Colin Rowe and Fred Koetter's *Collage City* (1984 [1977]) – which both stress the relevance of multiple historical layers to the shape of contemporary cities – to the notion of filmic image. Just like Piranesi's *vedute*, even when read as visionary accounts of the future of urban development, they are necessarily woven together from the architectural iconography of events long since passed.

References

Aureli, P. V. (2011), *The Possibility of an Absolute Architecture*, Cambridge, MA and London: MIT Press.

Bakhtin, M. (1999), *Problems of Dostoevsky's Poetics* (trans. C. Emerson), Minneapolis and London: University of Minnesota Press.

Ballard, J. G. (2005 [1975]), *High-rise*, London: Harper Perennial.

Blau, E. (1999), *The Architecture of Red Vienna 1919–1934*, Cambridge, MA and London: MIT Press.

Busbea, L. (2007), *Topologies: The Urban Utopia in France, 1960–1970*, Cambridge, MA and London: MIT Press.

Cook, P. (2008), *Drawing: The Motive Force of Architecture (Architectural Design Primer)*, Chichester: Wiley.

Coward, M. (2009), *Urbicide: The Politics of Urban Destruction*, London and New York: Routledge.

De Landa, M. (2000), *Thousand Years of Nonlinear History*, New York: Swerve Editions.

Deleuze, G. (1986), *Cinema 1: The Movement-image* (trans. H. Tomlinson and B. Habberjam), London: Athlone Press.

Ferriss, H. (2005), *The Metropolis of Tomorrow*, Mineola: Dover.

Freidrichs, C. (2011), *The Pruitt-Igoe Myth*, Columbia: Unicorn Stencil.

Gilliam, T. (1985), *Brazil*, Warsaw: Imperial CinePix.

Kitchen, T. and Schneider, R. H. (2002), *Planning for Crime Prevention: A Transatlantic Perspective*, London and New York: Routledge.

Koolhaas, R., Mau, B. and Werlemann, H. (1995), *S, M, L, XL*, New York: Monacelli Press.

Lathouri, M. (2013), 'A history of territories, movements and borders: Politics of inhabitation', in M. Weinstock (ed.), *System City: Infrastructure and the Space of Flows (Architectural Design)*, 224: 4, pp. 32–37.

Laurence, P. L. (2014), 'Modern (or contemporary) architecture circa 1959', in E. G. Haddad and D. Rifkind (eds), *A Critical History of Contemporary Architecture 1960–2010*, Surrey and Burlington: Ashgate, pp. 9–10.

Lima, A. I. (2003), *Soleri: Architecture as Human Ecology*, New York: Monacelli Press.

Lynch, K. (1960), *The Image of the City*, Cambridge, MA and London: MIT Press.

Nolan, C. (2012), *The Dark Knight Rises*, Warsaw: Galapagos.

Rossi, A. (1982 [1966]), *L'architettura della città/The Architecture of the City*, Cambridge, MA and London: MIT Press.

Rowe, C. and Koetter, F. (1984 [1977]), *Collage City*, Cambridge, MA and London: MIT Press.

Sadler, S. (1999), *The Situationist City*, Cambridge, MA and London: MIT Press.

Spiller, N. (2007), *Visionary Architecture: Blueprints of the Modern Imagination*, New York: Thames & Hudson.

Travis, P. (2012), *Dredd*, Warsaw: Monolith.

Walker, M. (2005), *Hitchcock's Motifs*, Amsterdam: Amsterdam University Press.

Notes

1. This adheres to Umberto Eco's notion of *overinterpretation*, as far as a typical reading of the filmic text is narrowed to the viewer's comprehension of the plotline and narrative ambiguities (especially if it involves flashbacks, futurospectives and other strategies that complicate the reading of a text), as it does not involve the apprehension of all intertextual references involving set design, profilmic settings or specific architectural references beyond simple affection through its mood (scale, lighting, texture, colour).

2. Yona Friedman envisioned a city suspended above Paris, resembling a network of rectangular tightly knit buildings (Busbea 2007: 34–55), although what most of the megastructural projects had in common was their reliance on vertical expansion and possibilities of structural engineering; unsurprisingly, the author of *Topologies* related these ideas to the Space Frames of Konrad Wachsmann and membrane structures of Frei Otto (Busbea 2007: 96).

3. *Arcology* is a term essential to Paolo Soleri's philosophy behind his projects for future alternatives to urban dwelling; as explained by Antonietta Iolanda Lima, '*ARCOLOGY is ARCHITECTURE as a materialization of the human ENVIRONMENT, and it is ecology as the physical, biological, and psychological balance of all aspects of a specific place and its existence overall*' (Lima 2003: 65; original emphases).

4. Hitchcock's term for an extraneous plot device, which drives the narrative forward. It may be an item that is of 'vital importance' to the characters in the film, although of little value to the director (and, by definition, also the audience), as from his/her perspective it is merely a 'means to an end' to resolve plot in a way that allows protagonists to be triumphant (Walker 2005: 296–306).
5. A massive plan by the Wiener Gemeindebauten of constructing 400 new apartment complexes, the pride of which was Karl Ehn's Karl-Marx-Hof (Blau 1999: 1). British critic George Eric Rowe Gedye compared them to citadels – 'islands of socialist power in a bourgeois city'.
6. This refers to the antagonisms set against architecture bearing distinctive ethnic style, termed by Martin Coward as *urbicide*. One of the cases brought up in his book concerned the Serbian attacks at the beginning of the siege of Sarajevo, or the attacks on Dubrovnik and Mostar, yet especially the initial phase of the siege during which mostly culturally and religiously significant buildings were targeted and strafed – the National Library, the building housing the newspaper *Oslobođenje*, churches, etc.

Section Two

Film as Spatial Research and Experiment

Chapter 6

Hollywood menace: Los Angeles and mid-century modern dens of vice

Gabriel Solomons

Introduction

A third of the way into Thom Andersen's 2003 video essay *Los Angeles Plays Itself*, the narrator (Encke King) voicing Andersen's words turns our attention to the ways in which architecture – specifically mid-century modern architecture – has been routinely portrayed with villainous associations by Hollywood film-makers since the 1950s: 'One of the glories of Los Angeles is its modernist residential architecture, but Hollywood movies have almost systematically denigrated this heritage by casting many of these houses as the residences of movie villains' (Andersen 2003: 41:00).

Andersen collects examples from a number of films to support this theory, weaving together a series of convincing references that include houses designed by, amongst others, John Lautner, Richard Neutra, Douglas Honnold and Frank Lloyd Wright.

Although Lloyd Wright's Ennis House cited in the film (and used so effectively in Ridley Scott's *Blade Runner* [1982]) is actually an example of Mayan Revival Architecture which utilized ornamentation more at odds with modernism's principles, the majority of Andersen's references highlight an intriguing precedent – and one which will be elaborated on with further examples later in this chapter.

The houses used – from Neutra's Lovell Health House (featured in Curtis Hanson's *LA Confidential* [1997]) and Honnold's Del Rio mansion in Santa Monica (featured in William Friedkin's *To Live and Die in L.A.* [1985]) to Lautner's Chemosphere in the Hollywood Hills (featured in Brian De Palma's *Body Double* [1989]) and his Sheats-Goldstein residence (featured in the Coen Brothers' *The Big Lebowski* [1998]) – are all the homes of dubious, shady characters: crime bosses, killers and high-class pimps. The original intent with which the architects looked to use space, sharp angles, materials and the surrounding environment to enrich the owner's sense of serenity and peace – aspects that will be discussed in further depth throughout this chapter – are all inverted when seen in these Hollywood films. Space creates tension, angles protrude with menace, materials seem cold and distant, and the surrounding environment seems to imprison rather than liberate.

It is interesting to note that many of the films cited in Andersen's essay conform to tropes and themes found in film noir, which had its roots in German expressionism. German silent cinema of the 1920s and 1930s was notable for its stylized use of irregular, distorted angles in its set designs, and contrasting shadow/light to create tension – techniques which would influence classic Hollywood film noir of the 1940s and 1950s. Many critics also see a direct link between cinema and the architecture of the time, with strong elements of monumentalism and modernism appearing throughout the canon of German expressionism, particularly in films like Robert Wiene's *The Cabinet of Dr. Caligari* (1919) and Fritz Lang's *Metropolis* (1927), which would in turn influence the work of Orson Welles (*Citizen Kane* [1941]) and Carol Reed (*The Third Man* [1949]).

Expressionist architecture – which developed in parallel with expressionist film of the early twentieth century – was characterized by an early-modernist adoption of novel materials, formal innovation and very unusual massing, sometimes inspired by natural biomorphic forms and sometimes by the new technical possibilities offered by the mass production of brick, steel and especially glass. Both Walter Gropius and Ludwig Mies van der Rohe were leading architects of expressionism and their influence on the International Style helps to further substantiate the link between expressionist film, modernist architecture and criminality in film noir.

In order to better understand the reasons why film directors would use a particular style of architecture in service of their narrative, and why Los Angeles in particular acts as the perfect city backdrop for 'dens of vice', it is worth looking at the origins of modernism and the International Style.

Whether as a result of social and political revolutions or primarily driven by technological and engineering developments, modernism was essentially optimistic, and pioneering European architects such as van der Rohe, Le Corbusier and Gropius saw an opportunity to improve living conditions and the environment we inhabit.

An international perspective

The International Style as a term was introduced to American audiences in the early 1930s by Henry-Russell Hitchcock, a leading American architectural historian, and Philip Johnson, the 26-year-old son of a wealthy Cleveland lawyer. Their document 'The International Style' – a term taken from the title of Gropius's 1925 book *International Architecture* – was written for the catalogue of the Museum of Modern Art's 1932 show of photographs and models aimed at introducing the work of Gropius and his contemporaries to New York, and would prove to be hugely influential in setting up a distinction between the European and American way of doing things. As Tom Wolfe would summarize in his essay *From Bauhaus to Our House* (1981):

> In Europe, Gropius, Mies van der Rohe, Le Corbusier, and Oud – the four great 'European Functionalists', as Hitchcock and Johnson called them – were creating *architecture*. In America, even the architects who thought they were being modern and functional were only engaged in *building*. Oh, there was always Frank Lloyd Wright, of course [...] and with a certain weariness Hitchcock and Johnson paid him homage for his work [...] in the distant past [...] and then concluded that he was merely 'half modern'. Which was to say, he was finished and could be forgotten. (Wolfe 1981: 30)

Hitchcock and Johnson's document, along with the emigration to the United States in 1937 of van der Rohe and Gropius, would be instrumental in introducing this 'international style' to architects strongly associated with the mid-century modern dwellings discussed below, and would help to popularize a particular brand of modernism in America that was more organic in form and less formal than its European counterpart.

While other émigré architects such as Richard Neutra (a contemporary of van der Rohe and Gropius, who studied under the influential European theorist of modern architecture Alfred Loos in Vienna) would infuse their work with a combination of styles as early as 1927 – including the Dutch De Stijl and Japanese minimalism – it was not until the mid-to-late 1930s that the International Style really took hold and exerted its full influence.

Émigré architects and designers arrived in the United States at a time of intense growth, when World War II was creating significant demand for innovative products and housing solutions. The choice of many to settle on the West Coast had much to do with the benign climate and informal living of California, both of which afforded them an opportunity to develop a new brand of modernism sympathetic to the surroundings yet rooted in European sensibilities.

From its inception, the movement had its detractors however, and critics were quick to address the threat which European minimalist domestic living posed to traditional American values. As Elizabeth Gordon, then editor of the popular *House Beautiful* magazine, wrote in her April 1953 editorial – 'The Threat to the Next America':

There is a well-established movement, in modern architecture, decorating, and furnishing, which is promoting the mystical idea that 'less is more.' [...] They are promoting unlivability, stripped-down emptiness, lack of storage space and therefore lack of possessions. [...] These arbiters make such a consistent attack on comfort, convenience, and functional values that it becomes, in reality, an attack on reason itself. [...] For if we can be sold on accepting dictators in matters of taste and how our homes are to be ordered, our minds are certainly well prepared to accept dictators in other departments of life. (Gordon 1953: 286–87)

Gordon's concerns about these 'dictators of taste', coming just a few years after America and its allies had fought to preserve freedom and democracy against tyranny of another form, were understandable, and similar sentiments would be expressed by the architect Robert Venturi in 1966. Venturi famously attacked Richard Neutra's missionary-esque zeal of clean precision in his book *Complexity and Contradiction in Architecture*, labelling Neutra's International Style brand as 'a form of aesthetic oppression [...] Its rigid geometry symbolized its inability to embrace the realities of life, its inevitable messiness' (Venturi 1997 [1966]: 18).

This 'inevitable messiness' of real life was a theme that the Los Angeles architecture critic Nicolai Ouroussoff would return to 30 years later. Reviewing a retrospective of Richard Neutra's work in 1997, Ouroussoff observed that whereas the architect's houses 'once suggested a perfectly ordered world, one where the curtains are drawn back to reveal children playing quietly on soft rugs, chaste couples sipping cocktails, where the curling smoke from a cigarette dissolves into a beautiful dreamscape', we now know that 'behind these large plate-glass windows couples cheat, kids do drugs, and cigarettes can kill. In an age where the layers of privacy are constantly being stripped away, Neutra's houses have become more like emblems of voyeurism' (Ouroussoff 1997).

Ouroussoff proceeds to draw parallels between this 'perfect compositional order of the work and the imperfection of life' by citing the use of Neutra's Lovell Health House in *LA Confidential* as perfect casting – owned as it is by 'refined peddler of porn' Pierce Pratchett (David Straithairn): 'The house's slick, meticulous forms seem the perfect frame for that kind of power. Spanish revival just doesn't have the necessary bite' (Ouroussoff 2007). Here, Ouroussoff is clearly referring to another villainous house from the movies – the Spanish Revival home of Phyllis Dietrichson and her husband in Billy Wilder's noir classic *Double Indemnity* (1944). In further comments about the Spanish revival style in his short critical review of the film from *World Film Locations: Los Angeles*, writer Jez Conolly (2011) points to the numerous portents of imprisonment that abide in this 'California Spanish house everyone was nuts about'. In comments on the film's protagonists, Walter Neff and Phyllis Dietrichson, he writes:

> the bars of the wrought iron staircase that Dietrichson sweeps down to greet Neff that first time, the ball-and-chain of her anklet that we see in close-up, the light filtering through the venetian blinds. In every sense Neff is a dead man walking (and talking – his confessional Dictaphone recording is the narrative's framing device) and the Dietrichson house is as much a mausoleum as it is a jailhouse. (Conolly 2011: 14)

In contrast to this, Neutra's Lovell Health House is diametrically opposed. Appearing both in day- and night-time scenes, the open expansiveness of the space and the split-level linear form of the house lends itself well to the multilayered, nuanced narrative of this modern film noir.

Once again, however, the appropriation of the physical space to suit particular cinematic ends is inconsistent with the architect's intention. The Lovell Health House – the first great manifestation of the International Style in Southern California – was built and completed in 1929 for the physician and naturopath Philip Lovell to 'act as a kind of manifesto for natural living, and it also became a centre for radical left-wing political meetings in the 1930s' (Andersen 2003: 41).

Neutra's belief that the human environment needs to address the senses was informed by the writing of experimental psychologist Wilhelm Wundt, particularly his most widely known work, *Principles of Physiological Psychology*, written in 1874, which placed great emphasis on linking body and mind, the physiological and the psychological.

In her introduction to Taschen's 2010 monograph of Neutra, Barbara Lamprecht elaborated on this philosophy, which the architect later defined as 'biorealism':

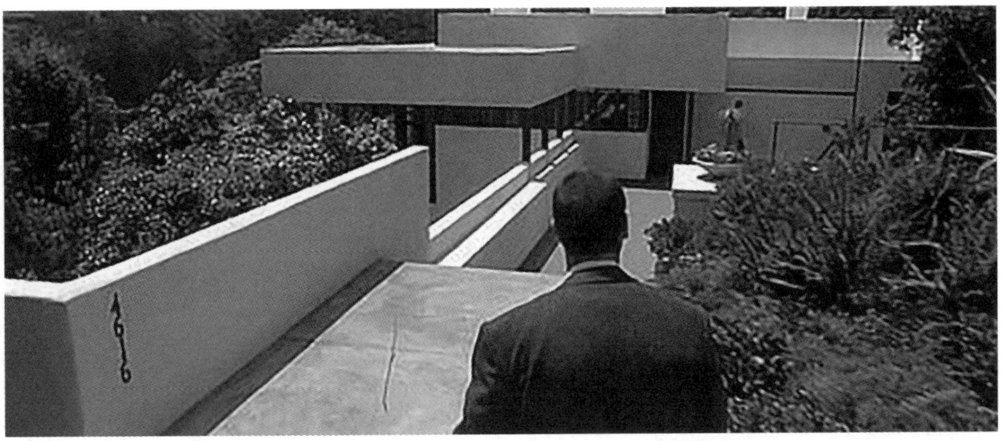

Figure 1. Detective 'Bud' White approaches the residence of Pierce Pratchett with suspicion. *LA Confidential* (1997), © Warner Home Video.

Neutra accepted the hypothesis that the human genetic code evolved on the savannahs of East Africa with its open plains interspersed with groups of trees. That hypothesis had dramatic consequences for his designs […] The theory provided a rationale for why people need physical contact with nature, even why they need to see the horizon. Embracing such a hypothesis was also one of the reasons Neutra went not just to America but specifically to warm, freedom-loving southern California. (Lamprecht 2006: 9)

A similar fate is accorded John Lautner's Sheats-Goldstein residence in the Coen Brothers' *The Big Lebowski*, which is home to pornographer Jackie Treehorn (Ben Gazzara). Supposedly located in Malibu, the house is actually on Angelo View Drive high in the Hollywood Hills, with enviable views across the expanse of Los Angeles. Completed in 1963 and growing from the hillside, the house's most striking feature is a coffered slab of concrete folded like paper, which forms the roof. The living room was initially separated from the outside by a simple curtain of blown air but, as seen in the film, glass was finally used for both security and insulation. Lautner's house is a prime example of what Frank Lloyd Wright termed 'Organic Architecture' that derives its form as an extension of the natural environment – and it was originally built for Helen and Paul Sheats, an artist and doctor respectively, and their five children. Lautner's early career was spent as apprentice to Lloyd Wright at Taliesin (Wright's School of Architecture in Spring Green, Wisconsin) from 1933 to 1938, where he developed a respect for the 'total concept' and methods for integrating a house into its surroundings, of creating an organic flow between indoor

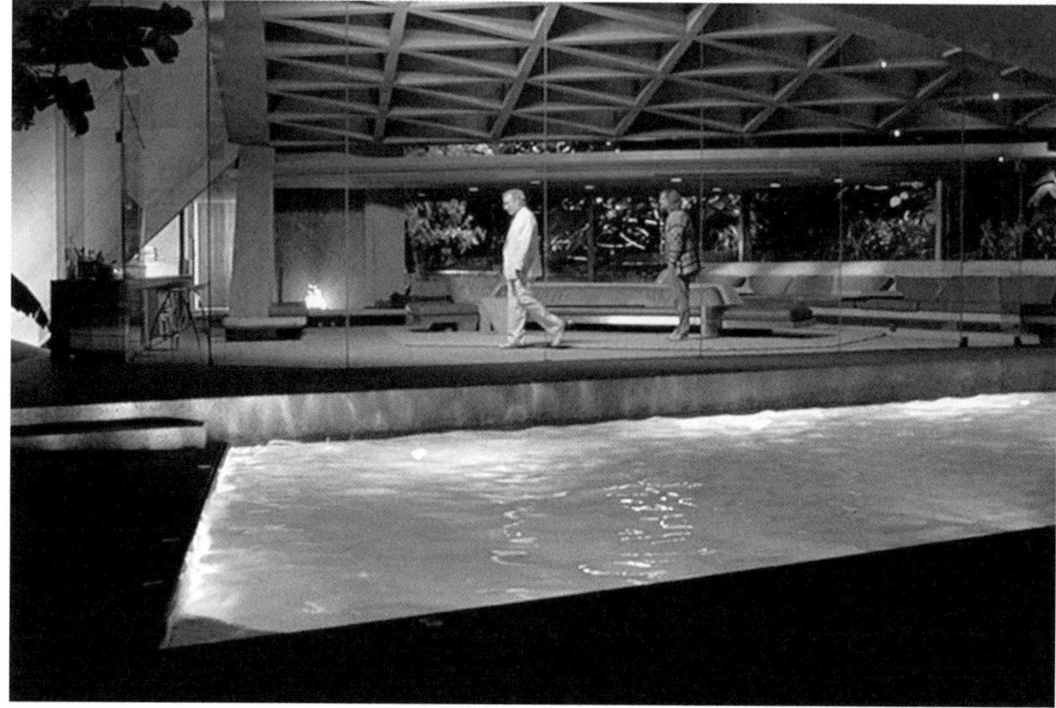

Figure 2. Jackie Treehorn is at home in John Lautner's Sheats-Goldstein residence. *The Big Lebowski* (1998), © PolyGram Filmed Entertainment.

and outdoor spaces. Although interviews reveal that Lautner had little regard for the International Style and its leading architects, many of his residential homes seem to retain a stripped-back minimalism more attuned to European modernism than the prairie monumentalism and ornamentation most associated with Lloyd Wright.

Whether situated in Malibu or the Hollywood Hills, the Sheats-Goldstein residence is not the sort of place that the laidback and slovenly Dude (Jeff Bridges) would frequent, being far more at home in his ramshackle Venice Beach bungalow.

It could be argued that the Coen Brothers are as much at odds with modernism as their central protagonist, if you consider that all of the film's 'villains' have some association with the trappings of 'streamlined', minimalist excess, from Jackie Treehorn's home and the leather Le Corbusier chairs found in Maude Lebowski's loft apartment, to the album cover of the fictional band (and villainous trio of nihilist thugs) 'Autobahn' that is an homage to Kraftwerk's 1978 album *The Man Machine*. These objects 'of desire' and their superficial, malicious owners act as stark contrast to the Dude and his band of bumbling sidekicks, adhering as they do to a more earthy and liberal way of life. Their clothes, cars, homes and habits are aligned far more closely to the average American's value systems, which positions them as the 'heroes' against the oppressive, conservative 'villains'.

The use of Brent Saville's Astral House as home to shady villain Terry Valentine (Peter Fonda) in Steven Soderbergh's *The Limey* (1999) is another example of a cinematic den of vice. On a singular mission to avenge the death of his daughter, Brit hardman Wilson (Terence Stamp) is oblivious to the lure of Los Angeles's excessive charms, and on arrival sees only a set of corrupt obstacles to overcome as he kicks, punches and shoots his way towards Valentine who is holed up in a pristine walled fortress. Wilson's rough-edged English vigilante set among the sleek curves of Astral House – a dream home financed by the curator Maurice Tuchman and completed just before filming began – makes for a powerful contrast when the two face off for the first time. While not built in modernism's heyday, the house, designed by museum architect Brent Saville, incorporates the clean lines, alternating scale and minimalist expansiveness so common in the International Style. The classic film connection between minimal interiors and emotional detachment is once again employed here, and – once again – the casting of such a house ignores the modernist philosophy that a building such as this was intended to liberate and enrich the

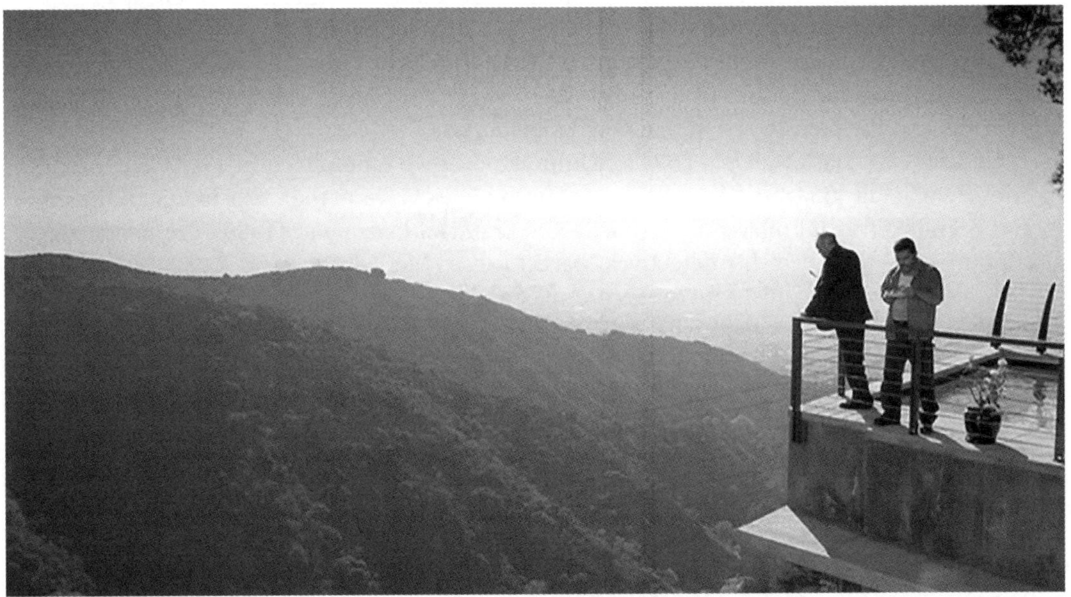

Figure 3. Wilson and Eduardo take in the view from Terry Valentine's lofty fortress. *The Limey* (1999), © Artisan Home Entertainment.

lives of the occupants. Here, Astral House acts as a prize possession, an ill-gotten gain of Valentine's shady drug dealings and criminal behaviour. The house protrudes perilously above the Hollywood Hills and likewise Terry Valentine's fate hangs in the balance, his life a ticking clock counting down to zero.

Looking out and looking over

The fact that so many of the homes discussed in this chapter are found in the Hollywood Hills makes perfect sense when considered within the context of cinematic myth-making. The familiar shot of a flat expanse disappearing into a (smoggy) distance or bed of twinkling lights beneath the stars has appeared in many of the films cited so far, often seen from panoramic glass-fronted buildings acting as veritable movie screens that appear to show its occupants everything the city has to offer. It is access to this view from John Lautner's Chemosphere that blinds the naive Jake Scully (Craig Wasson) to an obvious set-up in Brian DePalma's *Body Double* (1984). Situated on the San Fernando Valley side of the Hollywood Hills, just off of Mulholland Drive, the appropriately futuristic looking house was built for aerospace engineer Leonard Malin and completed in 1960. It offers a panoptic 360-degree view of the city and can be accessed by a funicular from street level or a bridged entrance from above. Scully's wide-eyed ascent to the house in the film is his metaphoric rise to 'the high life', but the house's location and vantage point encapsulates the film's central conceit: 'that even when we think we see everything, we can miss what is right in front of us' (Zeller-Jacques 2011: 54). The house is a trap made of concrete, steel and glass – luring the surface-obsessed protagonist into its clutches with luxurious interiors and the manifestation of an enviable lifestyle.

Lautner's Garcia Residence at 7436 Mulholland Drive (completed in 1962) is another house that boldly juts out of the hillside with unimpeded views of the city below. Standing in as the South African Embassy in Richard Donner's *Lethal Weapon 2* (1989), the apartheid-era film once again sees LA detectives Martin Riggs (Mel Gibson) and Roger Murtaugh (Danny Glover) up against a merciless group of bad guys, this time the threat coming from South African smugglers led with brooding menace by the country's racist, murdering ambassador (Joss Ackland). In one of the most memorable movie scenes to feature wanton destruction of a significant architectural site, Riggs – blocked from searching the property by claims to diplomatic immunity – ties a rope to one of the exposed pillars holding the house up, attaches it to his pickup truck, and pulls the immense structure (actually a full-scale model) down the hillside resulting in an epic series of explosions. Modernism comes crashing down to the wide-eyed glee and hysterical joy of an unhinged LA cop with nothing to lose. Further evidence that John Lautner is the architect Hollywood loves to hate, or simply the case that modernist homes look great on-screen?

Both the Garcia Residence and Chemosphere resemble futurist visions of the kind seen in *The Jetsons* – the animated cartoon show from the 1960s which was a distillation

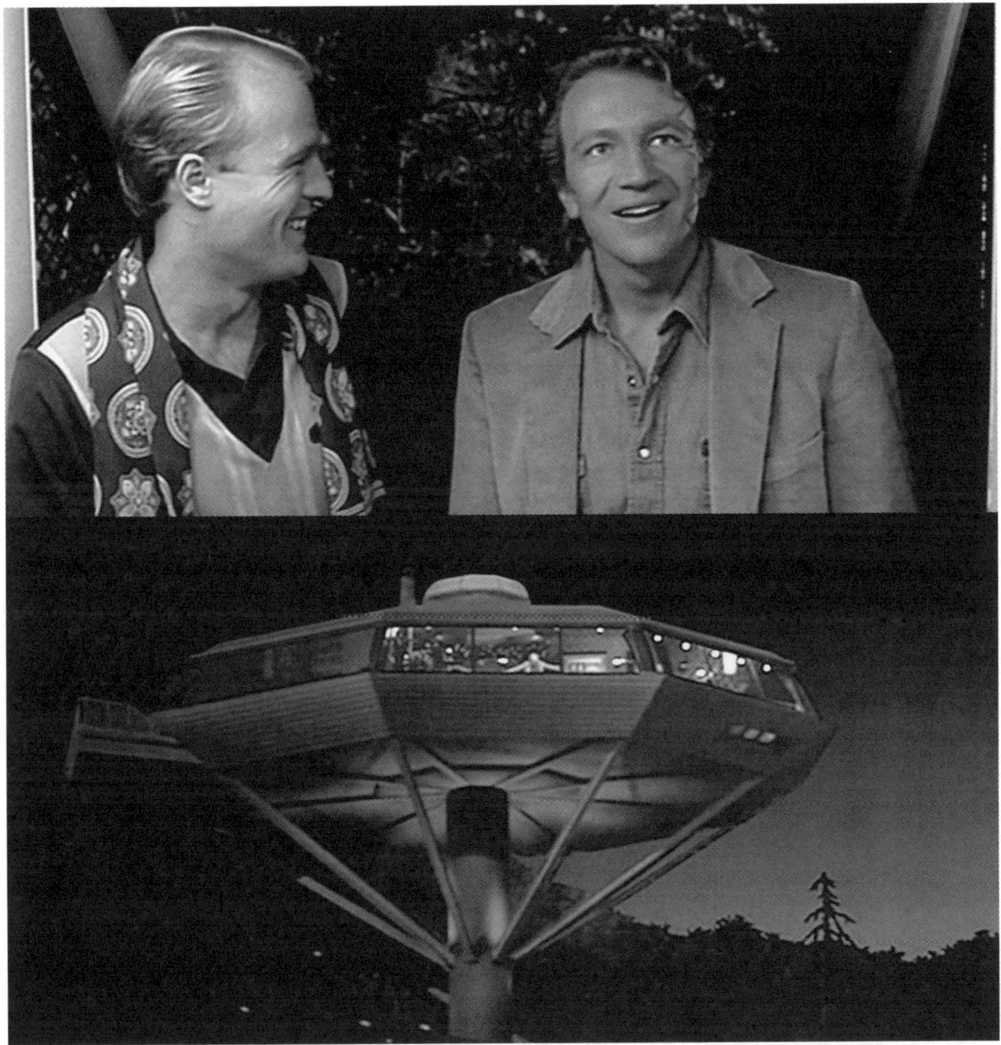

Figure 4. Jake is seduced by the trappings of a hilltop pleasure palace. *Body Double* (1984), © Columbia Pictures.

of every Space Age promise that Americans could muster. The show's artists drew inspiration from futurist books of the time, including the 1962 book *1975: And the Changes to Come,* by Arnold B. Barach, and borrowed heavily from the curvaceous, geometric 'Googie' aesthetic of Southern California – a term first used in relation to a now-defunct Lautner-designed coffee shop built in West Hollywood in 1949. Googie encapsulated the futuristic design found prevalent in the post-war sprawl of Los Angeles, and proved popular among coffee shops, motels and gas stations that were all increasingly becoming reliant on a burgeoning car culture.

Beyond the boundaries of Los Angeles proper, Lautner's Elrod House – based in Palm Springs and completed in 1968 – also features a curved UFO-esque dome that sits atop an imposing but naturally harmonious sprawl of chambers and glass-encased caverns. The house made a prominent appearance in *Diamonds Are Forever* (1971) in a fight scene between James Bond (Sean Connery) and two of Ernst Blofeld's 'bodyguards' Bambi and Thumper. The highly sexualized and at times brutal encounter takes the viewer on an alternative tour through the main atrium of the house as various pieces of furniture

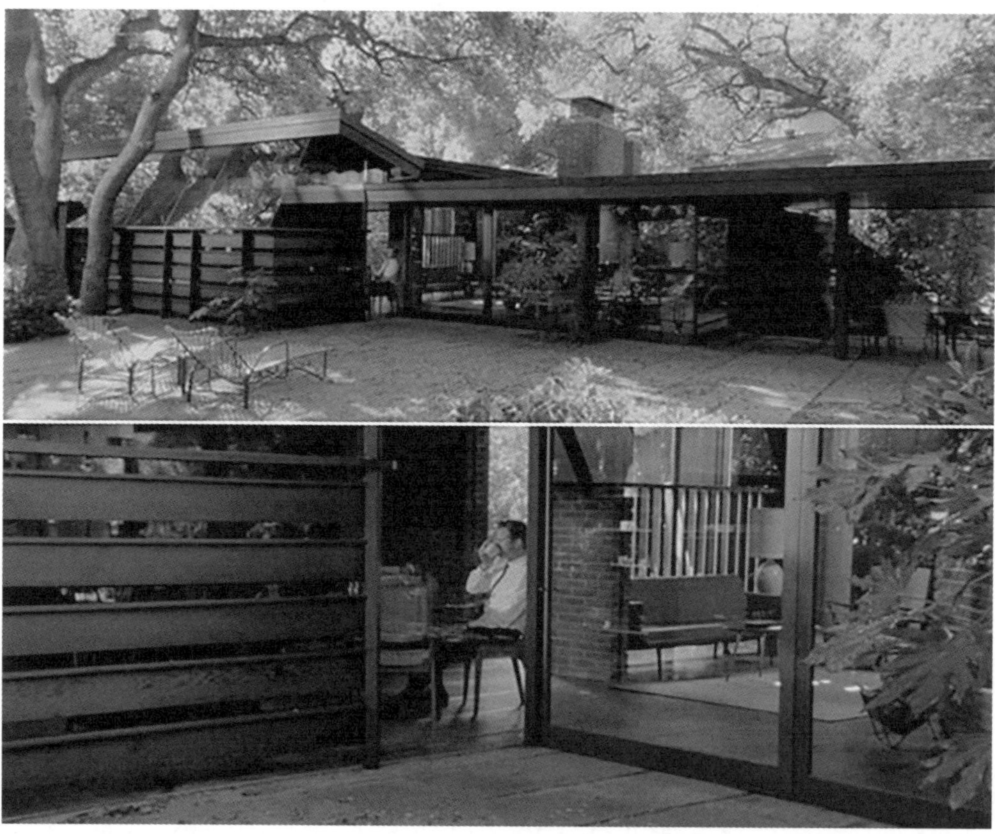

Figure 5. George contemplates the loss of love in Lautner's Schaffer residence. *A Single Man* (2009), © Sony Pictures Home Entertainment.

are swung from, smashed or tossed about, culminating in Bond being thrown into the outdoor pool before he finally gets the upper hand. Bond villains on the whole opt for outlandishly designed lairs from which to plot world domination, and in his piece 'James Bond: The enemy of architecture', Steve Rose (2008) suggests that the archetypal Bond villain is not dissimilar to a modernist architect: 'He is usually on a mission to "improve" humanity by wiping out the messy status quo and replacing it with some orderly, rational utopia of his own design.' He goes on to draw further comparisons between evil and modernism in other Bond movies: 'Osato's spacious office in *You Only Live Twice* is like Le Corbusier's work in Japan. Goldfinger's "rumpus room" is distinctly Frank Lloyd Wright, as is Hugo Drax's behind-the-waterfall lair in Moonraker, whose Mayan-patterned relief panels resemble those of Wright's Ennis House' (Rose 2008).

The penchant for casting LA's modernist architecture as homes for movie bad guys has waned somewhat in the past ten years, and there is an actual reappraisal by Hollywood for the merits of the movement's sympathetic origins. Lautner's Schaffer residence, built in 1949, plays a starring role as home to a gay man (Colin Firth) grieving the death of his partner in Tom Ford's *A Single Man* (2009); and the Lovell Health House recently appeared with far less menacing associations in Mike Mills's *Beginners* (2010), as home to a retired museum director (Christopher Plummer) who reveals that he is gay. The fact that both of these films deal with themes of alienation and mortality, and feature fragile protagonists with love in their hearts, seems to support the shifting perceptions of film-makers in casting these homes in their films.

Conclusion

Ultimate confirmation of this newfound favour for modernism is evidenced by Tony Stark's Lautner-inspired CGI cliffside mansion in the *Iron Man* films (2008–13) – home to a bona fide hero, scourge to evil-doers everywhere. Charlotte Neilson, in her article 'From psychopath lairs to superhero mansions: How cinema and modern architecture called a truce' (2012), suggests that our changing relationship with technology could play a part: 'It could be that, with the advent of smart phones and wireless technology, that we now consider it *preferable* and not psychopathic – to live in houses without the traditional trappings' (Neilson 2012). The downturn in the economy and the public desire for escapism into a 'monied, carefree world' similar to that experienced by audiences prior to the Great Depression is also proposed.

Whatever the case, it seems that LA modernist architecture has – for now – been granted a reprieve from its dubious associations in Hollywood productions, but I imagine it won't be long before we find a Blofeld-, Treehorn- or Pratchett-like character peering coldly out of a mid-century glass frontage across the vast Los Angeles expanse, while the rest of us exclaim 'wow, that's some pad'.

References

Andersen, T. (2003), *Los Angeles Plays Itself*, USA.

Barach, A. B. (1962), *1975 and the Changes to Come*, New York: Harper.

Broccoli, Albert R. et al. (1971 [2006]), *You Only Live Twice*, USA: Metro Goldwyn Mayer Home Entertainment.

Clarke, D. B. (ed.) (1997), *The Cinematic City*, London: Routledge.

Coen, Joel and Coen, E. (1998), *The Big Lebowski*, USA: Polygram Filmed Entertainment.

Conolly, J. (2011), 'Double Indemnity', in G. Solomons (ed.), *World Film Locations: Los Angeles*, Bristol: Intellect.

DePalma, B. (1984), *Body Double*, USA: Columbia Pictures Corporation.

Donner, R., et al. (1989) *Lethal Weapon 2*. USA: Warner Home Video.

Ford, T. (2009), *A Single Man*, USA: Fade to Black Productions.

Gordon, E. (1953), 'The threat to the next America', *House Beautiful*, April.

Gropius, W. (1975), International architecture. *Open University, Bletchley, England. History of Architecture and Design 1890-1939, Images 123, 1975; with Illus., Elevations, Sections.*

Hamilton, G., et al. (2006), *Diamonds Are Forever*. USA: Metro Goldwyn Mayer Home Entertainment.

Hanson, C. (1997), *LA Confidential*, USA: Regency Enterprises.

Hitchcock, H.-R., & Johnson, P. (1966), *The International Style*, New York: Norton.

Kaplan, W. (2011), *California Design, 1930–1965: Living in a Modern Way*, MIT Press.

Lamprecht, B. M., & Neutra, R. J. (2000), *Richard Neutra: Complete Works*. Köln: Taschen.

McClung, W. A. (2000), *Landscapes of Desire: Anglo Mythologies of Los Angeles*, University of California Press.

Mills, M., et al. (2011), *Beginners*, USA: Universal Studios Home Entertainment.

Neilson, C. (2012), 'From psychopath lairs to superhero mansions: How cinema and modern architecture called a truce', *Arch Daily*, 19 December, http://www.archdaily.com/309220/.

Ouroussoff, N. (1997), 'A new look, a look back', *Los Angeles Times*, 24 October, http://articles.latimes.com/1997/oct/24/entertainment/ca-46012.

Rose, S. (2008), 'James Bond, the enemy of architecture', *The Guardian*, 4 November, http://www.theguardian.com/artanddesign/2008/nov/04/james-bond-architecture.

Soderbergh, S. (1999), *The Limey*, USA: Artisan Entertainment.

Venturi, R. (1997 [1966]), *Complexity and Contradiction in Architecture*, London: Architectural Press.

Wolfe, T. (1981), *From Bauhaus to Our House*, New York: Picador.

Zeller-Jacques, M. (2011), 'Body Double', in G. Solomons (ed.), *World Film Locations: Los Angeles*, Bristol: Intellect.

Chapter 7

A second life for a second city: Tradition and modernity in *Guadalajara in the Summer*

Carmen Elisa Gómez-Gomez

Introduction

After a series of successful pastoral melodramas set in the countryside that made Mexican cinematography internationally renowned in the first half of the twentieth century, it was the city – and the arrival of modernity – that was to be presented in film during what was known as 'The Golden Age'. During this period, and especially during the late 1940s, the modern Mexican city was used as the background of many melodramas, thrillers and musical comedies.

In the film *Distinto Amanecer/A Different Dawn* (Bracho, 1943), set in Mexico City, the urban milieu is portrayed as a dangerous, difficult place, where the government's propaganda about the nation's financial success stands in stark contrast to the poverty of the working class. Following the formula of the film noir genre, the story is concerned with Octavio (Pedro Armendáriz), a political activist who tries to recover an envelope with secret instructions that could lead to thwarting a political plot by a corrupt union that wants to ensure the re-election of a corrupt governor. The action mostly takes places in a single night and reveals unflattering images of the threatening nightlife in Mexico City – highlighting its dangerous alleys amidst landmark Mexican buildings, such as the main post office or the Art Deco Bank of Mexico. Bracho's view of the city would change radically a couple of decades later however, when he directed the postcard-like comedy *Guadalajara en verano/Guadalajara in the Summer* (Bracho, 1964). This film could also be called an 'Ode to Modernity' due to its concern with showing the recently built sites of Guadalajara, and its acknowledgement of Mexico's thriving economy and optimism decades before globalization.

While the state Jalisco and its capital, Guadalajara, have been largely regarded as sites of essential 'Mexicanness' – as the birthplace of mariachi music, the *charro* (cowboy) and tequila – Bracho portrayed the image of a new, cosmopolitan city. Even so, Mexican stereotypes abound, and the traditional elements provide comic relief. It is thus a film that shows a reluctance to establish an opposition between tropes of modernity and tradition and, furthermore, gives the impression of travelling to touristic cities located in other places or in other times – a sensation created by the use of various narrative techniques evident in other Mexican films.

Following in the wake of other films that showcased the beauty of the city then, *Guadalajara in the Summer* offers a portrait of a modern city rooted in old traditions. In reality however, the city's modern face appeared some time before the production of the film (1947–62) when it underwent radical urban renovation, and Bracho's film elaborates on this as part of its main narrative. What follows, is an engagement and analysis of these interrelated urban and cinematic characteristics as they appear in the film.

Threading urban and cinematic narratives

Several authors have discussed topics related to urban narratives and the way in which cinema follows such narratives. The Russian film-maker and theorist Sergei Eisenstein was one of the pioneers in arguing that a parallel between urban narrative and cinematic narrative exists. Eisenstein discussed montage and argued that planning a building involves a similar process to designing the shots of a scene, as well as editing a scene (Eisenstein 1989: 111). Years later, other writers developed related ideas including, very recently, Richard Koeck, who suggests that there are several other characteristics that architecture and cinema have in common: 'Film and architecture share a number of properties, of which "narration" is arguably one of the most important agents in the transfer of spatially-embedded information' (Koeck 2013: 12).

The city, as portrayed in cinema, is the place where travelling narratives take place, not only for the foreign visitor, but also for inhabitants of the same location who can also 'travel' to the past through films that offer details of specific cities historically. This could be the case with the depiction of Rome in the 1950s, for example, in *Three Coins in the Fountain* (Negulesco, 1954). Giuliana Bruno explains that threading the past and the future in this way occurs in the cinematic representation of the city and that when the viewer is immersed in these narratives, he or she becomes a cultural traveller.

Acting as such a cultural voyager, the itinerant spectator of the architectural-filmic ensemble reads moving views – constructions of the flow of life. In the ciné city, the framing of space and the succession of sites organized as shots from different viewpoints, adjoined and disjointed by way of editing, constitutes a montage of forms of dwelling. (Bruno 2008: 23)

In other words, the film viewer becomes a tourist, a visitor to sites of cultural memory. In the case of *Guadalajara in the Summer*, today's spectator is thus immersed in the ambience and Zeitgeist of the Guadalajara of 1964.

Jalisco and the folkloric imagination

Since the beginning of cinema production in Mexico, Jalisco was regarded as an exotic location far from civilization. The most obvious example of this is the fact that the Lumière brothers, in the earliest days of cinema, sent the cameramen Claude Ferdinand

Von Bernard and Gabriel Veyre to Tequila, Jalisco, not far from Guadalajara. As part of several marketing strategies, these visits were intended to provide French audiences with images of other places around the world and, at the same time, serve as opportunities for the cinematographers to introduce the Cinematograph to new audiences. Jalisco was seen as sufficiently exotic to serve the first of these purposes for European audiences.

Von Bernard and Veyre arrived in Mexico in 1896. After paying a visit to President, Porfirio Díaz, they were invited to see his friend's hacienda in Jalisco and as a result, the first films in Mexico were shot in Jalisco in early November 1896 (Vaidovits 1989: 23). These brief films captured the countryside, the folkloric dances and rural activities of the horsemen in the hacienda – satisfying European curiosity for the exotic other.

In their article 'The Imperial Imaginary', Shohat and Stam (2002) reiterate that this ethnographic gaze started with the travelling cameramen of the Lumières:

If the culture of empire authorized the pleasure of seizing ephemeral glimpses of its 'margins' through travel and tourism, the nineteenth century invention of the photographic and later the cinematographic camera made it possible to record such glimpses. Rather than remaining confined to its European home, the camera set out to 'explore' new geographical, ethnographic, and archaeological territories. (Shohat and Stam 2002: 369)

Mexico's nationalistic cultural project

After the revolution that began in 1910 and ended in the late 1920s, peace finally came to Mexico after a period of instability. The government implemented several strategies to improve its own credibility and legitimacy, primary amongst which was 'artistic nationalism'. Anthropologist Jesus Machuca explains how this aesthetic/symbolic order was established: 'During the 1920s and 1930s the most prestigious Mexican intellectuals were set to design an iconographic discourse, with the purpose of constructing an image that would suit the hegemonic needs of the State' (Machuca 2005: 143).

The state encouraged the use of other art forms for the expression of nationalism as well, the most famous case being the support for the muralists Diego Rivera, Jose Clemente Orozco and David A. Siqueiros, who often drew on Mexico's history as an inspiration. Susan Dever explains how the man behind this ideological trend, Jose Vasconcelos, had a profound influence: 'Vasconcelos's strategies of imagining the nation and his techniques in promoting his visions reveal meaningful parts of the infrastructure of nationalism and the workings of the specifically Mexican cultural artifacts' (Dever 2003: 15).

As in many other emerging Latin American nations in the 1930s, Mexican mass media was becoming an industry consistently nationalistic in tone – a trend that remained prevalent for 40 years. Although many films displayed a cosmopolitan, modern face of Mexican life, strong nationalism came to be seen by local viewers – and foreign viewers –

as integral to the identity of Mexican national cinema, and the features of Jaliscan folklore thus became identified as the locus of Mexico as a whole. (The work of director Emilio Fernandez became a recognizable example of this approach.) For many years, Jalisco remained typecast in Mexican cinema and it became the stereotype of the homeland, most notably through the image of the 'big ranch': a rural environment that defied modernity to focus on traditional customs and, as such, offered a perfect backdrop for many comedies and melodramas.

However, from the early 1960s, with the arrival of more cosmopolitan trends linked to different historical and economic processes, Mexican film producers began trying to find new ways of approaching audiences, and cinema slipped into a crisis of creativity and productivity: 'By the end of the 1950s, it had entered a period of general decline. National film had become static and repetitive and lost in appeal to Hollywood. Audiences turned to North American and European cinema for their primary entertainment' (Maciel 1999: 200).

The same could be said at the urban level too with Mexican cities taking on North American forms through sprawl and an altered approach to zoning – characteristics considered synonymous with progress. The author of the book *Ciudad y arquitectura/ City and Architecture*, Silvia Arango (2012), states that in the 1950s, there was euphoria regarding new developments associated with the economic bonanza seen throughout North, Central and Latin America – the product of the industrialization that took place after World War II (Arango 2012: 276). From the late 1950s to the early 1970s, Mexico was experiencing an economic boom and under the presidency of Adolfo Lopez Mateos (1958–64), the country enjoyed an era of positive economic growth that came to be called 'The Mexican Miracle'. Gross Domestic Product grew steadily as the economy became ever more based on the industrial production of goods and services, and the population grew to 1 million by 1964. It was in this context that Guadalajara became the urban setting that would be portrayed by Branco.

Guadalajara, the second city: A new face, a new city

Guadalajara, the capital of Jalisco, is the second-largest city in Mexico. In 1962, the *New York Times* commented on the city's groundbreaking urban renovation, as well as the architectural eclecticism of its main sites and the pride of the locals for their landmarks.

Guadalajara, which was founded in 1531 by the Conquistador Nuño de Guzmán, was nearly demolished six years ago to make way for a big, new city. The result is an interesting blend – a touch of Florence, a dash of Munich, but mostly of the sprawling, fast-moving cities of the United States' western section, such as Phoenix. It has little left that is Mexican until one gets into the *barrios*, or neighbourhoods, and even these are punctuated with stunning displays of modern sculpture executed in volcanic stone, cantilever, reinforced concrete and other architectural virtuosity. (Miller 1962)

The *New York Times* article refers to the fact that a few years previously, the state government had caused a controversy when they permitted an urban design proposal involving tearing down buildings surrounding the cathedral to create four large, open plazas. Most of the demolished buildings dated from the eighteenth century, among them a church, the bishop's palace and other notable houses. For some, this modernization process was, from the outset, seen as destroying the prominent features of the colonial city centre and resulting in an unwelcomed urban palimpsest.

In this new urban narrative, modernity and new urban design produced a different – and new – foundational landscape of the city centre. The city acquired a newer, more sophisticated face related to processes of industrialization, and was seen as a product of a capitalist-driven amalgam of financial and political power. Hailing this in *Guadalajara in the Summer*, the film's producers, all natives of Guadalajara, portrayed the birthplace of Mexican cinema as a newly modern, cosmopolitan region, ready to embrace the modern age (Tuñón 1986: 110). Under the direction of Julio Bracho,[1] the film was given broad logistical support by local government and businesses. Federal, state and local buildings, along with other publicly owned sites, were opened for filming. Unlike many other touristic films, which are sponsored by the government, private producers funded *Guadalajara in the Summer* in its entirety. According to the producer Javier Torres Ladrón de Guevara, the film was made exclusively to 'showcase the beauty that the city could offer to the tourists. The main character was the city and the plotline was very plain' (Tuñón 1977: 17).

Indeed, the city takes centre stage in the production and for the viewer, the weak screenplay does little to detract from the scenery. Most of the film's locations are in the city's historic centre, conveying elements of tradition mixed with a new urban layout. It is also important to note the prominence given to the centre – as at that time much of the administrative, commercial and cultural activities were still carried out in the centres of Mexican cities. As the anthropologist Néstor García Canclini has pointed out: 'City life was organized, until fifty years ago, in a clearly defined territory, whose geographical, political and cultural center was in the historic center consisting of the colonial buildings' (García Canclini 2001: 169–70).

The plot of Bracho's film concerns a group of American students (Elizabeth Campbell, Lynn Karol and Dean Reed) who come to Guadalajara to take summer Spanish courses. During their stay, they make friends with Mexicans of their own age, indulge in romances and generally enjoy the city's lifestyle. Joining the group during their stay is Monica, an American reporter (played by Patty Hobbs) commissioned by her Los Angeles newspaper to write a story on the city. Fernando (Claudio Brook), the Spanish teacher, becomes her tour guide on this pretext and often mentions the history of the city in his classes. The film ends with the characters enjoying a performance of a folkloric dance ensemble at one of the newest public parks in the new urban complex.[2]

Like many other films, *Guadalajara in the Summer* wanted to appeal to the new generation while still making what is essentially a touristic documentary premised on the city's history, as much as its modern vitality. Consequently, under the comedy-melodrama plotline are numerous references to the history of the sites that the characters visit – a leitmotiv that informs the viewer of the rich indigenous culture and history of the region but which constantly interrupts the flow of the action, making even more apparent the lack of any principal dramatic conflict in the film.

It is not surprising then, that film critics rarely look on *Guadalajara in the Summer* favourably.[3] Jorge Ayala Blanco, one of Mexico's most influential critics, made a statement that was meant to be sarcastic, but, with the passing of time, has become complimentary: 'The ambition and brightness of the images of *Guadalajara in the Summer* moves in a vacuum. At the end, there is the impression that one has just watched a touristic documentary that was accidentally added a plot' (Ayala Blanco, quoted in García Riera 1986: 326).

Nevertheless, categorizing this film as a 'touristic documentary' actually highlights the best components of the film. Guadalajara is depicted as a stately, majestic town with attractive new urban spaces and, from the beginning of the film, the star, Guadalajara, is painted lavishly across the screen.

Walking the city through cinema

The film-makers, in their deliberate enabling of the viewers' own internal spatio-narrative structures, seem to be recalling Walter Benjamin's figure of the *flâneur*. In contradistinction to his figure of the stroller, Benjamin states: 'The man of the crowd is no *flâneur*. In him, composure has given way to manic behaviour. Hence he exemplifies, rather, what had to become of the *flâneur* once he was deprived of the milieu to which he belonged' (Benjamin 1988 [1937]: 172). In the film, it would appear that characters have enough time to stroll the streets in a relaxed way – as if it were a smaller provincial town. There are no traffic jams or scenes involving a madding crowd. The viewer/*flâneur* becomes immersed in sites of distinctive art and architecture of the past and the present – such as the murals of contemporary twentieth-century artist José Clemente Orozco.[4]

It is worth noting a particular scene in which aerial shots and human-point-of-view perspectives merge into one through unique camera motions. Monica and Fernando are visiting the State House and are admiring Orozco's mural located in the stairwell. In this beautiful shot, the camera, on a crane looking down from above, lowers to a close-up of the mural, assuming a remarkable perspective. While this angle might seem too high to reflect human scale, it allows the film viewer to take a closer look at the central image of the mural, which features Miguel Hidalgo (the father of Independence) who declared the end of slavery at this building on 6 December 1810. Subsequently in the shot, the camera moves gracefully to take up the viewpoint of the American reporter, Monica, and Fernando, in order for him to explain some details of the painting and Jalisco's history.

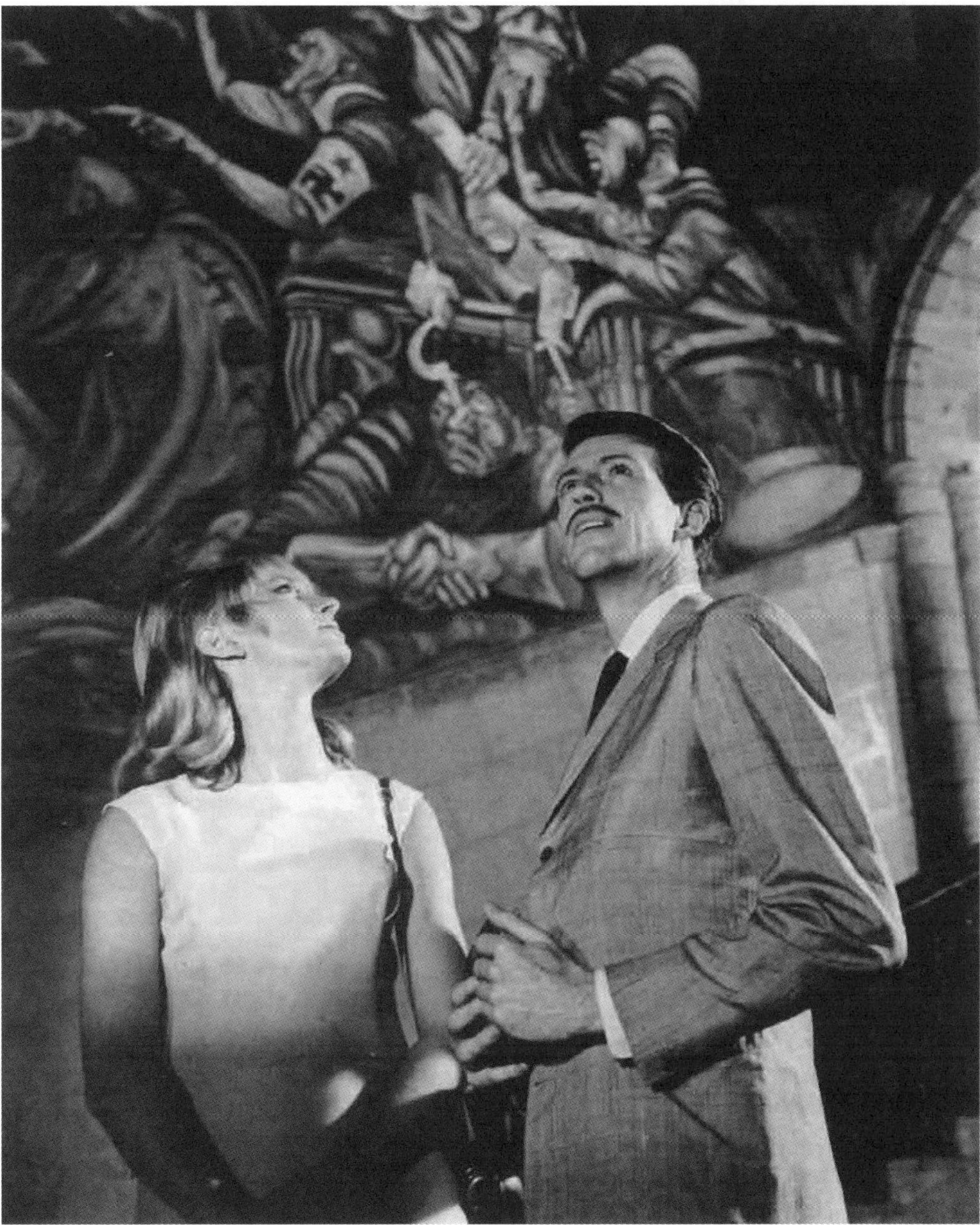

Figure 1. Views of the mural inside Jalisco's State House. *Guadalajara en verano/Guadalajara in the Summer* (1964), © Producciones Bueno, Javier Torres Ladrón de Guevara.

Modernity as a trope

Proud of the urban renovations and the construction of new streets and buildings in the city, there are several instances in which the film uses aerial shots of the city to underline the modernity of its architecture and urban layout. For example, there are several aerial scenes featuring the new squares surrounding the Cathedral. Even though this is an ancient building, the framing of shots reveals the radical nature of the urban plan by highlighting demolished buildings that are, or have been, supplanted by the new squares.

The film displays the city at its most modern then, and particularly uses the presentation of modern architecture to do so. In the process, it seems to assert that Guadalajara belongs in the international realm. An image of the tallest building in town is a perfect example of this. The Condominium – a large, unpleasant, office complex – figures prominently in the film's aerial sequence. Finished in 1962, with 25 floors it was considered the city's first skyscraper. It would not have been out of place in any other developed country in the world at the time.

The same sequence shows the other tall building, the new Hilton Hotel, only a couple of blocks away. This wide shot emphasizes the magnificence of the recently developed area in the south of the town, which included a recently constructed cultural complex with a new state library, theatres, art galleries, a large shop of local crafts and a museum. The imaginary is that of a financially powerful city where capitalism is ever present. Raymond Williams defines this kind of urbanism thus:

> I am willing to see the city as capitalism, as so many now do, if I can say also that this mode of production began, specifically, in the English rural economy, and produced, there, many of the characteristic effects – increases of production, physical reordering of a totally available world, displacement of customary settlements. (Williams 1993 [1973]: 331)

Reflecting on the origins of industrialization, Williams explains that this became a transnational trend in which the forces of improvement and development were the same in every local community around the world.

Another scene reiterating this reading is one featuring a sign that had become an important landmark in the city: an extremely large neon sign advertising Pepsi-Cola, which highlighted the folkloric icon of the *charro* and his female dancing partner, evoking the traditional Mexican hat-dance. It remained on the site for several years and was a clear example of a transnational brand, incorporating (even co-opting) a Mexican tradition, so as to merge the local with the global.

At this preliminary stage in globalization, the film shows how Guadalajarans were embracing the new internationalism while showcasing their own local cultural values. In fact, the preproduction stage of the film was directly linked to this conflict between the local and the global. Some hotel owners lent their facilities in the hope of having them placed in the film – as they were concerned that with the opening of the Hilton, their businesses would suffer.[5] The film thus acts, in a way, as a means of product placement for these hotels and a metaphor for the battle of local economies against shattering global power.

Although it highlights modern architecture, urbanism and ways of living, also important to the notion of modernity in the film is its presentation of concomitant mobility. Zygmunt Bauman (1998) clarifies the importance of the means of transportation at this historical period – a period in which concepts of 'near' versus 'far', 'inside' versus 'outside', and 'here' versus 'out there' made a real social difference:

> Modern history has been marked by the constant progress of the means of transportation. Transport and travel was the field of particularly radical and rapid change [...]. It was primarily the availability of means of fast travel that triggered the typically modern process of eroding and undermining all locally entrenched social and cultural 'totalities'. (Bauman 1998: 14)

This modern mobility is further underscored as the audience is introduced to the main characters of the film, each of whom arrives by modern conveyance. For example, one of the aerial cityscape shots represents the perspective of one of the main characters as they arrive by passenger jet. Other main characters come by train and others by bus, and it is thus through the motif of modern, technological mobility, that they are introduced to the audience.

The film-makers lavish the viewer with images of the long main avenues that lead to each of the city's recently built or remodelled stations. For instance, an overhead camera follows a bus entering the city through its famous arches in the south of town – near the distinctive statue of the Roman goddess Minerva (built in 1957). A jump cut then shows a character descending from the bus. In another sequence, the camera follows the steps of another woman who gets off a train and exits to the street through an underground passage.

In the private realm in the film, Guadalajarans similarly experience the modern narrative: the suburban houses that are featured are all modernist, that is to say large, square or rectangular spaces with lots of glass, stone and concrete. The use of space is functionalist, apparently in the style of Frank Lloyd Wright. Such houses conveyed a look towards modernity, and were luxurious by 1960s standards; they also conveyed a sense of economic prosperity that was within everybody's reach. As Raymond Williams explains, the suburbs of the city were taking over the rural surroundings: 'The concentrated city is in the process of being replaced in industrial societies by what is in effect a transport network: the conurbation, the city region' (Williams 1993 [1973]: 324). Guadalajara, in effect, was following these patterns of international sprawl.

In the public realm, the emphasis is on modern buildings like the library, the theatres in the south of town and sites of leisure. An attribute common to them all is the work of modern local artists – specifically of the early 1960s – such as the sculptures of Eric Couffal, the paintings of Gabriel Flores and the architecture of Julio de la Peña and Alejandro Zohn.

This insistence on the importance of modern local art is revealing of how the new values of the modern culture would embrace a new artistic language and, in a different sense, also reveals the openness of the Guadalajarans to these trends. Art seemed to offer a relatively conflict-free way to integrate with the global village while expressing local ideals, such as the use of specific construction materials, themes and colours.

The importance of tradition

In contrast to all the modernity of transportation thus far described, one of the female characters chooses to ride to her lodgings – an old boarding house of two colourful old ladies – on a traditional horse and carriage. These can still be found in downtown Guadalajara and are shown in the film to illustrate the city's ability to reconcile tradition and modernity without conflict. In a contrasting scene, a Mexican character drives around in his red Thunderbird convertible, which has a small television set built into

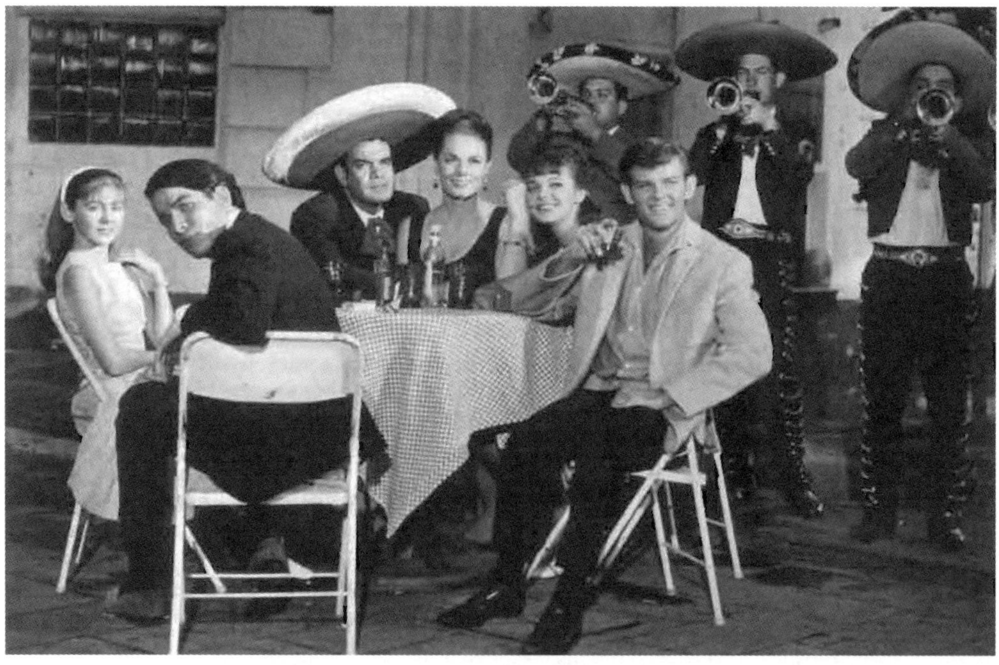

Figure 2. The singer Lola Casanova at Plaza de los Mariachis, 1964, © Agrasánchez Film Archive.

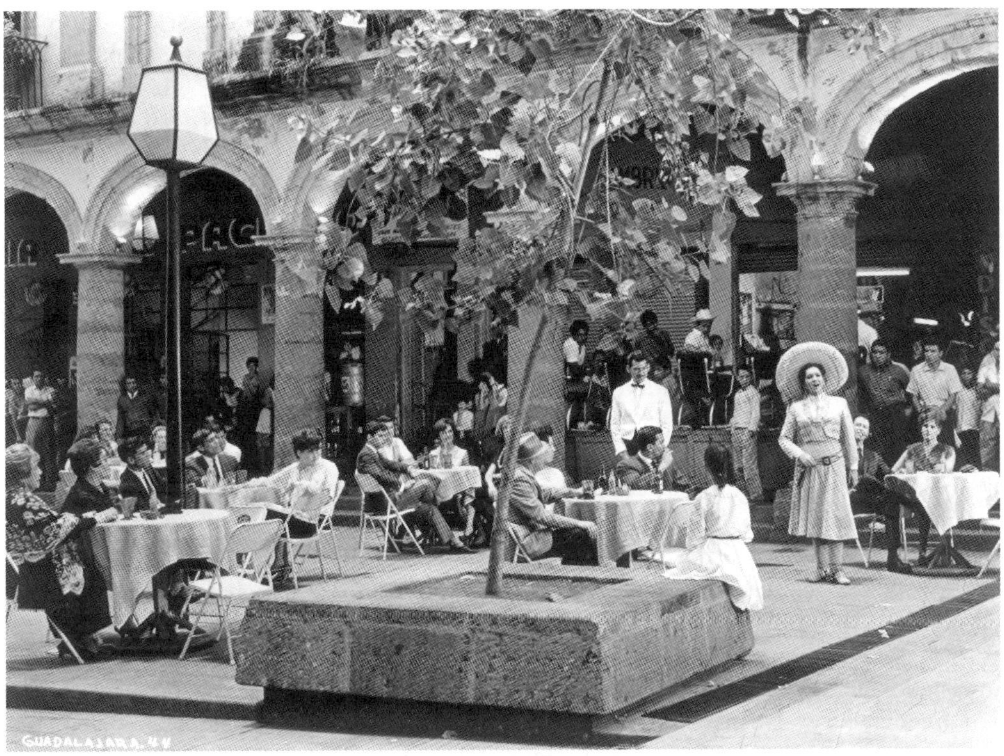

Figure 3. Mexicans and Americans enjoying a night in the city, 1964, © Agrasánchez Film Archive.

its dashboard. Illustrating how Mexico was embracing all sorts of new technology – and consequently the 'American Way of Life' – the car is a deliberate, if obvious, contrasting trope. Underlying the artifice behind these symbolic gestures is the fact that the film exaggerates the popularity of convertibles at the time – showing three different models, as if it was very common for young people in Mexico in the 1960s to have expensive, fast American cars.

Another 'traditional' scene occurs when the leading Mexican characters take their American friends for an informal dinner at the Plaza de los Mariachis, where they eat traditional food like *pozole* and listen to a folkloric singer. The scene further demonstrates the reconciliation of the traditional and pastoral innocence of the countryside with the experience of living in cosmopolitan Guadalajara, by showing rural remnants such as folklore and traditional music being used as a colourful accessory to modern life.

In *Guadalajara in the Summer* then, the notion of modernity as a disruptive force is entirely absent. Even though the colonial features of the historical centre were demolished and transformed, the film does not present this as at all problematic. Furthermore, it shows young Mexicans living a utopian lifestyle – even though that historic period had its own share of disagreements and contradictions, as Siegel explains: 'The moment also reaffirmed utopian notions that the social space of the city was a contested space, a living space, not necessarily immutable' (Siegel 2003: 139).

Conclusion

By 'reporting' on relevant, modern places to visit and things to do in Guadalajara (side-street cafes, public buildings and open squares), the film suggests cosmopolitan ways of inhabiting the city. Everybody in the film enjoys the harmonic, stress-free modernity of the city and locals and tourists alike dwell in an amicable environment. Despite the fact that the city had by then the distinctive landmarks of twentieth-century progress and modernity – and some of the social ills and conflicts that came with it – the film sought to show Guadalajara as an accessible site which, in Kevin Lynch's terms, was 'readable' (Lynch, 2012). It was presented as a city capable of attracting Americans through its cosmopolitan, vibrant atmosphere – a place that welcomed the culture of modernity and international capitalism. At the same time, these American 'exotic others' discover the uniqueness of a Mexican city and Mexican culture through its architecture, visual artists and composers and singers of mariachi music.

Guadalajara in the Summer then, features a city steeped in tradition while at the same time seeking to identify itself with modernity. It reflects the modern condition of its time, which, among other features, is open to the fusion of new cultural values – such as pop culture, foreign music and fashion. Even though the film is overloaded with tourist sites, and is a strange generic hybrid between a tourist documentary and teen comedy, it became a national hit at the time of its release and inspired the production of similar films throughout Mexico. It may not have been critically acclaimed, but in the state of Jalisco, more than 50 years after its release – and in the light of the current process of gentrification, globalization and real-estate bubbles – it still reminds us of times of relative financial stability, prosperity and innocence, and evokes a sense of pride and nostalgia in local communities.

References

Arango, S. (2012), *Ciudades y arquitectura: Seis generaciones*/City and architecture: Six generations, Mexico: Consejo Nacional para la Cultura y las Artes/Fondo de Cultura Económica.

Bartra, R. (1987), *La jaula de la melancolía. Identidad y metamorphosis del mexicano*/The cage of melancholy: Identity and metamorphosis in the Mexican Character, Mexico: Grijalbo.

Bauman, Z. (1998), *Globalization: The Human Consequences*, New York: Columbia University Press.

Benjamin, W. (1988 [1937]), 'In some motifs in Baudelaire', *Illuminations*, New York: Schocken Books, pp. 155–200.

Bracho, J. (1964), *Guadalajara en verano*/Guadalajara in the Summer, Mexico: Producciones Bueno, Javier Torres Ladrón de Guevara.

Bruno, G. (2008), 'Motion and emotion: Film and the urban fabric', in A. Weber and E. Wilson (eds), *Cities in Transition: The Moving Image and the Modern Metropolis*, London: Wallflower Press, pp. 14–28.

Dever, S. (2003), *Celluloid Nationalism and Other Melodramas: From Post-revolutionary Mexico to fin de siglo Mexamérica*, Albany: State University of New York Press.

Duque de Tlaquepaque (2009), 'Aquel inolvidable verano de 1964, o *Guadalajara en verano*… revisited', *El informador*, 8 August, p. 9-B, http://hemeroteca.informador. com.mx. Accessed 10 January 2012.

Eisenstein, S. (1989), 'Montage and architecture', *Assemblage*, 10, pp. 111–31.

Foster, D. W. (2002), *Mexico City in Contemporary Mexican Cinema*, Austin: University of Texas Press.

García Canclini, N. (2001), *La globalización imaginada*/Imagined globalization, Mexico: Paidós.

García Riera, E. (1986), *Julio Bracho 1909–1978*, Guadalajara, Mexico: Universidad de Guadalajara.

Koeck, R. (2013), *Cine-scapes: Cinematic Spaces in Architecture and Cities*, London: Routledge.

Lara Chávez, H. (2006), *Una ciudad inventada por el cine*/A city invented by cinema, Mexico: Consejo Nacional para la Cultura y las Artes/Cineteca Nacional.

Lynch, K. (2012), *La imagen de la ciudad*/The image of the city, Barcelona: Editorial Gustavo Gili.

Machuca, J. A. (2005), 'Reconfiguración del Estado-Nación y cambio de la conciencia patrimonial en México', in R. Béjar and H. Rosales (eds), *La identidad nacional mexicana como problema político y cultural*, Cuernavaca, Mexico: Centro Regional de Investigaciones Multidisciplinarias, UNAM, pp. 135–75.

Maciel, D. R. (1999), 'Cinema and the state in contemporary Mexico, 1970–1999', in J. Hershfield and R. M. David (eds), *Mexico's Cinema: A Century of Film and Filmmakers*, Wilmington, Delaware: A Scholarly Resources, pp. 197–232.

Martínez Assad, C. (2010), *La ciudad de México que el cine nos dejó*/Mexico city as seen by cinema, Mexico: Océano.

Miller, C. (1962), 'Guadalajara balances the old with the new', *New York Times*, 7 October, http://www.nytimes.com. Accessed 16 July 2013.

Muriá, J. M. (1994), *Breve historia de Jalisco*/Brief history of Jalisco, Mexico: Fondo de Cultura Económica/El Colegio de México.

Siegel, A. (2003), 'After the Sixties: Changing paradigms in the representations of urban space', in M. Shiel and T. Fitzmaurice (eds), *Screening the City*, London: Verso. pp. 137–59.

Shohat, E. and Stam, R. (2002), 'The imperial imaginary', in G. Turner (ed.), *The Film Cultures Reader*, London and New York: Routledge, pp. 366–78.

Tuñón, J. (1977), *Interview with Javier Torres Ladrón de Guevara* [Transcript], 18 January, Collection 'Proyecto Historia Oral', PHO/6/18, Library 'Ernesto de la Torre Villar', Instituto Luis María Mora, Federal District, Mexico.

—————— (1986), *Historia de un sueño: El Hollywood tapatío*/The history of a dream: The Hollywood from Jalisco, Guadalajara, Mexico: Universidad de Guadalajara/UNAM.

Vaidovits, G. (1989), *El cine mudo en Guadalajara*/Silent Cinema in Guadalajara, Guadalajara, Mexico: Universidad de Guadalajara.

Williams, R. (1993 [1973]), *The Country and the City*, London: Hogarth Press.

Notes

1. Director Julio Bracho of *Guadalajara en verano*, was a well-known film-maker whose career started in the 1940s, with several successful movies such as *Crepúsculo/Twilight* (1944). Later, he became a cult director when his film *La sombra del caudillo/The Shadow of a Leader* (1960) was censored by the government because it talked about treason and the assassination of a general. A decade later, Bracho would be filming in Guadalajara in some of the same places, when he made the film *En busca de un muro/In Search of a Wall* (1974), a biopic of José Clemente Orozco. In this other feature he did not apply the same elegance and attention to detail as in *Guadalajara en verano*.

2. A reference to the popular American beach movies of the period was also deliberately made in the film through the casting of American pop idol Dean Reed, who was enormously popular at the time in the United States and Latin America, where he would travel often. He spoke Spanish.

3. In an article from 2009 by Duque de Tlaquepaque, the author praises the work of the producers: 'The film is not quite a work of art, it is something better: primarily a historic document of what our longed Guadalajara was' (Duque de Tlaquepaque 2009). This article gives voice to the locals in their yearning.

4. Orozco was a native of Zapotlán, Jalisco (1883–1949).

5. The main hotels featured in the exterior and interiors were Hotel del Parque, Camino Real and Fénix, all of which remain in business. The Hilton opened in August 1964; years later it became, successively, Sheraton and Misión Carlton (the current one). The Hilton reopened in Guadalajara, decades later, at another location.

Chapter 8

The cinematic image as an architectural conductor: A mediated hint from future architecture

Aysegül Akçay Kavakoglu

Introduction

It has been almost a century since Fritz Lang imagined his modern city vision of the industrialized world, *Metropolis* (1923). It was a vision that committed itself to criticizing the effects of the Industrial Revolution by using architecture and city images as mediated conductors. Since then, *Metropolis'* representative power has been an inspiration for the disciplines of cinema and architecture in their various imaginings of the future.

Images of city and urban life on film can be considered as architectural or urban visions, or even in some cases designs, in the cinematic medium. From this perspective, it has often been argued that cinema uses architecture as a narrative tool, or that architecture uses cinematic images as channels, or 'conductors', for the development of future ideas in which the physical entities and dimensions of real buildings and cities vanish within the flat world of the screen. Although these dimensions disappear – and this is often seen as negative – new meanings and depths emerge within cinematic images of architecture in which spatial reconstitutions can and do occur. During this reconstitution images transform and generate outcomes for the future of architecture that enliven and enrich debate within the discipline. In some cases, this occurs in the context of real cities, such as in the films *Minority Report* (Spielberg, 2002) or *Renaissance* (Volckman, 2006). In some cases however, the architectural images created can be based in another universe where the 'real' city vanishes or transforms into a concept. Examples include *2001: Space Odyssey* (Kubrick, 1968) and *Elysium* (Blomkamp, 2013).

This chapter aims to explore the relationship of cinematic images and future architecture by considering science-fiction-genre movie set designs and their illustrated environments. In doing so, the author will discuss the possible real-life impact of these visions on city and urban life by comparing the films with each other and further argue that filmic set designs direct tomorrow's architectural images, and thus, urban life.

The mediated hint

There are many possible interpretations of 'science fiction'. It has been defined as being the 'literature of ideas' (Gilks, Fleming and Allen 2003), the 'literature of change, anticipation, and the human species' (Gunn 2004: 8) and 'the playground for the imagination' (Johnson 2011: iv). The *Oxford English Dictionary* defines it as 'Fiction based on imagined future scientific or technological advances and major social or environmental changes, frequently portraying space or time travel and life on other planets' (Oxford University Press 2015). It explores the consequences of these imagined ideas – of science and technology – within various media such as literature and painting, and those of interest here, cinema and architecture. It can be argued that these explorations often focus on three primary subjects – initially on the human; secondly, the environment inhabited; and thirdly, the alien. Annette Kuhn emphasizes that science fiction films, through these subjects/concepts, create 'fictional worlds which present themselves as other, or outside everyday reality – deep space. [They show] the inner geography of spacecraft, and the contours of alien planets' (Kuhn 1990: 6).

Embedded in all this is often a concern for the future of humanity, its environment and our daily lives. They are all concerns about the transformation of human life that are questioned via the imagination in science fiction. Consequently, the genre offers novel possibilities and variations of everyday life in the future, typically through speculations connected to our present reality. Outlining this, Kuhn suggests that these speculations are attached to iconographic conventions, which work as a catalyst between the spectator and the image. In fact, these attachments are tied up, primarily, in built and unbuilt environments. As a result, it can be said that in the science fiction genre, cinematic images act as a channel, or 'conductor', for the future by using architecture. Given that this cinematic – architectural relationship has a duality, in which architecture can also use the cinematic image as a catalyst, films become 'mediated hints' about the future of everyday life and architecture and vice versa. Consequently, both from the exclusive architect or urban designer's perspective, and that of film-makers and theorists, learning to read and analytically criticise these hints becomes crucial.

Key to reading these 'hints' is a consideration of architecture and cities in film as the materials of a cinematic science fiction experiment that operates architecturally, but also socially and culturally. This experimentation is based on the question of 'what if?', where James Gunn's definition of science fiction as 'the literature of discontinuity' (Gunn 2004: 8) comes to prominence in that it permits us to juxtapose hypothetical realities. However, this 'discontinuity' and its 'what if' hypothesis can in itself be interpreted as a signifier for a new world. At the same time, it can also refer to a restructuring or reorganizing of the old from a different viewpoint. Therefore, the cinematic visions of future architecture can be free of the past, or the realities we have at present. In this state, it reflects ideas of Sanford Kwinter who, talking of Sant'Elia's futuristic architecture, suggests the architectural project of the future 'cannot be subject to any law of historical continuity. It must be as new as our state of mind is new, and the contingencies of our moment in history' (Kwinter 1998: 597). However, the ceration of these images can take place in another context, as experiments conducted upon tradition – as in Kuhn's terminology – of iconographic conventions, which facilitate the perception of the new by familiarizing the spectator with the old/historical/usual in the cinematic image.

In both situations, the cinematic image 'possesses' the spectator and opens a gate towards the possible future, metaphorically injecting future memories about urban life and the city through using architecture. According to Juhani Pallasmaa, this situation creates mind spaces that articulate the experience of the world (Pallasmaa 2006: 10). Our understanding of space transforms through this experience that Pallasmaa calls 'lived space' – defined as the 'space that is inseparably integrated with the subject's concurrent life situation'. Pallasmaa emphasizes the inherent nature of this experience as a combination; 'material and mental worlds in which the experienced, remembered and imagined, as well as the past, present and future, are inseparably intermixed' (Pallasmaa 2001: 18).

Thus, the cinematic image becomes a conductor by restructuring the experience of both space and time by using architecture. Architecture becomes a protagonist, and its illustrations gain importance as a connector for the real and imagined, by ceasing to be just a cinematic background and transforming into a foregrounded and central theme. In the process of doing this, it reminds us of Pallasmaa once more – particularly his argument that architecture is a mediator, settling the spectator in space and place, and articulating the nature of the spectator's experience of both the past and the future. In his words: 'We understand and remember who we are through our constructions, both material and mental. We also judge alien and past cultures through the evidence provided by the architectural structures they have produced. Buildings project epic narratives' (Pallasmaa 2009: 17). They do the same in film.

Pallasmaa then, emphasizes architecture as a 'significant memory device' that paints time by projecting memories and stimulating the imagination. As he states:

Memory and fantasy, recollection and imagination are related and they have always a situational and specific content. One who cannot remember can hardly imagine, because memory is the soil of imagination. Memory is also the ground of self-identity; we are what we remember. (Pallasmaa 2009: 18)

The ability to project a narrative becomes an apparatus for the cinematic image in which memory is constructed through different future scenarios - each using urban life and the city as their key elements. This situation creates a cycle in which these 'mediated hints' reappear and redirect the spectator into a loop of familiarity regarding the imagined future, and thus, future architectures. It is suggested here that these 'mediated hints' primarily share two concepts: (1) time and (2) space. Although they involve various future scenarios, they are all linked together through time and space, depicting both the continuity and discontinuity of generated future images. This link can be a conscious and normalised one, or it can operate purely as inspiration. An architectural example of the latter is Pallasmaa's Portman Hotel which is based on Vincent Korda's visions in *Things to Come* (1936). Pallasmaa remarks that this inspiration is a negative statement on architecture, and he outlines that as an 'inspiration' it 'cold-bloodedly serves the economic interest of the developer; it utilizes the means of persuasion derived from stage sets designed for cinematic spectacles' (Pallasmaa 2001: 17). The reappearance of the cinematic hint here, affects the spectator reciprocally and the spectator gets used to these hints, accepting them as a part of his/her inherent memory. This acceptance can either be conscious or unconscious but it is easily normalised. Hence, the cinematic image influences how the spectator constitutes images of the real and the imagined.

Hint 1: The case of *2001: A Space Odyssey*

Imagining and depicting the future lies between the enigmatic layers of thought and representation constructed by and through science, art and architecture. Cinema articulates these layers through moving images, and employs both time and space as elements of synthesis of disjunction. According to Pallasmaa, the film director is like a magician evoking a lived situation from a distance by constructing an illusory narrative through projected images (Pallasmaa 2001: 20; 2006: 12). This description fits Stanley Kubrick and his generation of multidimensional readings of existence and the future in his cult science fiction film *2001: A Space Odyssey*. In this film, there are no visions of earth or daily urban life. The imagery of this film focuses on space colonization and the machinery of the future, albeit if strains of an early-1970s modernist aesthetic can be seen in some of the clothing, hairstyles, and assorted paraphernalia such as suitcases, etc. It can also be seen in the bright, sterile look of the red furniture held in relief by the white, grey and black interior backgrounds. That said, the design of the spacecraft, including both the interior and the exterior, is so detailed and sufficiently new that it directs the audience into a reality never faced before. This is epitomised by Hal (the unstable artificial intelligence) a symbol of the 'computerization of everyday situations', through its contradictory actions, judgments and decisions. Hal's behaviour towards the end of the film makes the audience question 'home' and the existence of daily activities, like dinner on the table and sleeping on a real bed. This is reinforced by Kubrick's symbolism, with green replacing red as the dominant interior colour. Besides causing tension in the audience though unexplained variations, this is intended to reflect the dominance of 'humanity' or human attributes. Beyond its representative power, *Space Odyssey* introduces the issue of living in a place other than Earth by presenting *Space Station V* as a complex that includes restaurants, hotels, offices and meeting spaces. In addition to drawing upon ideas of Arthur C. Clarke's and Kubrick himself, the design of this colonized space life involved consultations with NASA (Ordway n.d.). Beyond affecting the audiences' image of the future then, and engaging with the work of artists and architects *Space Odyssey* also drew upon technological institutions and the imaganisations of scientists. After the film's release in 1968, NASA's Ames Research Center started the 'Stanford/NASA Ames Space Settlement Studies' programme and established the 'Summer Study' initiative in 1975 (Davis 2007). The 'Summer Study' was a design study conducted by a broad interdisciplinary group that included engineers, architects, physicists, chemists, sociologists, economists, astronauts, artists and students from various disciplines.[1] Amongst the results of this study was a toroidal-shaped space colony design concept, called the 'Stanford Torus', (Davis n.d.) (Figure 1).

Subsequent NASA funded studies covered a range of environmental, agricultural, architectural and structural projects that drew upon and influenced the modernist movement of the era. Their definitions and illustrations of architectural projects were heavily influenced by the topology of the Stanford Torus and some of its associated physiological, psychological and material considerations on habitation, society, construction and transport. (Design 1977). In this imagined new world, housing was to be built on a modular structural system with dwellings at a maximum of five stories high (Design 1977). The work defineable as architecture by the NASA Ames Research Center did not stop in the 1970s however. As recently as 1994, it launched a design competition

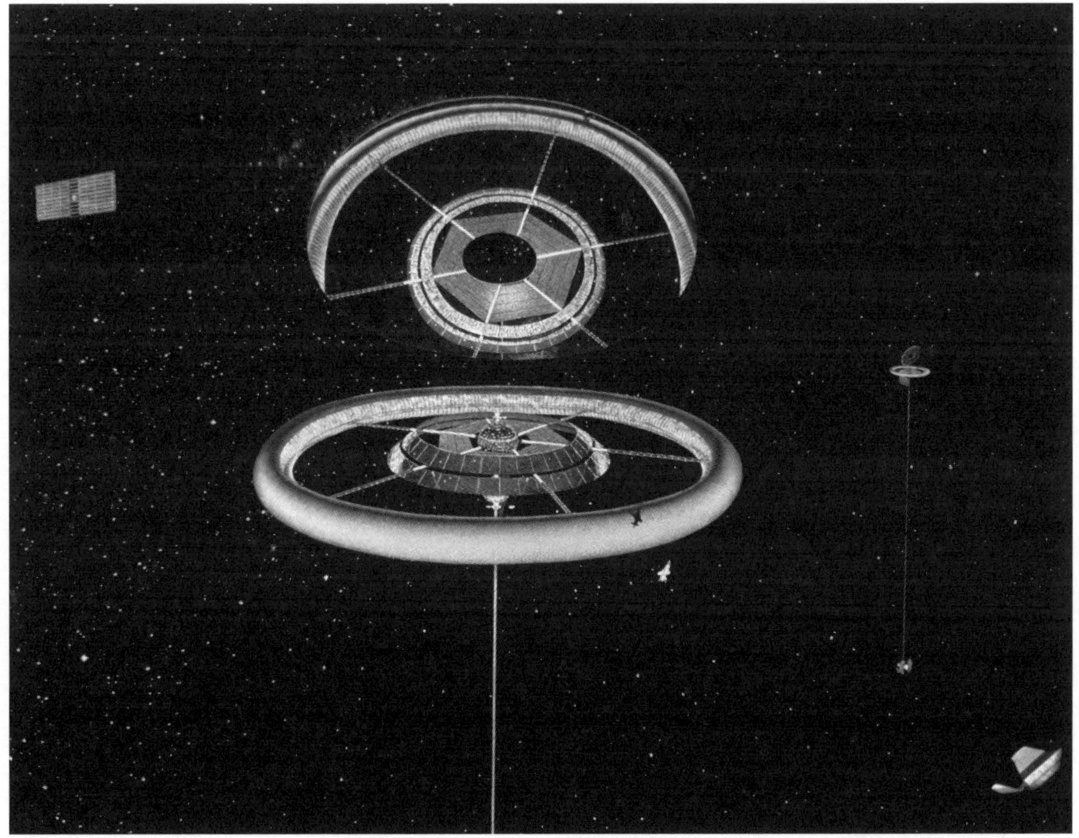

Figure 1. The exterior view of the Stanford Torus illustrated by Don Davis in the 1970s, © NASA Ames Research Center.

for students. Since then, there have been 21 competitions and numerous awards for projects that focus on the sustainability of a space colony.

Both concepts imagined, and the imagery that accompanies them, at NASA have clearly used fiction to structure a relational loop scientifically, architecturally and socially, another example of which is the work of Don Davis. Davis, a space artist working for NASA, illustrated the icons of future environments in drawings that act as an image data bank for an alternative urban life and, at the same time, operate as a 'conductor' by carrying information between disciplines to bind the relationships in the above-mentioned loop. His images have a multi-layered essence in which the past, present and the future exist at the same time. In other words, although these illustrated environments refer to their epoch, the 1970s, they – like Kubrick's epoch tinged imagery – are ageless. The epochal style vanishes as the audience spends more time looking at them, and thus become normalized to them.

Hint 2: The case of *Minority Report* in 2054

Steven Spielberg's *Minority Report* is set 53 years after Kubrick's film. Its action takes place on Earth in the year 2054. Specifically using the context of Washington DC Spielberg's film shows us the technological future of the city. Alex McDowell, the production designer of the movie, explains this from Spielberg's point of view in one of his interviews (Brew 2010). According to Spielberg, people live in yesterday's future, where many of our buildings are 100 years old, and although we change our cellphones every year, the way technology affects our lives is relatively small (Brew 2010). During the conceptualization of *Minority Report*, Spielberg and McDowell tried to predict the future by investigating the developing projects and studies at the technology departments of big companies. In addition, Spielberg gathered some researchers, scientists, technologists and architects, including urban planners like Peter Calthorpe, to predict the future of our technology, our architecture and our cities in a brainstorming session over one weekend (Wired Staff 2012). The pre-cogs of Speilberg's film - people who possesses 'precognition' as a form of extra-sensory perception – and the city of touch-screen technology we see in the film, were the result. (Wired Staff 2012) On the film, Spielberg and McDowell conceived the future imagery and architecture of Washington DC as two separately operating worlds – one serving the wealthy and business elite, the other serving those who cannot afford the high-tech future. While buildings transform into vertical highways in one part of the city, the film simultaneously shows us the informal housing districts of the city built by the have-nots. (Figure 2). When we add to this mix historic row-houses we are presented with a clearly postmodernist view of architectural and social poles (Rishabhhajela 2011).

Instead of adding new layers to the city, as was done in Ridley Scott's *Blade Runner* (1982), Spielberg constructed a new identity for the future urban conglomeration similar to Fritz Lang's *Metropolis*. In this new city we see criticism of modernism and

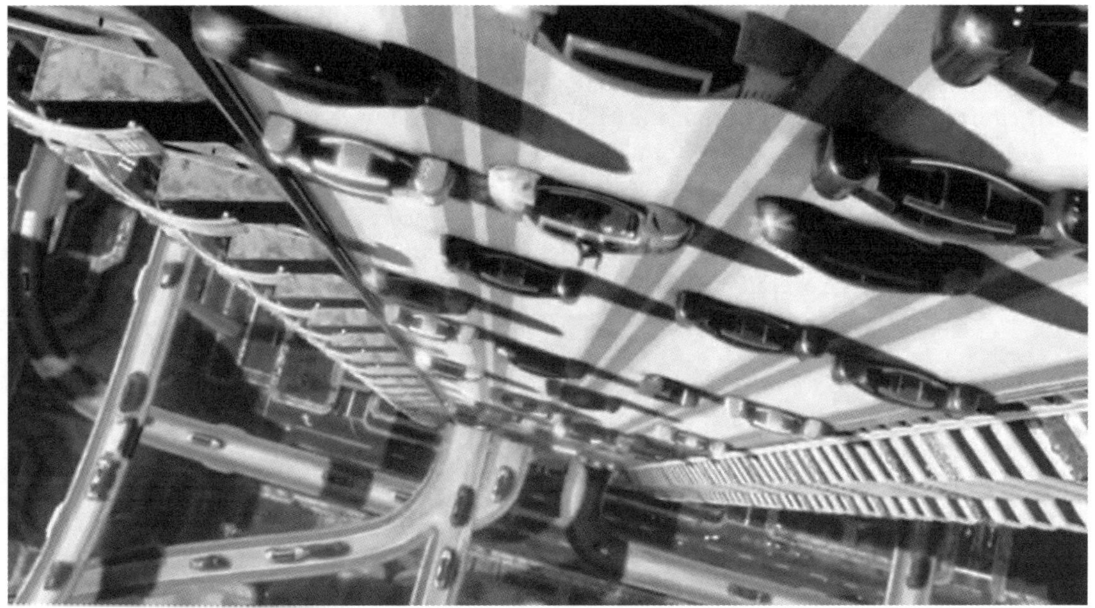

Figure 2. The vertical highways at the new city centre. *Minority Report*, (2002), © 20th Century Fox.

its implications. The architectural and city concepts employed, steel, glass and grass, direct the audience into symbolic colour schemes of grey, blue and green that fade into each other as if they were part of a grand corporate, kinetic structure. As facades turn into highways or news bulletin boards, negative and positive spaces are regenerated and inverted through a form of kinetic structure that has eyes and ears - and which serves as a living mechanism watching and recording every situation and every person. The city thus turns into a ubiquitous amorphous corporation and physical entity in which nothing can be hidden. Advertisements in the city are directed at individuals through collected information via surveillance. They are projected as an ambient intelligence that senses people and responds to their actions and attitudes. Not only that, in this future world, people lose their autonomy. Drivers cede control of their vehicles for example, but more significantly, people lose the power to act as they are hunted by the pre-crime police department before they get a chance to commit a misdemeanour.

Although *Minority Report* envisions 2054, many of the ideas in the film were realized prior to 2015. Touchpad screens are now indispensable tools for many in business, communication, education and daily life. Personalized advertisements are popular via the Internet, especially through social portals in which the system records every website that the user enters and ads pop up on webpages like e-mail programs without the authorization of the user. In approximately two years, driverless cars are expected to be on the roads. (Torr, 2014; Litman, 2014: 42). Through previsioning these concepts, *Minority Report* asks questions and criticizes information management and technological development, and their impact on society and urban life. However, at the same time, the film promotes future designs and embeds the produced images in the audience's memory. Besides initiating the realization stage of future images for film-makers and the audience then, the illustrated future environments in films like this facilitate the process of actualization in real life. Consequently, it can be argued that every detail in this imagined world gains importance for constructing the overall mood and ambience of future urban life.

Hint 3: The case of *Renaissance* in 2054

Nezar AlSayyad defines cinematic space as an analytical tool for criticism of the city as reel and real, in terms of its perception and experience through a flat screen (AlSayyad 2006: 4). The boundary between the real and the virtual has eroded and a mutated constitution has emerged within a paradigm of a 'real–virtual continuum' (AlSayyad 2006: 5). This continuum hosts a variety of alternative instances and situations from urban daily life that were designed as cinematic images which become both facts and dreams, overlapping in the form of memories through these images. Christian Volkman's *Renaissance*, which takes place in 2054 Paris, is a perfect example of this due to its status as an animation constructed on the real and transformed into the virtual. Even though it is an animation, the audience gathers all of the information from this 'real–virtual continuum' and composes his/her own mental image of Paris – another possible future of the year 2054. This futuristic film noir is clearly situated on a continuum with the architectural and spatial heritage of Paris; Haussmannian urbanism and the five points of Le Corbusier still dominate the city's future image. The 'terraced roof gardens' and the lifted movable modules supported by 'pilotis' look like steel structures attached on nineteenth-century dwellings' rooftops. It is an image of the city that can be traced to the 'free facades' and integrated 'horizontal windows' repeatedly found in the sketches by Alfred Frazzani, an architect, and the art director of *Renaissance* (Figure 3). *Renaissance* then, creates a future through multilayered urban visuals in which nineteenth-century architecture binds with high modernist ideas. While trying to respect these historical layers however, the film problematises the heritage of the city through its interpretation of space via critical modern paradigms.

Janet Staiger states that the designed cities in science fiction films can be understood as utopian commentaries on hopes and failures, or on the contrary, can be understood as dystopian propositions criticizing modern urban life and its associated economic system (Staiger 1999: 99). The multilayered city in *Renaissance* can thus be read as a critique of today's Parisian images, in which the historical and the modern are separated, literally, with the historical being inside and the modern being outside - on the peripheries of the city. In reference to this definition, Staiger has commented on Terry Gilliam's *Brazil* (1985)

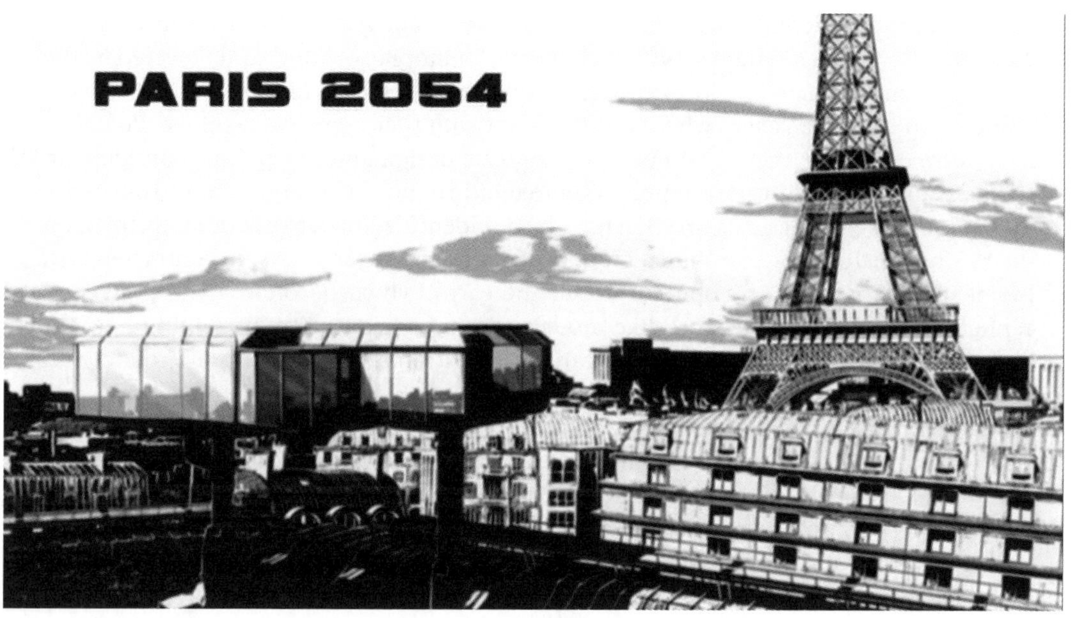

Figure 3. The attached 'pilotis' look like structures. *Renaissance*, (2006), © Miramx Films.

evoking Le Corbusier's 'a machine to live in' metaphor (Staiger 1999: 113). Through these associations, the city in *Renaissance* becomes a protagonist acting as an organism and spying on its inhabitants through constant surveillance – it becomes a living machine. Similarly, in *Minority Report*, the highly modern city is envisioned as a living machine – but one that turns out to be a ubiquitous corporation. In these cases, the city as a machine goes beyond being a concept and becomes reality and, as a result, the notion of a city itself starts to evolve – its machine-like entity becoming more relevant than its physicality as place or geography.

Hint 4: The case of *Elysium* in 2154

Science fiction is just a filter to look at real life.

Erik Sofge

The above quotation is from an article by Erik Sofge about Neill Blomkamp, the director of *Elysium* (2013). In this film Blomkamp reimagines daily life and the city in 2154. The film's central idea is the fight for a better life in which everybody will be equal in terms of socio-economic conditions. Set in the context of emigration from Earth to space, Elysium is a space settlement serving rich people - a utopia governed and powered by the same company, Armaydne, since 2097. It is a space-urb designed for the elite in which the wealthy can heal themselves whenever they want with their personalized Med-Pod 3000 healthcare machines; they live in villas of exquisite design and exceptional construction standards; and live with the support of humanoid robotics (Elysium Home Tour n.d.). This space-urb even has its own citizens, who are identified by DNA codes imprinted on their skins which act like combined identity cards, passports and keys. In contrast to this, Blomkamp envisions a dystopic future for the earth, which becomes a twenty-second century slum. Poor people work like modern slaves to keep Elysium running but lack basic human rights or access to health care. It is a vision that has common ground with twenty-first century gated communities and slums.

Marketing the 'perfect life' image remains the same for the future society in 2154 as for 2054 in the other films previously discussed. Indeed, the official website of the movie is like a real estate website, selling the perfect space – urban life – to the audience through the phrase, 'Elysium: You won't find a better home on Earth'. This 'perfect-life' idle has, since the Industrial Revolution, been used as a popular selling strategy in politics and business and is played out through all media, including cinema, advertisements, photographs, newspapers, television etc. Thus, although cinema can produce films that criticize everyday-life situations, politics and the economics of urban life, along with its infrastructures, it also does the opposite – it creates a strategy for avoiding these criticisms by selling representations of the 'ideal'. According to Brian Wallis, these representations are posed as natural 'facts' and their misleading plenitude directs people towards a foggy field where reality-comprehension transforms, or even vanishes, in constructed representations (Wallis 1984: xv). These constructed representations, whether positive or critical, tend not be be formed in isolation, but rather borrow from other images and ideas and subsequently feed into other notions and visions. This is clearly true of the films discussed here and is central to the overall argument being laid out. For example, Elysium, which is designed as a space-urb, shares elements with Kubrick's *2001: A Space Odyssey*, in which the concept of space colonization was explored via cinema. *Elysium* takes Kubrick's vision as a reference in order to conduct its future image of 2154 (Figure 4; Figure 5) but also draws upon NASA's studies inspired, in part, by Kubrick. Elysium, as a habitat for space colonization, references the Stanford Torus produced during the 'Summer Studies' by NASA, and constructs its own conceptual designs through these studies.

This borrowing of ideas and influences however, goes beyond the sci-fi genre in film itself – and beyond its immediate influences. *Elysium* comments on today's urban life and architecture by merging ultramodern dwellings, postmodern suburban features and neo-futuristic elements of today's architecture. For instance, Santiago Calatrava's 'City of Arts and Sciences in Valencia' turns into Elysium's Marine Opera House; a real villa from Mexico, Puerto Vallarta, serves as an Elysium citizen's villa; and the Sony Center in Berlin becomes the setting of high-rise residences in Blomkamp's utopic vision.[2] Although urban life in space is a new entity then, Blomkamp adopts historical styles rather than design a totally new futuristic vision. Using well-known buildings from the 1990s and 2000s, as well as unknown housing projects, Blomkamp directs the audience towards a 'normalised' perception of the future that does not need high-tech structures, robots and futuristic torus like design.

All this sits alongside a dystopic view of life on earth based on a real mega-slum in the district of Iztapalapa in Mexico – an area with a population of 4 million people (Mora-Torres 2013). This is not unusual. Juan Mora-Torres (2013), a history professor at DePaul University, identifies that many recent sci-fi movies point out a miserable future grounded in pandemics, ecological devastation and social corrosion of today. According to him,

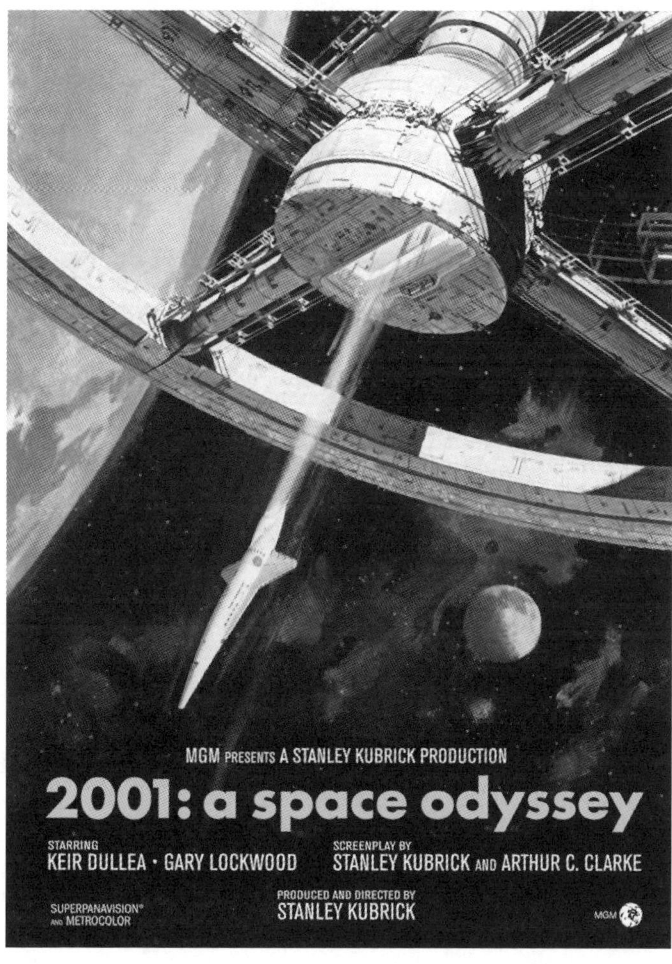

Figure 4. The official movie poster for *2001: A Space Odyssey*, (1968), © Metro-Goldwyn-Mayer.

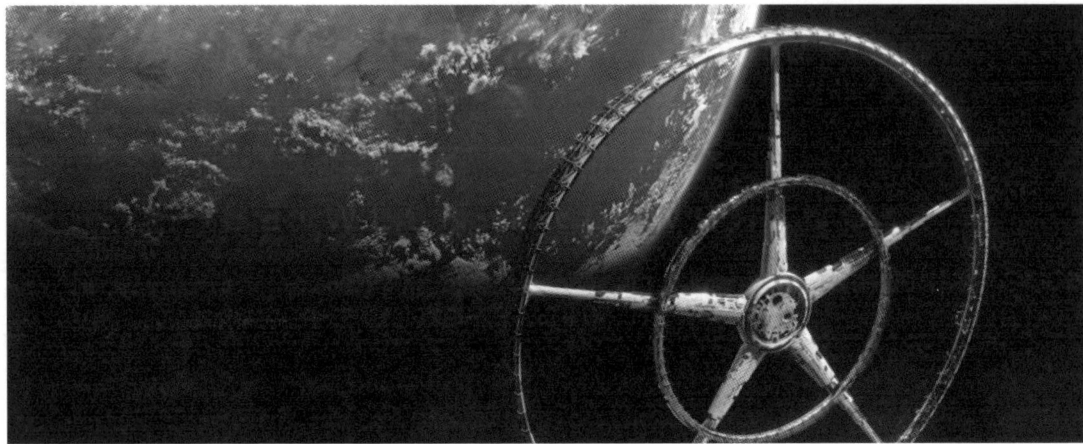

Figure 5. The exterior view of Elysium. *Elysium,* (2013), © TriStar Pictures.

Blomkamp uses the 'idea of progress' - within a political subtext in *Elysium* - and suggests that under capitalism this 'progress' will take humanity in two opposite directions (Mora-Torres 2013). One will be the unaffordable ultra-luxurious life directed by science and technology, and the other will be the ecological disaster curated by capitalism's desire for profits. This process has already started with the iconic architectural object being seen as the symbol of wealth and success operating in a 'context free' condition contrasted with slums and other residential areas of the working classes appearing to be more like 'concrete farms' than places to live. The fact that those living in these areas support the capitalist system as service industry providers means they are definable as spaces required to capitalism's continued expansion.

Conclusion

The films studied in this chapter present overlapping future images through depictions of politics, economics, social and urban life. They all, with the exception of *2001: A Space Odyssey*, rely on the core idea of a rich and poor dichotomy in which health, beauty and security are the main topics of a period spanning one century (2054–2154). They also prioritise issues of information management and technological development – and their impact on society. Similarly, they mostly focus their questions on these issues in the context of urban life. Other similarities include the fact that their architectural images of the future take their cue from high modernism juxtaposed with the heritage of the cities in question.

All of this, it is suggested, reflects the fact that cinema is an experiential realm in which the architecture created for the cinematic spectacle relies on perception and previous experience, and that this opens a gate between the image and the imagined – the cinematic image and the architecture we seek to develop in film and in reality. This gate serves as a passage for the audience to capture memories through cinematic experiences and perceptions, resulting in spatial reconstitutions appearing in the mind of the observer/audience. It is by conceptualizing the relationship between cinema and architecture in this way that we end up with an interpretation of the cinematic image as an architectural 'conductor' that both literally and metaphorically orientates the observer/audience towards developing and accepting future architectural ideas and projects.

In addition to this however, this chapter has also suggested that the visions of the future created and developed in these films not only prepares the audience for the future by overlapping memory traces in the eye/mind, it suggests there are real affects for architectural production. These can be seen through *Minority Report*'s touchpad screens referenced in ongoing studies and architectural projects of the 2000s. It was clearly evident in *Space Odyssey*'s influence on NASA researchers and designers in the 1970s and can can also be seen in *Elysium*'s envisioning of 2154's space urban life. This is perhaps a more recognised way in which cinema, through science fiction films, engages with architecture and the city but, when placed alongside a reading of the public's acceptance of the future city as influenced, by film, gives us strong reasons to see the cinematic image as an architectural conductor and its imagery as a series of mediated hints about future architecture and cities.

References

AlSayyad, N. (2006), 'Introduction: The cinematic city and the quest for the modern', in N. AlSayyad (ed.), *Cinematic Urbanism*, New York: Routledge, pp.1–19.

Blomkamp, N. (2013), *Elysium*, USA: TriStar Pictures.

Brew, S. (2010), 'Alex Mc Dowell interview: Designing *Minority Report*', 12 May, http://www.denofgeek.com/movies/15773/alex-mcdowell-interview-designing-minority-report. Accessed 9 June 2015.

Corbusier, L. (1927), *Towards a New Architecture*, London: Architectural Press.

Davis, D. (n.d.) 'Public domain works done for NASA', http://www.donaldedavis.com/PARTS/allyours.html. Accessed 9 June 2015.

———— (2007), 'Hope for survival and the growth of human potential by space migration', http://www.donaldedavis.com/2007NEW/SPACEMIGRATION.html. Accessed 9 June 2015.

Sony Pictures (2013), Armadyne, http://armadyne.net/. Accessed 10 January 2016.

Gilks, M., Fleming, P. and Allen, M. (2003), 'Science fiction: The literature of ideas', http://www.writing-world.com/sf/sf.shtml. Accessed 9 June 2015.

Gunn, J. (2004), 'Towards a definition of science fiction', in E. J. Gunn and M. Candelaria (eds), *Speculations on Speculation: Theories of Science Fiction*, Maryland: Scarecrow Press, pp.5–12.

Hajela, R. (2011), '*Minority Report*: Architecture and the movie', 30 April, http://futuristicarch.wordpress.com/2011/04/30/minority-report-architecture-and-the-movie/. Accessed 9 June 2015.

Johnson, D. B. (2011), *Science Fiction Prototyping: Designing the Future with Science Fiction*, San Rafael, CA: Morgan & Claypool Publishers.

Kubrick, S. (1968), *2001: Space Odyssey*, USA: Metro-Goldwyn-Mayer.

Kuhn, A. (1990), 'Introduction: Cultural theory and science fiction cinema', in A. Kuhn (ed.), *Alien Zone: Cultural Theory and Contemporary Science Fiction Cinema*, 7th ed., London: Verso, pp.1–14.

Kwinter, S. (1998), 'La citta nuova: Modernity and continuity, Zone 1–2', in K. M. Hays (ed.), *Architecture Theory Since 1968*, Cambridge, MA: MIT Press, pp. 586–614.

Litman, T. (2014), 'Ready or Waiting', Traffic Technology International, January 2014, pp. 36-42.

Mora-Torres, M. J. (2013), 'Movies: "Elysium" – the year 2154 is 2013', 18 August, http://www.pilsenportal.org/news/2580. Accessed 9 June 2015.

NASA (1977), 'Space settlements: A design study', http://www.nss.org/settlement/nasa/75SummerStudy/Chapt5.html#HAB. Accessed 9 June 2015.

Ordway, I. F. III (2001), '*2001: A Space Odyssey* in retrospect', http://www.visual-memory.co.uk/amk/doc/0075.html. Accessed 9 June 2015.

Oxford University Press (2015), 'Science fiction', http://www.oxforddictionaries.com/definition/english/science-fiction?q=science+fiction. Accessed 9 June 2015.

Pallasmaa, J. (2001), 'Introduction: Lived space in architecture and cinema', *The Architecture of Image: Existential Space in Cinema*, Helsinki: Building Information, pp. 11–37.

—————— (2006), 'Lived space in architecture and cinema', in B. Uluoğlu, A. Enşici and A. Vatansever (eds), *Design and Cinema: Form Follows Film*, Newcastle: Cambridge Scholar Press, pp. 10–32.

—————— (2009), 'Space, place, memory and imagination: The temporary dimension of existential space', in M. Treib (ed.), *Spatial Recall: Memory in Architecture and Landscape*, New York: Routledge, pp. 16–41.

Sofge, E. (2013), 'Before directing 'District 9,' Neil Bloomkamp illustrated for popular science', 18 July, http://www.popsci.com/science/article/2013-06/directing-district-9-neill-blomkamp-illustrated-popular-science. Accessed 9 June 2015.

Spielberg, S. (2002), *Minority Report*, USA: Twentieth Century Fox Film Corporation.

Staiger, J. (1999), 'Future noir: Contemporary representations of visionary cities', in A. Kuhn (ed.), *Alien Zone II: The Spaces of Science Fiction Cinema*, New York: Verso, pp. 97–123.

Torr, F. (2014), 'Next-gen Audi A8 drives better than you,' Motoring, 22 October, http://www.motoring.com.au/next-gen-audi-a8-drives-better-than-you-46963/. Accessed 9 January 2016.

Volckman, C. (2006), *Renaissance*, Paris: Miramax Films.

Wallis, B. (1984), 'What's wrong with this picture? An introduction', *Art After Modernism: Rethinking Representation*, New York: New Museum of Contemporary Art, pp. xi–1.

Wired Staff (2012), 'Inside *Minority Report*'s idea summit (2012)', 21 August, http://www.wired.com/2012/06/minority-report-idea-summit/. Accessed 9 June 2015.

Note

1. The entire participant list can be seen at the official website of NASA Space Settlements: http://www.nss.org/settlement/nasa/75SummerStudy/partslist.html. Accessed 14 June 2014.
2. These buildings are used for the Armadyne Corporation website launched by Sony Pictures to explore and develop ideas expressed in Elysium: http://armadyne.net/company/about.php. Accessed 10 January 2016.

Chapter 9

Berlin on film: A mediated and reconstructed city

Graham Cairns

Introduction

The moment the still image was imbued with life through film, a new visual language was born. Radical in its forms and profound in its consequences, that language represented what may now be called an 'optical revolution'. In 1895, Louis and Auguste Lumière astonished the first cinematic audiences in Le Salon Indien du Grand Café. The following year, Georges Méliès fragmented space and time through the optical trickery of the cut. By the close of the nineteenth century, our view of the world had changed forever. Art now had at its disposal a new visual language. It had a new and radical formal vocabulary. From now on, the modern eye would filter momentary and multiple stimuli. It would process a new optical experience. It would navigate a strange and complex visual world. It would have to learn to read anew. The human eye was now faced with the phenomenon of movement – constantly.

This new scenario did not take long to influence architecture, and film would be fundamental to the vanguard of the early-twentieth-century design influences and theories. Film led to a questioning of how we perceive the space around us. It offered new possibilities in our understanding and representation of buildings. It presented architects with a platform for experimentation – at the scale of the interior and at the scale of the city. Theories arose that considered the practice of film as analogous to the practice of architecture. Dziga Vertov called himself Kino Eye – which he defined as 'an eye that constructs'. Sergei Eisenstein correlated cinematic montage with architectural experience. Soviet architects Vladimir Tatlin and the Vesnin brothers all proposed a cinematic-typology for both set design and architecture – spaces of real and perceptual movement. Architecture could now be seen, imagined and perceived not only as space, but also as time and motion. Film was a kindred spirit.

The genre of film that most obviously reflected this new cinematic-typology for architecture was, of course, the 'city symphony'. A form of visual montage in movement, the city symphony marked not only the emergence of a new type of film, but also the obsession of modern architecture with the city as a concept and social phenomenon. At the turn of the twentieth century, the architectural issue par excellence – the city – had a new way of being seen to go with it. Perhaps its most obvious manifestation was Dziga Vertov's masterpiece, *The Man with a Movie Camera* (1929). Another, however, was Walter Ruttmann's *Berlin: Symphonie einer grossstadt/Berlin: Symphony of a Great*

City (1927) – a film that gave its name to the genre and took as its subject matter the same city that would be examined by Tom Tykwer some seventy years later in *Lola Rennt/ Run Lola Run* (1998). It is the relationship between Tykwer's contemporary, narrative version of the city symphony and contemporary architectural concepts regarding the metropolis that is examined here. It will be suggested that *Run Lola Run* not only updates the city symphony genre, but that it reflects some of today's most notable theories on filmic representation, the city, its life and its architecture. It will be approached through the prism of several other films and the works and theories of several writers and thinkers of urbanism and architecture.

Run Lola Run: A narrative through the city

Run Lola Run has become a cult classic. Starring Franka Potente as Lola and Moritz Bleibtreu as Manni, it offers a high-octane, goal-focused form of *dérive* through the streets of the German capital, in which everything revolves around an incredibly simple narrative objective: Lola needs to find 100,000 marks and get it to Manni on the other side of the city in twenty minutes. Narratively, the film could not be simpler or more conventional: it has a conflict that has to be resolved and everything that follows on-screen is directly related to the resolution of that conflict. It becomes a race against time that we are symbolically reminded of by the repeated insertion of clock images as Lola runs through the streets of Berlin. This extreme narrative focus is made sharper than normal by a filmic structure that breaks down the story into three twenty-minute variations of the same events. As a result, it offers three short films, each of which is resolved in a different way.

Tykwer's film, then, is narratively conventional and acutely goal-based. However, the way in which the film evolves towards the resolution of that goal is anything but conventional: overlaying three similar event sequences in three distinct spatio-temporal strata. Structurally, it offers a literal tripartite layering of narratives, spaces and simultaneous times whose circular, repetitive and mutating spatio-temporal framework folds nuances into our reading of the sequential stories as they emerge. It is clearly experimental in its presentation of space and time and, in that sense, takes its place in a catalogue of films from the past two decades that have, albeit in very different ways, attempted similar things.

One example of this approach to the space–time construction of film is Alexander Sokurov's, *Russian Ark* (2002). In direct contrast to *Run Lola Run*, this is a single-shot, 96-minute film recorded on uncompressed high-definition video by one continually moving camera. Spatially, it passes through the 33 rooms of the Winter Palace in the State Hermitage Museum, St Petersburg, and narratively it passes through various layers of Russian history, presenting the viewer with images of Peter the Great, Catherine the Great, Tsar Nicholas I, the Shah of Iran, Joseph Stalin and various contemporary figures in modern dress.

Coordinating over 200 actors to move, interact and weave narratives together through a single unified time and space sequence, *Russian Ark* also completely rejects standard narrative techniques and the goal-orientated rules of continuity. It layers spaces, events and movements in an incredibly fluid and sophisticated filmic construction. Characters, narratives and times all merge with one another, flow alongside each other, and evolve out of each other. It is a film that perfectly reflects Deleuzian notions of the folding, the fluid and the morphing.

Another film that does something analogous in spatio-temporal terms is the Douglas Gordon and Philippe Parreno-directed *Zidane: A Twenty-first Century Portrait* (2006) – a film that uses seventeen cameras developed by NASA, complex diegetic sound effects, advanced zoom lenses, superimposed text, and the introduction of diegetic actions in its particular presentation of events and spaces (Dauncey and Morrey 2008). As with *Run Lola Run* and *Russian Ark*, it follows one principal character through the continuous and unbroken storyline: in this case, a footballer playing a single game of football. Rejecting standard narrative and plotline in favour of a 'real-time experience', it takes the enclosed space of the football pitch and fragments it through multiple extreme close-ups. The fragments are never fully disjointed, however, with the proximity of the footballer's body imposing an intense unity of space throughout. *Zidane: A Twenty-first Century Portrait* is another recent film that employs both advanced technologies and radical thinking to create a spatio-temporal filmic experience that is multilayered, intricately fragmented and complexly continuous.

One thing that distinguishes *Run Lola Run* from these films, however, is its intense narrative structure. Despite the fact that its reduced twenty-minute storyline would seem to negate the possibility of making a fully engaging narrative film, Tykwer finds ways to make the film's plot function in much the same way as the plot of a full-length feature film would. He uses photo flash-forward sequences to condense subplots into a series of seconds (Whalen 2000) while flashbacks allow something similar to occur with regard to the characterization of the protagonists – their fears, hopes and aspirations are revealed explicitly in short clips (Bergen-Aurand 2005). In addition, we get various moments of dramatic intensity in which narrative and character information arrives in a matter of seconds.

Thus, despite the temporal limitations imposed by the film's structure, *Run Lola Run* is read narratively in very conventional ways. Each twenty-minute segment follows Lola as she runs along more or less the same geographical path across the city on three successive occasions; each trip functions like a game on a video console in which the protagonist makes another attempt at achieving her goal. It is prevented from becoming repetitive by ensuring that the repeated events are subtly changed, and thus fall slightly out of sync with each other in each successive attempt. The result of these dislocations of times, spaces and events is a series of slightly different encounters between the film's protagonists and the spaces they inhabit (Bordwell 2002). These events cascade into a series of subsequently altered encounters that, in turn, explode the number of narrative variations possible within the framework of the individual subplots. The film is a tour de force in the exploration of narrative and plot structure that revolves around momentary connections of time, space and events that are easily recognizable as a daily occurrence, albeit without the tension of the film's drama.

Run Lola Run: The visual fragmentation of the city

The fragmentary nature of the narrative and plot game created by this approach to narrative construction is emphasized by its filming techniques. The spaces of each of the three segments are filmed from different angles and in different formats and ways: dolly shots mix with handheld camerawork, which is overlaid with crane shots, etc. This cinematic combination of techniques multiplies perspectives by changing viewpoints within the context of a single journey and simultaneously varies the aesthetic feel of each sequence. The disjunction that occurs through this sub-fragmentation is further emphasized by the speed and quantity of the editing, the multiple views produced through repetition, and the use of more than one camera. All these are jumbled at such a speed that the final effect can appear dizzying. The visual tempo this sets up is matched by the underlying soundtrack, which again emphasizes tension and disjunction. It is a combination of techno-like tracks that sets up a repetitive and seemingly relentless forward drive to the events (Hexel 2010).

Breaking up and disjointing all of this even more is the combination of various types of film footage: black and white for flashbacks, photographic stills for flash-forwards, video for scenes without the protagonists, standard 35mm film stock for when the protagonists do appear, and animation for the opening shots of each of the three stories. In combination with the 'three game structure' (Whalen 2000: 33–34) of the film, these techniques underline the film's gaming culture references by calling upon a variety of visual tropes not commonly associated with mainstream cinema.

Structurally and cinematographically, then, *Run Lola Run* is a complex collage of events and images in which time and space jump around in apparently random patterns. The film's cinematographic and structural characteristics allow the director to replay actions and to emphasize minute differences between them. These characteristics allow him to emphasize the disruption of our sequential understanding of events and to introduce the idea of parallel realities – or at least parallel alternatives to courses of action. *Run Lola Run* is a film whose visual techniques emphasize all of this through the multiplication of aesthetic and formal effects. Thus these visual techniques permit and underline the film's examination of the nature of time, space and events – and the relationship between them.

All of these spatio-temporal and cinematic experimentations are of course physically located in a very definite site: the city of Berlin. That city is, however, also caught up in the narrative and filmic disjunctions that operate throughout *Run Lola Run*. The physical places across which we see the protagonist literally run are, in reality, impossible to link in a continuous twenty-minute route. Just as the narrative and its protagonists build up their

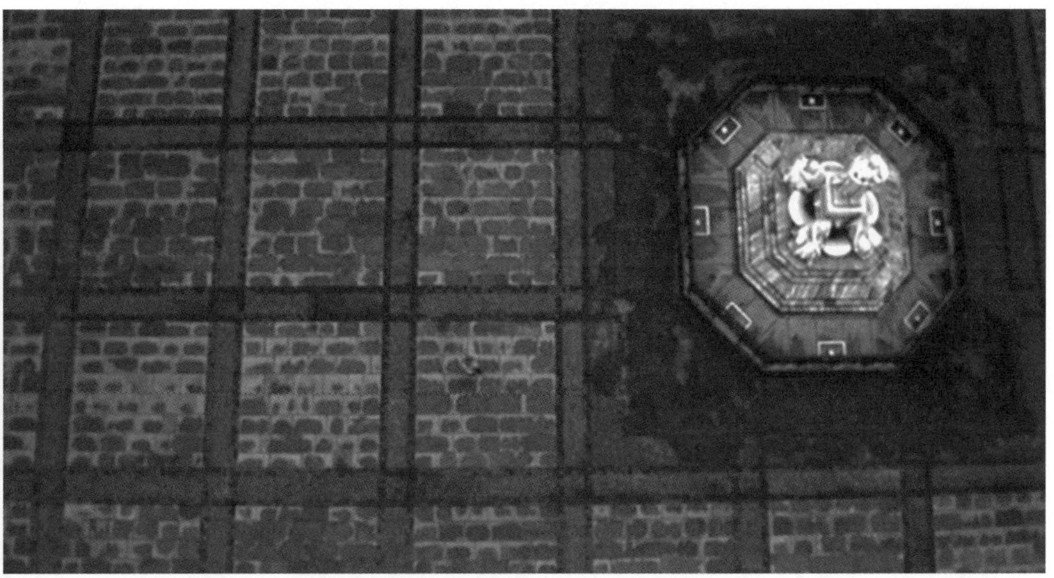

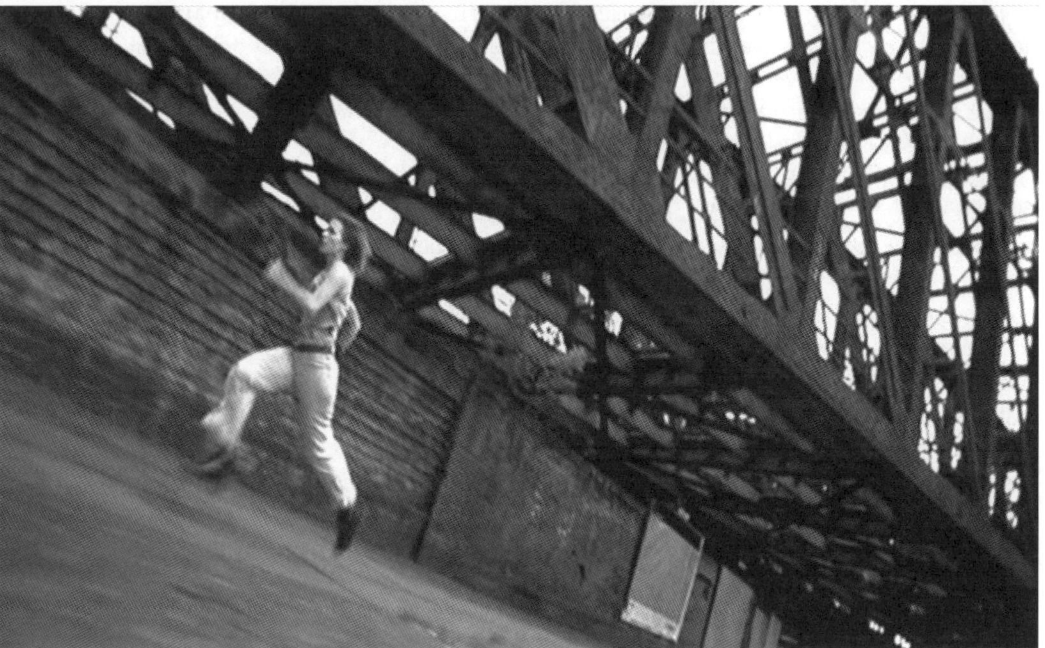

Figures 1–2: The fragmentation of the city in *Run Lola Run. Lola Rennt/Run Lola Run* (1998).

own impossibly fragmented and repeated stories, so too does the city. Directly paralleling the film's narrative, it rejects its real topography and becomes a 'filmic simultaneous city' in which time and space implode into a geographical urban montage. *Run Lola Run* is not only aesthetically and narratively daring; it reworks the city through the formal possibilities of the cinematic medium.

Run Lola Run: A city symphony

In the fragmentation of the city it presents on-screen, *Run Lola Run* clearly engages with the architectural-cinematic tradition of the city symphony. For many, the city symphony has its origins in the work or the earliest experimental film-makers of the Russian-Soviet period: Vsevolod Podovkin, Lev Kuleshov and, of course, Sergei Eisenstein and Dziga Vertov. For Podovkin, film offered the opportunity to creatively rupture space and time in order to dramatize events. For Lev Kuleshov, this ability to fragment space and events gave film the possibility of unleashing a new visual language and a new approach to narrative construction. For Vertov, it would alter 'our perception of the world' and everyday events (Vertov, Michelson and O'Brien 1984: 49) whilst also manipulating the 'mechanics of the eye' (Petrić 1993: 139). Vertov differed from Pudovkin and Kuleshov, however, in one crucial way. For Vertov, film was a documentary medium, whilst for the others it was a narrative form.

The film-maker with whom Vertov was to clash most notoriously on this point was Eisenstein, who would go on to be the most influential of the Soviet-era directors and whose shadow would lurk in the background of the architectural avant-garde for decades (Tschumi 1994). Eisenstein's relationship with film was most notably evident in his 1938 text, *Montage and Architecture*, in which he uses the work of architectural historian Auguste Choisy to propose that architecture operates as a form of sequential narrative montage (Eisenstein, Bois and Glenny 1989 [1938]). In this reading, architecture offers an understanding of events as things we perceive, experience and engage with along both a spatial and a temporal path. Referencing Choisy's interest in the nature of architectural experience as a phenomenon involving a moving viewer, Eisenstein describes the imagery of architecture captured by the eye and the lens as a form of peripatetic vision.

Quoting extensively from Choisy's *Histoire d'architecture* (1899) in which the historian describes the visual experience of a walking visitor to the Acropolis, Eisenstein (1989 [1938]: 112) suggests that the viewer's engagement with architecture becomes one of glimpses, partial views and momentary glances in sequence – a form of 'montage computation within an architectural ensemble' (Bruno 1997: 14). This description does not only fit, almost perfectly, Vertov's *Man with a Movie Camera*, but is also an apt description of Ruttmann's *Berlin: Symphony of a Great City* – the most famous cinematic examination of the city of Berlin to date, and the film to which *Run Lola Run* owes much of its formal characteristics.

Although Ruttmann came from a purely abstract filmic background, the team he worked with on his 1928 film would go on to work on some internationally renowned commercial successes. Ruttmann himself, however, remained firmly in the more abstract camp, with both *Berlin: Symphony of a Great City* and his later collaborations with Leni Riefenstahl being cinematic experimentations in the visual, narrative, temporal and spatial possibilities of the new medium. His 1928 masterpiece is a 'documentation' of the city, its space–time relationships and the lives of 'everyday people' (Vertov 1984). Focused on life in Berlin during the course of a 'typical day', it essentially follows the ebbs and flows of the city for a single 24-hour period and is arranged in five 'acts', each one foregrounding the multiplicity of events, spaces and times that characterize the modern urban experience. It takes the viewer from the early hours of the morning as the city wakes, through the activities of the working day, and ends with scenes of the city's social life in the evening.

Despite its ordered structure, however, *Berlin: Symphony of a Great City*, fragments its presentation of space and time within its clearly defined segments. It is filmed from various viewpoints, is full of dynamically composed shots, is edited to produce graphic matches or deliberate graphic disjunctions, and employs a number of transitional techniques (Bernstein 1984). Sometimes, the camera is mounted on top of buildings, while at other times, it is located on the ground. Notably, it is often carried on cars, trains and trams so as to continually emphasize movement. Indeed, mechanized transport becomes a form of leitmotiv that continually appears in each of the film's five acts. Thus in its use of Berlin and in its aesthetic of conflicting cinematic tropes, *Berlin: Symphony of a Great City* represents a form of historical precedent that Tykwer's film will pick up and modify at the end of the twentieth century.

Siegfried Giedion: The filmic view of the city

Central to these similarities between *Run Lola Run* and *Berlin: Symphony of a Great City* are two themes that have been key issues in architectural theory throughout the twentieth century: the city and the notion of architecture as an experience premised on a simultaneous space–time relationship. The year Ruttmann's film was released, 1928, saw the first international Congrès internationaux d'architecture moderne (CIAM) conference in La Sarraz, and thus marked the point at which modern architecture addressed the question of the city face-on (Mumford 2000). What was to become central to the thinking of CIAM was the controlled, rational planning of the city at an urban scale, as indicated in CIAM's 1938 *Athens Charter*. Described by Eric Mumford as 'the most important contribution to urban design thinking ever' (2000: 59), the consequences of CIAM would later be defined by Henri Lefebvre as the imposition of abstract space, 'a space in which the division of labour seen in the capitalist mode of production repeats itself in spatial organisation at a city wide scale' (Lefebvre 1991). In 1928, however, the city was still seen as an uncontrolled menagerie of industrialization, movement and activity that excited the imagination of architects who, as yet, did not seek to 'control it', but rather to rejoice in it.

A key figure at the 1928 conference was Siegfried Giedion, whose first book, *Building in France, Building in Iron, Building in Ferroconcrete*, was published that same year. Part historical document, part eulogy for modernism, it was a book that foregrounded the space–time argument as a key concept in the understanding of modern architecture. Discussing this argument was to become Giedion's modus operandi in the years to come, and with the publication of *Space, Time and Architecture: The Growth of a New Tradition* (1941), it was not only presented as a key question in modernism, but was given a historical foundation. In this work, Giedion traces out the evolution of the city from the Renaissance to the twentieth century through an 'operative historical approach', and argues that the development of the city reflects an evolution in notions of space and time.

The culmination of this development is read as the conflation, juxtaposition and simultaneity of space and time in the contemporary architectural and urban 'experience' (Giedion 1967 [1941]). Nowhere is this more evident than in Giedion's description of the Rockefeller Centre, New York – a project he proposes as a form of 'precedent' for urban development in the contemporary city of the first half of the twentieth century. A conglomeration of fourteen buildings in the heart of Manhattan between Fifth and Sixth Avenues and 48th and 51st Streets, he describes the Rockefeller Centre as 'cutting out a new form in New York's checkerboard grid'. It is akin to a Mondrian painting in its repeated use of similar elements, and Giedion identifies that, 'seen in plan, nothing is revealed of its dynamic form and the dynamic sensation it produces on the eye'.

As one moves around the complex however, Giedion suggests that it optically begins to explode:

> its three largest structures rise in different directions and to different heights. They cannot be grasped from any single position or embraced in any single view. There becomes apparent, a many-sidedness in these simple and enormous slabs. From these well calculated masses one becomes aware of a new fantastic element inherent in the space-time conception of our period. (Giedion 1967 [1941])

The nature of the architecture – its urban scale and its asymmetrical arrangement of buildings – turns the Rockefeller Centre into an example of modern urban architecture which, according to Giedion, 'can only be comprehended in terms of space and time analogous to what has been achieved in modern scientific research as well as in modern painting' (1967 [1941]: 845–53). This space–time analogy, which can be summed up in one word – 'simultaneity' – is aesthetically reinforced by Giedion's presentation of the Rockefeller Centre in the photographic collage format.

Artificially manipulating his presentation of this urban complex, Giedion's collage underlines his central argument of a combined, conflated, superimposed and simultaneous

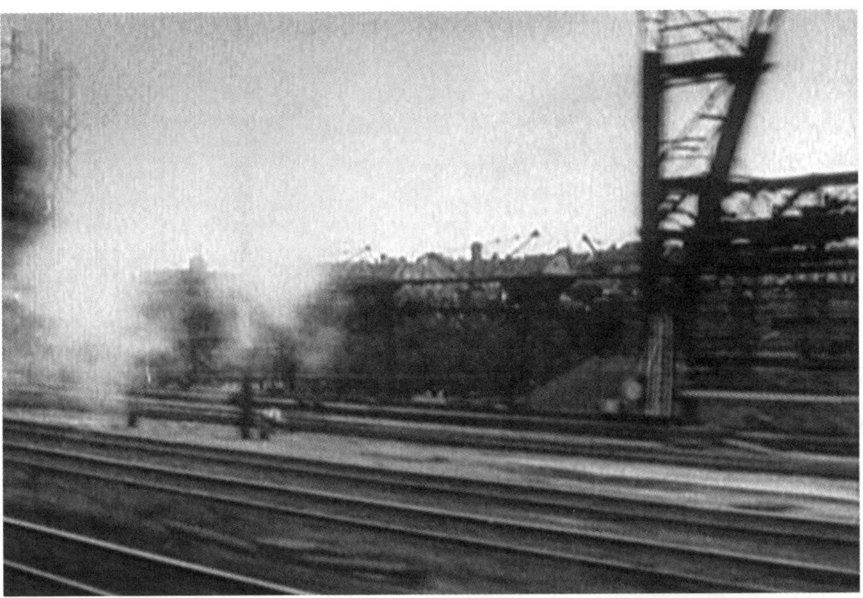

Figures 3–4: Ruttmann's multiple-cutting opening sequence and Giedion's photographic montage of the Rockefeller Centre.

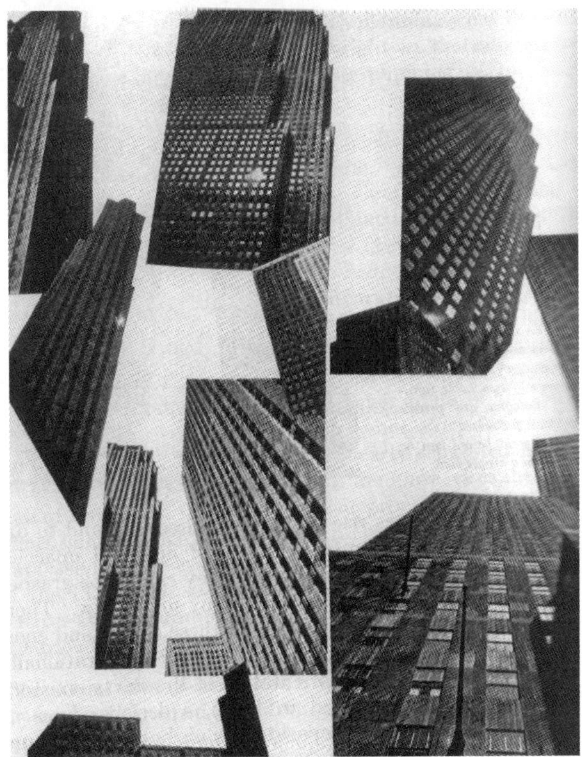

notion of space and time. Beginning his engagement with these ideas in 1928, Giedion's space–time architecture found its cinematic brethren in *Berlin: Symphony of a Great City*, a film that also fragmented, conflated and juxtaposed spaces and times into an on-screen visual collage. In reading these two works as analogous and related, we find an example of a mutual set of interests emerging in both architecture and film in the early twentieth century. These interests were theoretical on the one hand and aesthetic on the other. They were also social. The theory was, of course, based on the twentieth-century space–time concept explored by Giedion throughout his career, and particularly in his 1941 text. The shared aesthetic concerns revolved around the formation of a new fragmentary visual effect, whilst socially both works picked up on the question of the city and modern urban life.

Rem Koolhaas: A contemporary Giedion?

When considered in this historical context, reading *Run Lola Run* as a contemporary reworking of Ruttmann's film – albeit in a more commercial and narrative form – leads us to ask another question: does Tykwer's film find echoes in contemporary architectural theories and practitioners in the way *Berlin: Symphony of a Great City* did through the writings of Siegfried Giedion? Using the criteria of theoretical, aesthetic and architectural-social concerns to ask the question, a number of possibilities come to mind: Peter Eisenman, Thom Mayne, Daniel Libeskind and others – architects generally associated with deconstruction. Amongst these, it may well be Bernard Tschumi – whose early theoretical writings explicitly referenced film – who seems the most appropriate.

The films of Eisenstein became a form of cinematic precedent for Tschumi's event-space architecture, in which events, spaces and movements all overlap, conflict and cross contaminate. It was an influence most expressly manifest in his *Parc de la Villette* project of the 1980s, and resulted in a series of buildings (follies) composed of multiple fragments violently forced together in an architecture of aggressive asymmetry and formal rupture. In its planning, too, *Parc de la Villette* asymmetrically superimposed one set of infrastructures on another, resulting in the most emblematic deconstructive building of the period (Tschumi 1987). Tschumi's 'deconstruction' of the conventions underlying architectural thought, then, was not only reinforced through references to film, but was accompanied by an aesthetic and formal deconstruction that produced some of the period's most notable, controversial and memorable architecture. It was certainly an architecture whose aesthetic would seem analogous to that of *Run Lola Run*.

Despite the apparent suitability of Tschumi's work as an architectural parallel to the conceptual, formal and aesthetic character of *Run Lola Run*, it is also possible to consider the film alongside the work of Rem Koolhaas and the Office of Metropolitan Architecture (OMA). Given their greater focus on questions of the city, they become an even more suitable point of reference for this cross-disciplinary argument. Koolhaas first came to notoriety with his 1978 publication, *Delirious New York: A Retrospective Manifesto*. Taking on the city dealt with by Giedion in his description of the Rockefeller Centre, Koolhaas develops variations on the arguments of simultaneity and the conflation of time, space and events that are central to *Space, Time and Architecture: The Growth of a New Tradition*. Whilst Giedion concentrated on the modern urban experience as one of conflated space and time and thus 'simultaneity', in a primarily optical sense, Koolhaas mines a somewhat different field.

In Koolhaas's reading, the density of New York is such that single buildings become home to multiple activities – the skyscraper easily being an office, a gym, a restaurant and a hotel all in one, for example (Koolhaas 1994 [1978]). A corollary of this folding of events and spaces is an analogous conflation of times: events normally associated with the morning, afternoon and evening merge in a single space and unregulated time sequence. Life in the modern city, as epitomized by New York, is a complex, overlaid menagerie of events, activities, times and locations. Furthermore, it is also a site of continual change. The speed of technological and urban change at the end of the twentieth and beginning of the twenty-first centuries is such that Koolhaas argues it has become simply impossible to conceive of the type of pre-planned approach to urban design that was possible in the CIAM period. Echoing comments found in the later editions of Giedion's *Space, Time and Architecture*, he proposes an approach to urban design that is based on facilitating continual evolution and multiple redevelopments (Koolhaas 1994 [1978]).

These themes were evident is some of Koolhaas's earliest projects, such as his own proposal for the *Parc de la Villette* competition, Paris, 1984. Although the competition was eventually won by Koolhaas's former teacher, Bernard Tschumi, the Koolhaas proposal for *la Villette* employed the deconstructive approach of his tutor. Described as a 'strategy' rather than a design proposal, the scheme presented by Koolhaas envisaged dividing the site into strips of spaces and activities that would be overlaid and juxtaposed on each other. Use was to be indeterminate. The architectural 'objects' envisaged as scattered around the site would not define function or use a priori. They would thus become a series of independent architectural forms similarly intended to juxtapose themselves with one another and to facilitate change and adaptability for the overall ensemble.

Central to this conflation of events and spaces was the question of scale, a theme Koolhaas dealt with in *Delirious New York* and would return to some twenty years later in *S, M, L, XL*, co-authored with Bruce Mau. In *Delirious New York*, Koolhaas suggested that as buildings become ever larger, any sense of disparate spaces for distinct events becomes irrelevant. Multiple locations and activities coalesce in a unified entity: the mega structure or skyscraper. In *S, M, L, XL*, he argues that a subtext to the ever-increasing scale of buildings permitted by a range of technological developments is, quite simply, 'fuck context' (Koolhaas 1994 [1978]: 502).

'Fucking context', however, is not limited to the imposition of ever-larger forms on the existing urban fabrics of modern cities. It is something that frees the architectural object from stylistic limitations – a notion perfectly in tune with the deconstructive tendencies of Koolhaas's former tutor and with his own earlier projects. Amongst the projects that display his parlance for fragmentary architectural form, material juxtaposition and spatial fragmentation are the CCTV building, Beijing; the Casa da Musica, Porto; the Seoul National University Museum of the Arts; and the Seattle Public Library, to name but a few of the more emblematic. Smaller projects displaying similar tendencies, as well as the idea of overlaying multiple and conflicting activities in a single space, are his projects for Prada in New York, San Francisco and Los Angeles between 1999 and 2004 – projects in which OMA also experimented with the use of various technologies and new construction and interior materials (Koolhaas et al. 2001).

Koolhaas's projects, then, can be complex visual and disjunctive forms, sites of multiple conflicting activities and aesthetically rich collages of colours, textures and materials. This aesthetic sensibility not only echoes Koolhaas's more generalized theories – his constructed architecture and his arguments about the city – it is also repeated in his books. Taking the cover of a book such as *Content* (2004), for example, we have a teenage-boy-like collage of action heroes, politicians, female bodies and logos: a front cover that is a punchy visual commentary on contemporary throw-away culture. Inside, a similar feel continues with a layout that is seemingly a random arrangement of stories, graphic formats and images of different types, sizes and themes.

S, M, L, XL does something similar. It is a combination of typefaces, images and graphics that is often difficult to read and eschews the easy sequential reading of a single theme. Both books operate as textual manifestations of the approach, aesthetic and theories underlining the buildings and urban design concepts proffered by Koolhaas and OMA. At the level of the city, that means a consideration of the urban condition as one of continual change, fragmentary experiences, multiple human narratives and conflicting events. Repeated on a daily basis, these phenomena are, however, never the same – the sheer complexity and density of the city prevents any literal repetition of plot on consecutive days. The city, the architecture that composes it and the activities this architecture houses, come to be seen as a veritable urban collage reminiscent of *Run Lola Run* on various levels.

Conclusion

Clearly, what emerges from this examination of the work of Koolhaas, Giedion and Ruttmann alongside Tom Tykwer's *Run Lola Run* is an interpretation of the film that links it with both historical and contemporary issues in architecture. Metaphorically, Tykwer presents Berlin as a city in which events, actions and spaces are continually malleable and open to the layering of multiple different, repeated and altered scenarios. He also presents events, spaces and times that are fragmented and disjointed. In addition, he creates a chaotic but rich aesthetic through a complex mix of visual styles: animation, video, black

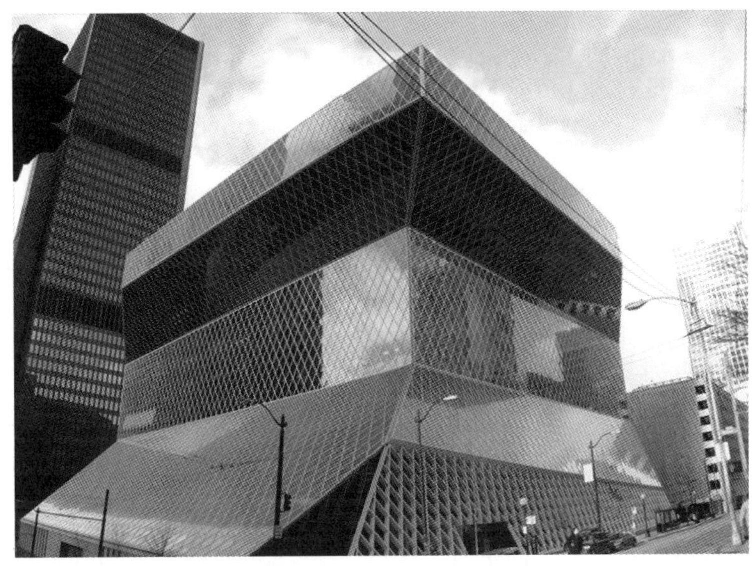

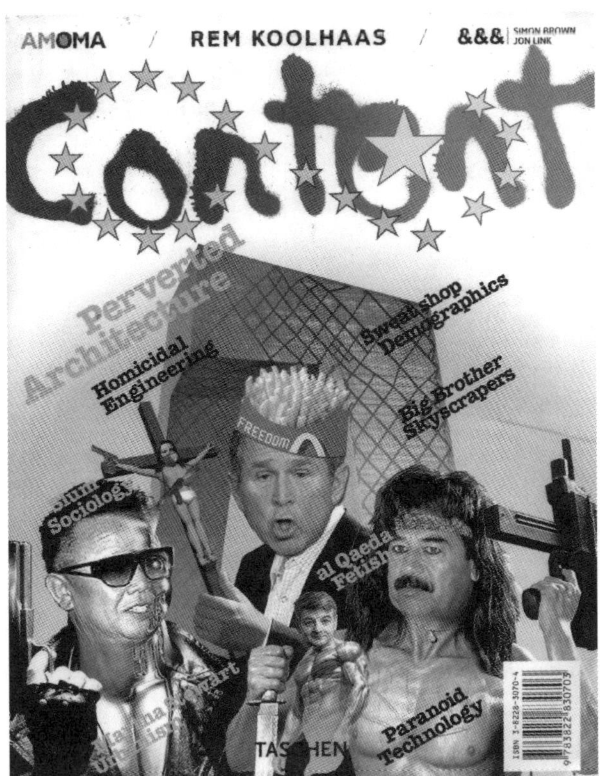

Figures 5–6: Seattle Public Library. OMA, Rem Koolhaas, 2004 and the front cover of *Content* (2004).

and white and standard 35mm film stock. Just as Ruttmann's *Berlin: Symphony of a Great City* paralleled Giedion's theories of architecture and his photographic montage aesthetic in the first half of the twentieth century, it is arguable that *Run Lola Run* parallels issues raised by Koolhaas and OMA in the late twentieth and early twenty-first centuries, albeit unintentionally.

Placed within the tradition of cinema's engagement with architecture through the space–time question then, *Run Lola Run* becomes not only a film analogous to Ruttmann's 1927 cult classic – it becomes a film that we can read in parallel with some of the most controversial and high-profile architectural themes of today. Furthermore, just as Koolhaas's work involves an inevitable 'modernization' of the aesthetic and debates set out by Giedion, so, too, *Run Lola Run* 'modernizes' the themes and aesthetic offered by *Berlin: Symphony of a Great City*. In doing so, it modernizes its own medium's relationship with architecture.

Examined in this way, we begin to see *Run Lola Run* as much more than a film about love and the power of the will, much more than a film about coincidence and about chance, and even much more than a film about Berlin. We begin to see it as a film about contemporary architectural and urban theory, a film about spaces and events, and a film about the contemporary conflated, contradictory and complex urban condition. It becomes a film that takes its place in the historical lineage of its medium's engagement with architecture, a film that shows us that the century-old engagement of film with architecture is still active, and a film that captures contemporary architectural theories about the city. It is a film that shows us that the camera, the lens and the screen still have the power to rework, represent and reflect the modern condition – and its architecture.

References

Bergen-Aurand, B. (2005), '*Run Lola Run (Lola Rennt)*', *The Radical Teacher*, 74, pp. 42–43.

Bernstein, M. (1984), 'Visual style and spatial articulations in *Berlin, Symphony of a City* (1927)', *Journal of Film and Video*, 36: 4, pp. 5–61.

Bordwell, D. (2002), 'Film futures', *Sub-stance*, 31: 97, p. 88.

Bruno, G. (1997), 'Site-seeing: Architecture and the moving image', *Wide Angle*, 19: 4, p. 8.

Dauncey, H. and Morrey, D. (2008), 'Quiet contradictions of celebrity: Zinedine Zidane, image, sound, silence and fury', *International Journal of Cultural Studies*, 11: 3, pp. 301–20.

Eisenstein, S. M., Bois, Y.-A. and Glenny, M. (1989 [1938]), 'Montage and architecture', *Assemblage*, pp. 111–31.

Giedion, S. (1967), *Space, Time and Architecture: The Growth of a New Tradition*, Cambridge, MA: Harvard University Press.

——— (1995), *Building in France, Building in Iron, Building in Ferroconcrete*, Santa Monica, CA: Getty Center for the History of Art and the Humanities.

Hexel, V. (2010), 'The use of dance music and the synergy of narrative vehicles in *Run Lola Run*', *The Soundtrack*, 3: 2, pp. 83–96.

Koolhaas, R. (1994 [1978]), *Delirious New York: A Retroactive Manifesto for Manhattan*, New York: Monacelli Press.

—————— and Mau, B. (1994), *S, M, L, XL: Small, Medium, Large, Extra-Large*, Rotterdam: 010 Publishers.

——————, Hommert, J., Kubo, M. and Chiara, M. (2001), *Prada*, Milan: Fondazione Prada.

—————— and Office for Metropolitan Architecture (2004), *Content*, Köln: Taschen.

Lefebvre, H. (1991), *The Production of Space*, Oxford, UK: Blackwell.

Mogwaï, Gordon, D., & Parreno, P. (2006), *Zidane: A 21st century portrait*, S.l: Pias.

Mumford, E. P. (2000), *The CIAM discourse on urbanism, 1928–1960*, Cambidge, MA: The MIT Press.

Petrič, V. (1993), *Constructivism in Film: The Man with the Movie Camera: A Cinematic Analysis*, Cambridge, UK: Cambridge University Press.

Tschumi, B. (1987), *Cinégramme folie: Le Parc de La Villette, Paris nineteenth arrondissement*, Sevenoaks: Butterworth Architecture.

—————— (1994), *Architecture and Disjunction*, Cambridge, MA: MIT Press.

Tykwer, T., Potente, F., Bleibtreu, M., Knaup, H., Petri, N., Sony Pictures Classics, & Columbia TriStar Home Video (1999), *Run Lola Run*, Culver City, CA: Columbia TriStar Home Video.

Vertov, D., Michelson, A. and O'Brien, K. (1984), *Kino-Eye: The Writings of Dziga Vertov*, Berkeley: University of California Press.

Whalen, T. (2000), 'Run Lola Run', *Film Quarterly*, 53: 3, pp. 33–40.

Section Three

Film as Spatial Practice

Chapter 10

The grey area between reality and representation: The practices
of architects and film-makers

Gemma Barton

Introduction

Movies, music, plays – it's all time-based art. There's a beginning, middle and an end. And you have to see it from beginning to end. You're restrained to that time line, that way of experiencing it. But then there's paintings, no beginning, no middle, no end. You see what you want to see when you want to see it. No restrictions. It's just there.

Sam Esmail, *Comet*

Although cinema and architecture are distant arts, dynamic and static respectively; their complex relationship gives life to each other. Sharing a mutual respect for the parallel processes involved in producing their works, the creators behind these two expressions have an understanding that one will always benefit the other.

Murray Grigor, *Space in Time: Filming Architecture*

There is a well-documented relationship between cinema and the city. Schonfield, in her book *Walls Have Feelings: Architecture, Film and the City* (2003), educates us on the use of film as a means of decoding architecture and the built environment; Bruno, in her *Atlas of Emotion* (2002), examines the geography of the moving image through spatial constructs and film theory; and Penz (1994) describes the counterpoints and overlaps between the film industry and architecture student experiments in his 1994 contribution to *Architectural Design* (vol. 64). This chapter does not seek to reproduce this territory but rather to add to it by focusing on the space shared by the creators behind the worlds of cinema and the city, the architects and the film-makers. It is a well-known fact that both architects and film-makers imagine future realities for inhabitation; compose spatial sequences; and communicate multiple narratives through the use of representation, inspired by the past and present condition – but what insights can they share about operating in the 'grey area' between reality and representation?

Act 1 of this chapter looks to set the scene – establishing the characteristics, presence and parameters of the grey area occupied by architects and film-makers. Act 2 investigates this shared territory through the frames of 'the city' and 'the narrative' – chosen for exploration as these are the exchange points, the positions of interaction, and the methods by which each can be recognized and explained. Here, the nature of practising in the third space is explored through interviews with those currently producing work in this territory. Through practice as an academic, editor and writer, the skills and knowledge of this author lie in communication, thus the methodology employed derives directly from experience of the dissemination of conversation, and by association considers the role of the architect and the film-maker as 'temporal commentators'.

Act 1: The grey area: Presence and parameters

Everything that exists was once imagined. In seeing all things, you are exposed to the thoughts, dreams, decisions and visions of others who have gone before you. Yet events take place, are (re)imagined and remembered all in one moment. The philosophical dualisms discussed in this chapter: body/mind; real/imaginary, are extensions of the thinking of Durkheim, who asserts that the mind is a set of representations; and Kant, who believes representations to be produced by a faculty of the mind. For the purposes of this chapter, the term representation is considered to be both metaphysical (the idea and the vision) and physical (tangible communicative product). 'One of the problems of the dualism, reality/representation, is that representation may be mistaken for the reality' (Pickering 2002) – the grey area.

Deciphering where creating, thinking and communicating begin and end is challenging and makes the discourse between reality and representation a deep and perplexing one. Separating representative imagery from the actualities that inspire them would be a difficult task. However, this does not mean that representation does not have the ability to be an extension or manipulation of existent realities. Both films and spatial constructions are complex entities, each one being delicate and different from the next. There are architectures that fall outside of this narrative foothold, such as digital form-finding techniques and auto-authorship, yet in order to understand the core themes behind the creative process we must begin to formalize the structure. Architectural and film-making processes take place across the reality/representation spectrum, and as they do so, the output they produce can also exist across this threshold. In its simplest format the different phases of architectural design and film-making production swing between reality and representation. The first exists in the mind, the vision or idea. The second exists on paper/models/screen as drawings, scripts, storyboards and mock-ups. The third exists as the stage or the building site, for rehearsals and development, live exploration and realization. The fourth exists as documentation projected onto surfaces as images and/or prints. Buildings, once complete, exist in real time and space; however, photographs of them, in journals and the press, are continually developing representations of the fact.

To paraphrase Roland Barthes – the reality of an object is not exhausted by its phenomenal existence, but extends into each and every representation of it. In other words, we have works, and we have photographs, and it is not that the photograph is simply a poor substitute for the work, but rather that it is another facet of the world's being, and one that can be thought about in its own right; as a result of course, the work is never 'finished' – as long as images of it continue to go on being produced, it will, so to speak, always still be in development. (Forty 2014)

Robin Evans famously asserted, 'Architects do not make buildings; they make drawings of buildings' (Evans 1989) and fourteen years later Neil Spiller added

Architects do not make buildings; they make a range of different types of representations that may be used in the construction of buildings or they may be used in a number of ways to create a wide array of spatial possibilities. (Spiller 2013)

In addition to this composite conversation, it can be argued that, in a similar way to film-makers, architects do not make buildings: they envision future life in a space/place, which is translated through architectural convention, without which the building could/would not become a reality, thus extracting that the value of architecture is not only found in the reality of the built form but equally in its representational components. Communicating vision effectively is as important as the vision itself. Along with other prestigious names (Alexander Brodsky, Lebbeus Woods, Neil Denari) Perry Kulper works in this field of 'visionary architecture' or 'paper architecture' where representations, through technique and content, incite critical debate and also communicate a message without the need for construction (Pohl 2012). As Brodsky says,

From the moment a structure is built it becomes a real thing and it stops being paper architecture. Before the realization of the building is the border between what I am drawing and what I am building. I am always trying to destroy this border. (Brodsky 2013: 14)

The border Brodsky describes here is the grey area, the expanding threshold challenged by those architects, artists and film-makers who believe boundaries to be flexible, fluid and ripe for manipulation. This ability to cross borders and blur boundaries signifies the implication of a playful emancipation, a freedom to prod, challenge and speculate outside of traditional and professional margins – an outreach that enables greater communication and haptic discovery.

Film-making projects exist as representation in construct and in process – both the planning and realization of film exists across multiple media: storyboards, scripts, stills, moving images. Outside of props, sets and locations there is no primary tangible output/product – further drawing attention to the greying area. Film-makers therefore find themselves alongside architects and directors 'caught' in the realm between things that exist physically and things that do not. Figure 1 describes these relations between traditionalist definitions of the products of architects and film-makers and their position on the reality/representation spectrum. Pallasmaa once described the physical space created within film as 'architecture without architect' and the film-maker as the 'architect without client' (Pallasmaa, quoted in Khorshidifard 2009). The idea of the 'architect without client' lends somewhat to the romantic notion of ideology in film-making, the freedom of the artist outside of the realities of industry restriction, a notion shared only with visionary or paper architects and not the experience of those operating within commercial landscapes.

Visionary architecture performs as a hybrid, in that the critical image is the output itself. In film-making, the screening of the product is pure (re)presentation but the constituent parts can be a combination of real-life locations, fictional characters and inspired-by-a-true-story plotlines. In exploring the extents of this territory, it becomes clear that it could be considered less of a 'grey area' and more of a 'grey scale', as the edge definition between reality and representation appears both perforated and fluid. The architect makes proposals for a (biographic/prosthetic) narrative that might come into existence. The film-maker constructs worlds to make sense of narratives that will exist only in the film and not (yet) in reality. In film-making, a real space (the site, the location) featuring in an artificial narrative becomes imagined by association, a differing yet real representation

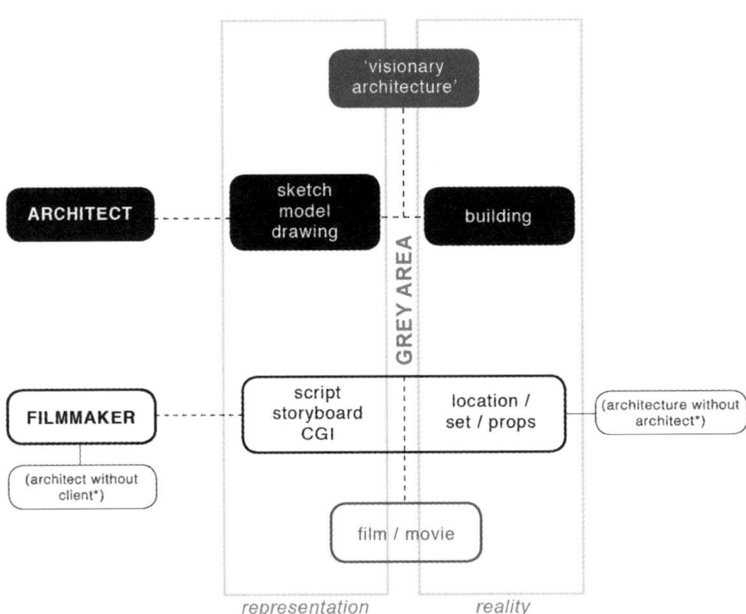

Figure 1. Reality + Representation, G. Barton, 2013.

for each audience member. In an interview, Perry Kulper says 'I think of architecture as having multiple levels, or families of representation, all real; the plan, a story told about a building, data collected from it, photographs. The levels of representation play different roles in structuring the "whole"' (Kulper 2014). Both architect and film-maker dwell side by side in this transience between reality and representation – where buildings are facilitative, vehicles by which stories are orchestrated and/or where lives are lived. In essence, fiction can be grounded by reality and conversely a reality can be displaced by fiction.

Act 2: The city and the narrative: Authenticity, articulation and ideology

Act 2 draws on the affective qualities of both narrative and space as an articulated process/focus and begins with a filmic analysis of the city. 'The city is big, the image is small' (*Los Angeles Plays Itself* [Andersen, 2003]). As a collective, the material presence of the city exists in reality without question; however, it also appears among fictional characters, both human (actors) and as augmented reality (CGI creations). By changing this built landscape, the meaning and the representation of the city becomes altered, even prosthetic in part. Narrative appears in different manifestations throughout architecture and cinema. Narrative offers architects a way of engaging with the way a city feels and works, as well as with its people. It does not dilute the discipline to aesthetic, material or technical specialism and instead champions the experiential dimension of architecture. Broadly speaking, in architecture, the narrative is the organization of story-based components, the defining and inspirational thread, be it derived from a historical site context, a political manifesto or a childhood memory; this concept drives decision-making and allows a language to appear and a creation to be legible. An architectural programme can also be an imagining of narrative, the fiction of the imagined life. In film-making, the narrative could be the plotline, the tempo at which the story is unravelled and the way in which it does so. The narrative comes in the form of words, images, music and cinematography, something the entire film attends to. Film-making began as a method to communicate to the masses 'actualities' or scenes of things they had heard about on the radio or read about in newspapers, but never actually seen. The Lumière brothers' pioneering work in documentaries paved the way for experimentation with the more playful side of popular culture, developing the trend for narrative storytelling, which continues and thrives today.

'Memory's images, once they are fixed in words, are erased' (Calvino 1997). Architectural narrative is present in the built environment and the medium in which this is visualized varies greatly from city to city. As identified by Massumi in his essay, 'The Autonomy of Affect' (1995), there is an interesting relationship between fact, emotion and narrative-intensity in film-making. The purpose and power of the narrative can become ineffective if not readily interpreted; therefore, at times the moving image and

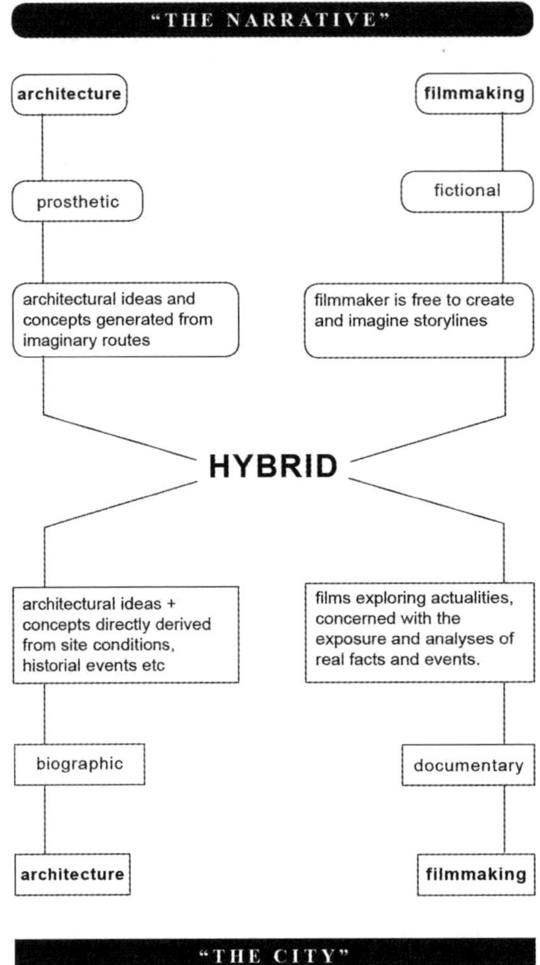

Figure 2. City + Narrative, G. Barton, 2013.

built form are stripped back to ensure a clear message can be communicated. In films such as *Koyaanisqatsi*, directed by Godfrey Reggio in 1982, there is no verbal narration to support the time-lapse footage of cities and natural landscapes. Dubbed a visual-tone-poem, Reggio states, 'It's not for lack of love of the language that these films have no words. It's because, from my point of view, our language is in a state of vast humiliation. It no longer describes the world in which we live' (Reggio 1982). This resonates clearly in the world of narrative and architectural representation, where words cannot sufficiently describe the intention, expression or feeling that a space and a story can generate. Kulper asserts, 'The conventional use of language – words – for spatial design purposes is largely antiquated. Proactively, words can initiate, trigger, and thicken spatial possibilities. The use of language can be an active form of representation and design' (Kulper 2015). In *Koyaanisqatsi*, by removing verbal content (and with it auditory assertion) the narrative lays itself open for interpretation and participation. The 'scenery' and footage is real, but the speed at which it is displayed has been manipulated: slowed down, or sped up into a time-lapse. This manipulation of tempo and order of delivery alongside a Philip Glass score leaves the content open for personal analysis. This approach tends to be reserved for the artist rather than the director, who by virtue of his/her title aims to direct the thoughts and feelings of the audience using both dialogue and moving image.

Architectural narratives too hold a sense of ideological power. WAI Architecture Think Tank, who focus on the understanding and execution of architecture from a panoramic approach (from theoretical texts to architectural artefacts, narrative architectures, buildings and urban and cultural conditions) published *Narrative Architecture: A Manifesto (WAI Architecture Think Tank)*. This investigatory work bases the characteristics of its existence upon non-existence. Existing as pure representation ensures the criticality of the image, and allows for genuine conjecture of composition and meaning. This has a direct impact on our understanding of architectural principles that are holistically connected. "There is a form of architecture that aims at not getting built [...] Narrative Architecture, as we call this form of critical architectural project that relies on narrative to construct a critique of architectural ideology, exists beyond the realm of the mind' (Frankowski and Garcia 2013). Many architects working in commercial and industry-led practices reportedly struggle to see the value attributed to these purely unbuilt speculations; however, architects such as Lebbeus Woods have made progress in communicating the potential worth in such hybridity. In 1999, Woods created the image 'Lower Manhattan' – an example of this fantastical and propositional ideology that illustrates the composition of both real and representative content within a single image. Authenticity of place here makes the vision more critically plausible and allows for an in-depth analysis of social and architectural possibility. Woods explains

> I wanted to suggest that maybe lower Manhattan – not lower downtown, but lower in the sense of below the city – could form a new relationship with the planet. So, in the drawing you see that the East River and the Hudson are both dammed. They're purposefully drained, as it were. The underground – or lower Manhattan – is revealed, and, in the drawing, there are suggestions of inhabitation in that lower region. (Woods 2007)

Woods uses certain recognizable elements such as the New York plan formation and high-rise density to communicate the reality in the image. This familiarity allows space for the representation in the image; in this case, the proposition of the underground and the 'what if' consequences of spatial and social decisions. Film-makers regularly adopt this approach to hybridity; they use certain spaces, places, landmarks and skylines to literally set the scene and generate emotion, familiarity and understanding in their audience. This is a key tactic which architectural teams are beginning to deploy more regularly in short films created to convey spatial narratives to clients and funding bodies when pitching for competition work. This type of film-making is often outsourced to specialists with an understanding and background in architectural communication; however, a move towards more traditionally cinematic approaches here would indicate the progression of a common voice.

The role and presence of buildings within cinematic space has been widely written about, from the architecture of Alfred Hitchcock in Jacobs's book *The Wrong House* (2007) to Lamster's book *Architecture and Film* (2001), but this relationship is also analysed using moving image. *Los Angeles Plays Itself* is a seminal video-essay by CalArts professor of film composition Thom Andersen, in which he discusses the representation of the city of Los Angeles in movies: 'Of course I know movies aren't about places, they're about stories. If we notice the location, we're not really watching the movie' (Andersen 2003). Conversely, Robert Mallet-Stevens suggested some seventy years earlier in the 1925 article 'Le Cinema et les arts: Architecture'/'Cinema and the arts: Architecture' (Becherer 1996) that architecture in film, should not simply frame but become a part of the narrative action, become an actor. It is no surprise here that the architect places a greater significance on the role of the city than the film-maker, but could this also suggest a decline in the importance and/or impact of the representation of the city between the 1920s and 2003? I contacted Andersen to discuss my thoughts with him, this was his response:

> *Los Angeles Plays Itself* is, of course, primarily about places, and only incidentally about stories. The line you quote is an acknowledgment that its analysis goes against the grain, which it is not a conventional film that it appeals to the viewer's voluntary attention, as I say later. I think it shows that architecture is an actor. [...] The unexpected success of my modest movie demonstrates that the representation of the city on film is more a concern now than ever before. (Andersen 2014)

And of course he is right: in our digital age, the medium cannot be questioned, our cities are exposed daily in films, documentaries, TV shows and commercials; the question remains, however, whether or not the audience is indeed seeing. Andersen talks of voluntary attention, the content that the mind permits oneself to focus on. Our cities are also 'represented' daily in sequences of fiction, imagination, dreams, hallucinations and mythical projections. This curating of our vision requires participation – in these 'prosthetic' representations we are no longer spectators, we become stars in our very own screenplays (actors, directors and cinematographers). Beatriz Colomina says of this, 'Architecture is not simply a platform that accommodates the viewing subjects. It is a viewing mechanism that produces the subject. It precedes and frames the occupant' (Colomina 1992). Thus suggesting that the human in this relationship forever cycles between observer and participant.

For architects and film-makers, existing on the same creative spectrum offers up many advantages brought about by shared skillsets, allowing one to move freely between the vocations. Many trained architects and designers transition into film-making, such as Anshuman Prasad, Tino Schaedler and Joseph Kosinski, indicating that the movement is somewhat mono-directional. Recognized as a valid and experiential offshoot from architecture, it is not to be considered abandonment but rather specialization. Attracted by the diversity, magic and freedom that being involved in the creation of cinematic space can offer, these 'transistors' recognize the benefits that their architectural training provides; skills which they now showcase and exercise in an (ideal) world not hampered by the limits of construction, but expanded by the openness of imagination.

Joseph Kosinksi, director of *Tron Legacy* (2010), studied at Columbus University where he is now an adjunct professor of architecture. Kosinski created an entirely new city for the 2010 *Tron* remake, 'I saw the opportunity to build a universe from scratch, not only with the architecture, but also with the character and vehicle design' (Kosinski 2010), utilizing his architectural training and a great deal of imagination. This new 'city' may only ever be a representation of Kosinski's imagined reality. The elements: the sets, the digital and physical models, have a synergy with the stage at which an architectural project would be presented to an investor or client, the very moment before it gets the go-ahead to be built, to become a reality. In this scenario, *Tron's* 'realization' takes place on-screen, rendering it 'screen architecture'. Similarly, cities can be adapted in film, changed for the better or worse, on the screen or in the mind.

Three architecture graduates from The Bartlett, UCL, formed Film Company Factory Fifteen. Their 'brand' of animated films or 'synthetic architecture', which includes *Robots of Brixton* (2011) and *Jonah* (2013), has received high acclaim from both the architecture and film industries. Jonathan Gales of Factory Fifteen says, 'We work to create projects that engage in narrative and envisage space. [...] All projects engage in some way with the built environment, posing "what if" scenarios, or using the visualized environment to aid the narrative of the story' (Gales 2013). Their films play out with an intentional focus on utilizing and/or reimagining the existing city. In both *Jonah* and *Robots of Brixton*, the city and the narrative are intertwined perfectly; for example, in *Robots of Brixton* 'biographic' happenings such as the 1981 riots in Brixton are said to have inspired the prosthetic narrative and augmented locality of the film. Incidentally, the release of *Robots of Brixton* in June 2011 came just months before the London Riots, placing their architectural/ social insight on the cusp of actualism. Art imitates life imitates art, the boundaries and definitions blur further. Engaging with architecture to generate these more temporal and ephemeral outputs rather than traditional buildings, allows creation and critique without the imposition of responsibility and/or longevity.

As Kosinski and Factory Fifteen evidence, architecture training provides numerous transferable skills, which opens the doors between the two fields, and arguably lays the ground for the conception of the grey area. Yet, there is an extremely unique exchange that takes place when architects and film-makers work together. An example of this

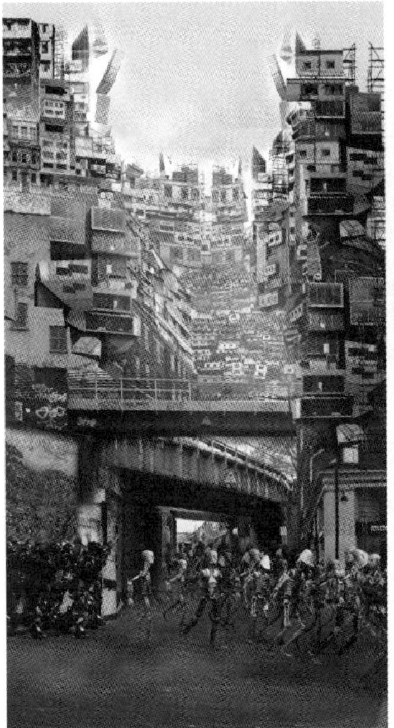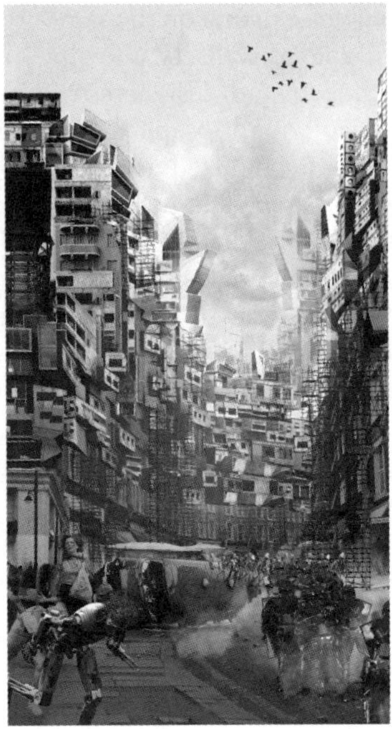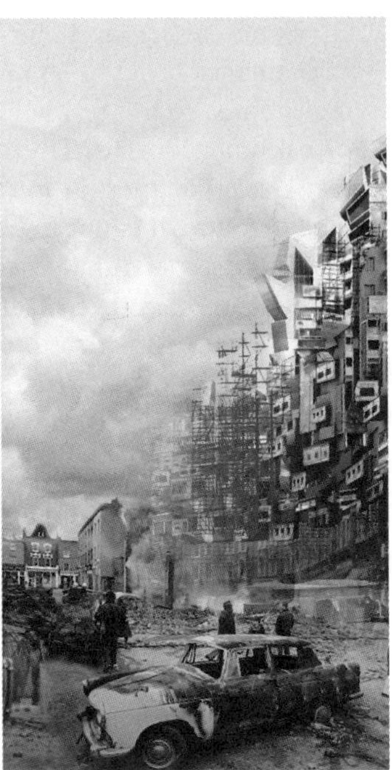

Figure 3. *Robots of Brixton* © Factory Fifteen, 2011.

collaboration was released in October 2013 when French film-maker Benjamin Seroussi and French architect David Tajchman made *Kaplinski*, a film showing different structures, made from the same repetitive wooden element, gathered around the human body. It is aimed at communicating the ideas of construction, repetition, mobility, articulation and demolition. In interviews, Seroussi (2013) and Tajchman (2013) can offer varying textures in their answers. When asked how they would describe their roles within the collaboration, Seroussi, for example, talks of his ability as a director to reinvent and reimagine the existing, manipulating time and space to alter the perception of reality in his films. Tajchman considers his role as an architect to envision the future, with a lesser focus on the manipulation of the existing and a greater emphasis on creating a vision of the unknown, through the illusionary power of digital media. As representatives of their vocations, both individuals have the ability to deal creatively (yet differently) with unseen reality. 'I'm always searching for a way to extract things and people from reality. Film lets me do this by stopping time and stretching space' (Seroussi 2013). Both Seroussi and Tajchman believe their roles have a magical strength. When talking of the power of digital technologies used to create his imagery, Tajchman says, 'I can achieve an illusion of reality. I am a sort of "illusionist"'.

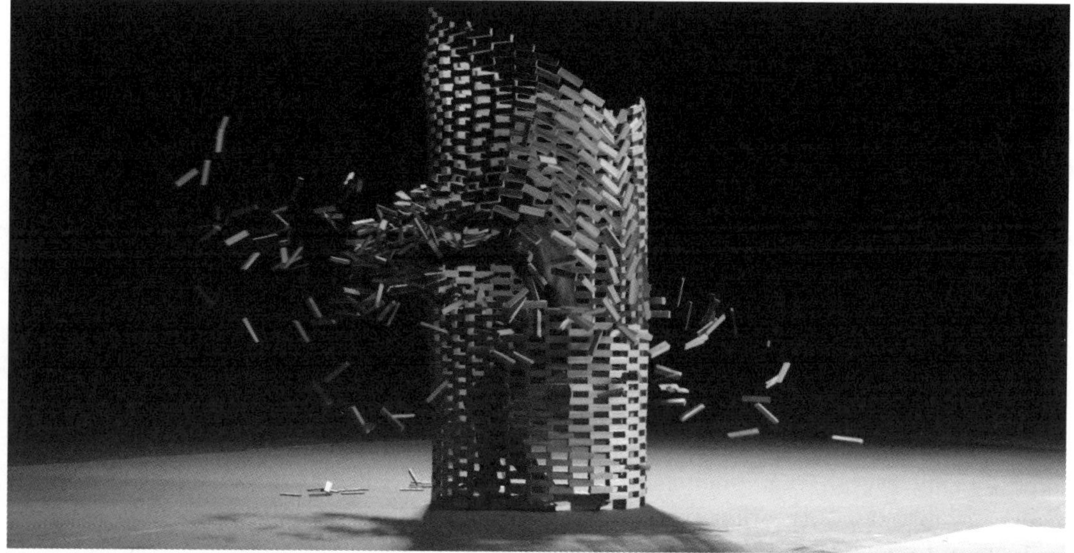

Figure 4. *Kaplinski* © Tajchman and Seroussi, 2013.

Act 3: Final statements

From the research undertaken and documented here, it could be said that the key difference between architects and film-makers is that film-makers use their 'art' to create imaginary worlds by manipulating space and time with the aim of changing others' perceptions of reality through cognitive interaction – akin to a mass call to action – either as a delicate instigator or an explosive catalyst. Architects, on the other hand, use their drive and imagination to envision and then build a future, taking control of the pathway, creating a new reality for others to inhabit – an inward call to action. When these powers meet in a creative capacity, the output has the potential not just to transcend the limits of each discipline but to create a new one, where medium and creation are both one and the same. One film-maker who has successfully turned their hand to architecture and design is the stylistically and symmetrically driven Wes Andersen who, alongside Office for Metropolitan Architecture (OMA) has recreated familiar scenes from his seminal films into Café Luce, a Milanese cafe, for Prada. Wes Andersen uses a magical mix of narrative, imagination and real-life elements to generate the plots and scenes for his films. The films themselves then inspire real architectural projects – reality > representation > reality goes full circle – closing this loop however, opens up even more dialogue and possibility. This poses an interesting cyclical relationship and highlights the blurring of the boundaries between reality and representation even further, becoming greyer and ever more diluted – the possibility for future collaboration between architects and film-makers, for generations of new genres, becomes possible.

The nature of the film preproduction process (scripts, storyboards, casting) is to formulate and ensure the successful execution of the preordained outcome. In (most) films, eventualities are tested and explored in advance, and deviation from the agreed path is avoided at all costs. Film-makers rely upon architectural conventions to instil familiarity, authenticity and empathy into a film. They rely upon the visual conditioning of the built environment as a mode of entry into their imagined world. Where the two disciplines really differ is in their intention: architects imagine life, and plan for the realization of their designs, but they cannot preordain its end use; families' split, plots are divided, rivers flood and developers swoop. Planning for the final outcome is thus not an easy task for an architect. In many cases, longevity and flexibility are considered preferable, but often the outcome of this approach can lack the desired narrative or personality. People are unpredictable; they use space differently and will interpret films in their own way. This variety is powerful – stairs are designed to aid movement between floors, yet they become reappropriated in many ways: as a place to sit and talk on the phone or a place to make love (in Hollywood movies). These alternate functions are rarely considered when choosing materials and following building regulations, yet these are the 'realities' or the 'subplots' of spatial occupation. These 'subplots' are occurrences or memories generated by historic or filmic events, and they have the power to make a place 'significant'. This sense of place can be both made and destroyed through portrayal on the screen or in the hands of an architect's decision. The spectacle of an on-location movie shoot can make a street or a cafe a landmark. Architects and film-makers could learn from each other about the role that narrative plays in curating reputations, place-making and their joint duty to continue to be innovative.

The representational mediums, techniques and design methods architects conjure are approximate, indirect, and sometimes downright mischievous. Trading in tropes, metaphors, half-truths, and distortions, we pick the pockets of truth, acting like con artists leveraging sleight of hand tactics, poking around for possible worlds in the act of the design. Using languages and visual accomplices of all manner, architects are metaphorical Houdini's escape artists, fictitious and duplicitous writers on spatial dreams, invoking imagined worlds riddled with a politics of communication on the lookout for architecture that advocates for real cultural agency. (Kulper 2015)

Kulper here describes the methods of the architect in the same fantastic way one imagines the daily chores of the film-maker: choosing locations, cutting seamlessly between cities, changing actors' characteristics and voices with the press of a button. But what Kulper is suggesting here is that the two approaches are very similar – it is all about perception and visibility; the architect often makes serious his role, he plays down the elements of emotion and gut instinct in favour of justification and value engineering. The more architects that recognize their inner Houdini, the more cinematic life might be. Film-makers place their focus on the people in their creations and their ability to communicate a storyline or narrative, putting the spotlight on life, humanity and experience. Too often architecture is centred on the built form or the ego as the lead, focusing on the container of an experience rather than the creation of the experience itself. Architects might place an equal amount of attention on the end user, their 'leading lady', in order to connect more with the community.

Anything is possible, the imagined future is endless, and architects and film-makers are at the heart of the production > communication network. The responsibility is heavy but the true advantage of representation is its ability to be consumed and interpreted by many. As the 'city' demands more information (activities, typologies, people and cultures) the production of imagery, representation and conversations is increasing to generate a new backdrop and story. Perhaps the future will hold more cross-disciplinary collaborations, interchangeable professionals exploring the joint responsibilities and the new possibilities that shared skills can afford. The role of the architect and the film-maker is to provide platforms for further critical insight into the world we believe we know and the city we believe can become reality. Architecture and the city are a dependable constant, irrespective of quality, which collide with stories daily, both real and imaginary. At the fore, architecture can deflect and affect the trajectory of the storyline, as well as frame and incubate narrative processing. Films get edited, cut and mediated. Buildings weather, get re-purposed and amended. Reality is not a fixed condition, it is continually analysed in relation to time, distance, and its vital representational counterpart. This temporal nature of the reality of the built environment places it evermore on the spinning spectrum of cinema and the moving image. Architecture is so much more than a backdrop for cinema. Film is so much more than an outlet for unrealizable scenarios. When explored wholly by New Wave pioneers, the architecture/film dualism will conceive of temporal, kinaesthetic, emotive and experiential opportunity. The medium of analysis will continue to change and we may never be able to extract the black and white from the grey; in turn, this welcome ambiguity will ensure a future of profound consideration, and critique of what is 'real' and 'possible'.

References

Andersen, T. (2003), *Los Angeles Plays Itself*, Thom Andersen Productions.
———— (2014), Interview, January. (Interview with author via email, Jan 2014).
Archinect (2013), 'The Kaplinski project is an experimental film collaboration between a filmmaker and an architect', *Archinect*, 22 October, http://archinect.com/news/article/84778343/the-kaplinski-project-is-an-experimental-film-collaboration-between-a-filmmaker-and-an-architect. Accessed 24 October 2013.
Becherer, R. (1996), 'Past remembering: Robert Mallet-Stephens's architecture of duration', *Assemblage*, 31, pp. 16–41.

Brodsky, A. (2013–14), 'The place of paper' [Interview by B. Ronngren], *AArchitecture* 21.

Bruno, G. (2002), *Walls Have Feelings: Architecture, Film and the City*, London and New York: Verso Books.

Calvino, I. (1997), *Invisible Cities*, London: Random House.

Clarke, A. (2012), *Spatial Experience, Narrative and Architecture*, Sydney: Byera Hadley.

Colomina, B. (1992), *Sexuality and Space*, New York: Princeton Architectural Press, p. 83.

Evans, R. (1989), 'Architectural projection', in E. Blau and E. Kaufman (eds), *Architecture and Its Image: Four Centuries of Architectural Representation*, Montreal: MIT Press, pp. 18–35.

———— (1997), 'Translations from drawing to building', *AA Document Series*, The MIT Press, Cambridge, Massachusetts, pp. 55-91.

Fitzgearld, N. (2010), 'Paper architects and the razing of Moscow' [Interview by Yuri Avvakumov], *Russia Beyond the Headlines,* http://rbth.com/articles/2010/02/24/240210_avvakumov.html. Acessed 22 October 2013.

Forty, A. (2014), 'Future imperfect', in B. Iain, M. Fraser and B. Penner (eds), *Forty Ways to Think About Architecture: Architectural History and Theory Today*, Chichester: Wiley, pp. 17–32.

Frankowski, N. and Garcia, C. (2013), Interview, November. (Interview with author via email).

Gales, J. (2013), 'Beyond built architecture' [Interview by E. Baraona Pohl and C. Reyes Najera], *MAS Context*, http://www.mascontext.com/issues/20-narrative-winter-13/beyond-built-architecture/. Accessed 24 October 2013.

Gioni, M. and Avvakumov, Y. (2012), 'Paper tigers', *Domus*, 21 March, http://domusweb.it/en/architecture/2012/03/21/paper-tigers.html. Accessed 9 April 2015.

Haldane, J. and Wright, C. (1993), *Reality, Representation & Projection*, Oxford: Oxford University Press.

Jacobs, S. (2007), *The Wrong House: The Architecture of Alfred Hitchcock*, Rotterdam: 010 Publishers.

Kant, I. (1855), *Critique of Pure Reason* (trans. H. G. Bohn), London: H. G. Bohn.

Khorshidifard, S. (2009), 'A film studies approach in architectural research: Urban space in three Iranian films', Architectural Research Centers Consortium, *Proceedings of the 2009 Annual Research Conference on the Architectural Research Centers Consortium: Leadership in Architectural Research, Between Academia and the Profession*, College of Architecture, University of Texas, April 2009, pp. 189–98.

Kosinski, J. (2010), 'Building the grid: A conversation with *Tron Legacy* director Joe Kosinski' [Interview by C. Lamar], 23 November, IO9.com, http://io9.gizmodo.com/5697228/building-the-grid-a-conversation-with-tron-legacy-director-joe-kosinski. Accessed 9 January 2016.

Kulper, P. (2014), Interview, June. (Interview with author via email).

———— (2015), 'The precision of promiscuity', *Sci-Arc Offramp: Lies*, 9.

Lamster, M. (ed.) (2001), *Architecture and Film*, New York: Princeton Architectural Press.

Massumi, B. (1995), 'The autonomy of affect', *Cultural Critique: The Politics of Systems and Environments,* 31: Part II, pp. 83–109.

Massumi, B. (2002), *Parables for the Virtual: Movement, Affect, Sensation*, Durham: Duke University Press.

Parsons, D. L. (1999), 'Review of the cinematic city', *Film-Philosophy*, 3: 39, p. 252.

Penz, F. (1994), 'Cinema and Architecture: Overlaps and Counterpoints: Studio-Made Features in the Film Industry and Studio-Based Experiments in Architectural Education', *Architectural Design*, 64, Academy Editions, London.

Pickering, W. (ed.) (2002), *Durkheim and Representations*, London: Routledge.

Pohl, E. B. (2012), 'From line to hyperreality', *Domus*, 12 March, https://www.domusweb.it/en/architecture/2012/03/12/from-line-to-hyperreality.html. Accessed 3 January 2013.

Reggio, G. (1982), *Koyaanisqatsi*, IRE Productions.

Schonfield, K. (2003), *Walls Have Feelings: Architecture, Film and the City*, London: Routledge.

Seroussi, B. (n.d.), *Benjamin Seroussi*, http://www.benjaminseroussi.com. Accessed 24 October 2013.

—— —— (2013), Interview, November. Interview via email with the author.

Spiller, N. (ed.) (2013), *Drawing Architecture AD*, London: John Wiley & Sons.

Tajchman, D. (n.d.), *David Tajchman Architects*, http://www.davidtajchman.com. Accessed 24 October 2013.

—— —— (2013), Interview, November. Interview via email with the author.

Thinktank, WAI. 'What about WAI?', http://waithinktank/about. Accessed 30 October 2013.

Toy, M. (ed.) (1994), *Architecture & Film AD*, London: John Wiley & Sons.

WAI Architecture Think Tank (n.d.), 'What about WAI?', http://waithinktank.com/About-WAI-Think-Tank. Accessed 30 October 2013.

Webb, M. (1987), 'The city in film', *Design Quarterly*, 136, pp. 1, 3–32.

Woods, L. (2007), 'Postopolis – Lebbeus Woods', *City of Sound*, 8 June, http://www.cityofsound.com/blog/2007/06/postopolis_lebb.html. Accessed 30 December 2013.

—— —— (2007), 'Without walls: An interview with Lebbeus Woods', *BLDG BLOG*, 8 March, http://bldgblog.blogspot.co.uk/2007/10/without-walls-interview-with-lebbeus.html. Accessed 30 October 2013.

Chapter 11

Electric Signs revisited

Alice Arnold

> What, in the end, makes advertisements so superior to criticism? Not what the moving
> red neon sign says – but the fiery red pool reflecting it in the asphalt.
>
> Walter Benjamin, 'This space for rent'

In 2005, while filming advertising signs for a documentary on street art, *To Be Seen* (Arnold, 2006), a new type of sign proliferating in Times Square could be observed. These signs were very large and bright (they could be seen in daylight from several blocks away, and they featured moving images) – video on a scale rarely seen at that time in an outdoor environment, let alone hanging from a skyscraper. From a technological perspective, the image quality of these signs was impressive. From a visual perspective, they were seductive – even when the content was uninspiring, they commanded attention.

Times Square, situated at the crossing of Broadway and Seventh Avenue in midtown New York City, is famous worldwide for its signs, and has been since the 1920s, when the first neon signs and sign spectaculars began to light up the night sky. Sign spectaculars are a type of advertising sign that developed in the late nineteenth century and early twentieth century, alongside the growth of cities, the development of mass manufacturing and mass consumption, and the advent of an electrical infrastructure to support outdoor lighting (Nye 1992). The early sign spectaculars used neon light, which created coloured light and could be fashioned into words and shapes; and electronic switching mechanisms, which enabled the sequencing of lights on and off to create animated images; and they utilized the design element of scale in their construction (Starr and Hayman 1998). The signs towered over people, combining electric light, text, images and colour to create a powerful message in the sky. The visuality of these electric signs eclipsed the textual messages they carried, a phenomenon grasped by Walter Benjamin in Berlin in the 1920s (Benjamin 2004: 476) and alluded to by Marshall McLuhan in his famous phrase, 'the medium is the message'.

By the 1920s, Times Square was attracting large crowds of people, who came to look at the signs and be entertained. Sergei Eisenstein, the Russian film-maker and innovator of montage theory, who visited Times Square in 1930, wrote: 'All sense of perspective and of realistic depth is washed away by a nocturnal sea of electric advertising [...] It was thus that people used to picture stars – as glittering nails hammered into the sky' (McQuire

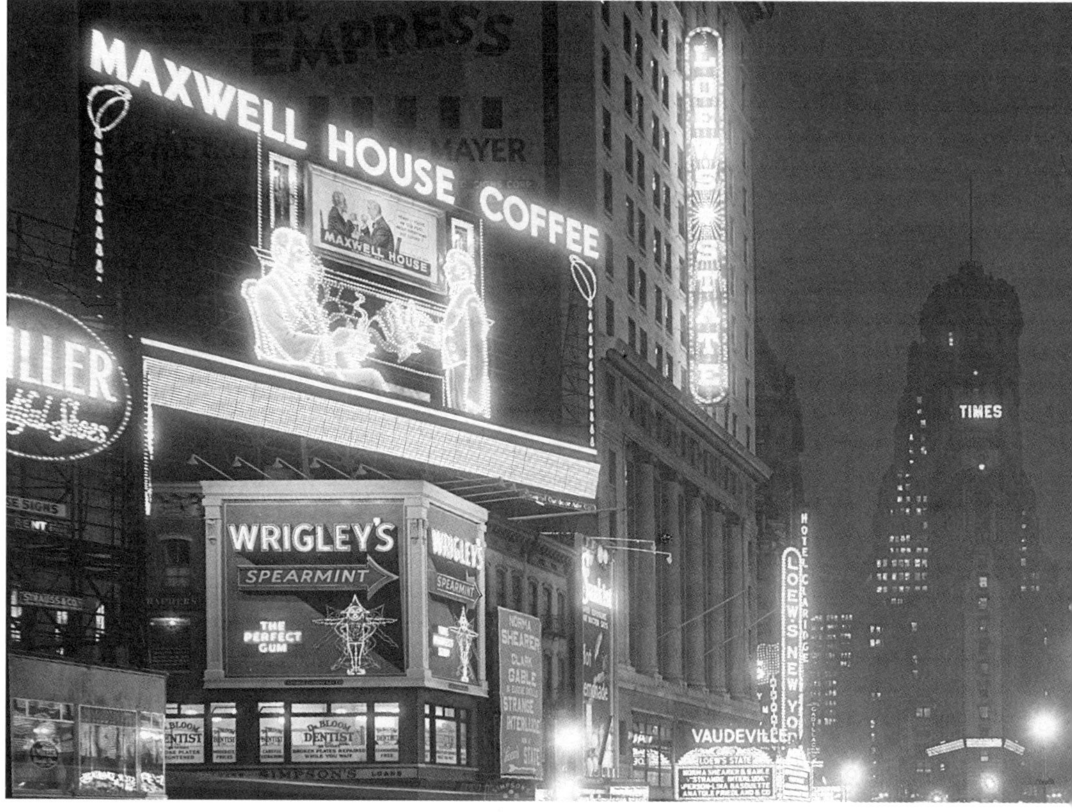

Figure 1. Times Square sign spectaculars, 1933. Image courtesy of the Library of Congress.

2008: 121). Eighty years later, one can be equally dazzled by the twenty-first-century version of the sign spectacular, and that led to my next project, *Electric Signs* (Arnold, 2013) , a documentary on signs, screens and public spaces.

Electric Signs is a visual study of the new video-based sign systems that began appearing in global cities in the early 2000s. The film investigates how this new 'economy of signs' impacts urban environments around the world. How do these screens, which add a sophisticated level of mediated experiences to the urban environment, change the way people interact with and experience the city? As public spaces become more highly concentrated with commercial messages, will this dilute the political nature of public spaces? How do the screens (both the large-scale outdoor ones and the smaller mobile ones), combined with new image and communication technologies, affect people's communications, impact visual culture and shape people's perceptual experiences? And as these devices, as well as cities, become more networked, what are the connections between screens and surveillance? These are the questions that propelled this film project, which started with a Fulbright Fellowship in 2007. This chapter extends the film in a new medium: it discusses ideas and strategies about filming the city; summarizes some of the key ideas and places explored in the film; and revisits three of the cities, so as to better understand how large- and small-screen-based media devices are impacting urban environments today.

Filming for *Electric Signs* began in Hong Kong because it is a city with a long tradition of electric lighting and outdoor advertising signs (there are streets in the Mong Kok district where the density of signage creates a canopy overhead). More recently, it has become a hub for LED manufacturing and finance. Upon my return from Asia to the United States in 2008, the majority of signs in Times Square were now digital and they were becoming larger and more visually complex. For example, Forever 21, a fast-fashion retail chain, installed a large video billboard on the facade with a camera inside, so that it could record and project in real time images of the crowd below looking at the sign. In Los Angeles, citizens were fighting the city and the outdoor advertising industry over the installation of digital billboards and super graphic signs. A year later in 2009, Prague celebrated the twentieth anniversary of the Velvet Revolution. Under Communism, there were hardly any outdoor advertising signs, but now digital signs were visible on tram rides throughout the city centre. And in many other cities in Europe, Asia and the Middle East, new buildings integrating programmable LED lighting technology into architectural facades created a new type of media surface in the city: the media facade. By 2010, however, the real estate market in the United States had crashed under the weight of speculation. Financial markets in the United States and other areas in the world were in turmoil. The Occupy protest movement, which grew out of the recession, gained momentum in New York City in 2011.[1] The protestors, fighting for greater economic and social equality, occupied Zuccotti Park, a privately owned public space in the financial district.[2] Their encampment brought a new awareness to the public about the political importance and social value of public space.

Since the film was released in 2013, the economy in New York City has rebounded. Real estate prices have returned to their previous highs and Times Square-style sign spectaculars are spreading southward along Seventh and Eighth Avenues, to 34th Street. Los Angeles's sign war continues, propelled by legal fights and sign district proposals. In Hong Kong, pro-democracy protesters occupied major roads and businesses in Autumn 2014. And one of the most interesting developments since this project started is the expansion of small mobile, networked screens. The first iPhone was released on 29 June 2007 and since then over 700 million iPhones worldwide have been purchased (Protalinski 2015). These seamless, illuminated electronic surfaces are the devices through which most people now frame their experiences.

The city symphony

With Walter Benjamin's work as a guide, I started to investigate this economy of signs and the new urban space of the media city.

Narrator, Electric Signs

Electric Signs is structured as a documentary essay film in the spirit of city symphony films and 'stars' Hong Kong, Los Angeles and New York. The spine of the film is a voice-over narrative by a 'city observer' who takes us on a journey through a variety of urban landscapes and weaves together the film's themes, cities and various personalities. The narrator, who appears on-screen throughout the film as a shadow (the opposite of light), references Walter Benjamin's writings, so that he becomes a presence in the film. Benjamin wrote about city life and media in the 1920s and 1930s, a time period analogous to ours when new forms of advertising media and distribution technologies, such as electronic signs, reshaped urban public spaces – and people's experiences in them (Benjamin 2004; McQuire 2008; Nye 1992).

The film is structured with three layers of content: interviews, vox pop interstitials and *vérité* film segments. The interviews are with lighting designers, advertising and marketing professionals, urban sociologists, visual culture experts, community activists, and a public space artist whose work offers alternative ideas about the use of media in the public sphere. The vox pop sections feature people in the city who walk, sit, work, shop and daydream in these urban lightscapes. And the *vérité* layer's function is to show the city – the rhythms and spatial dimensions of urban public spaces and the unique lighting style of the electric signs. Super 8mm time-lapse cinematography was used as the main visual strategy for this layer.

The standard frame rate of a film camera is 24 frames per second. That is, every second of film contains 24 still images, or frames. At this frame rate, cinema audiences experience a continuity of motion in the projected image, creating an illusion of real time (Kittler 2010: 149). Film-makers generally strive to create a narrative structure that conveys a unity of time (and space), known as the continuity system, so that audiences can more easily immerse themselves in the film story. The story the film is telling, however, is rarely in real time. Film-makers condense days, months and years into two-hour narratives. Or they stretch tiny fragments of time into more substantial minutes, so as to heighten the drama of the situation.

With time-lapse cinematography, though, the camera takes, for example, one frame every second. For the audience, this technique creates a gap in time between the sequential images (as they are projected and seen), so that the viewers' perception of time and space is not smooth or contiguous. As Lefebvre noted, cities, and the people in them, experience different rhythms throughout the day, based on biological (or mechanical) functions and on social interactions (Lefebvre 2007). The use of variable time in *Electric Signs*, through different time-lapse settings and editing techniques, was

188

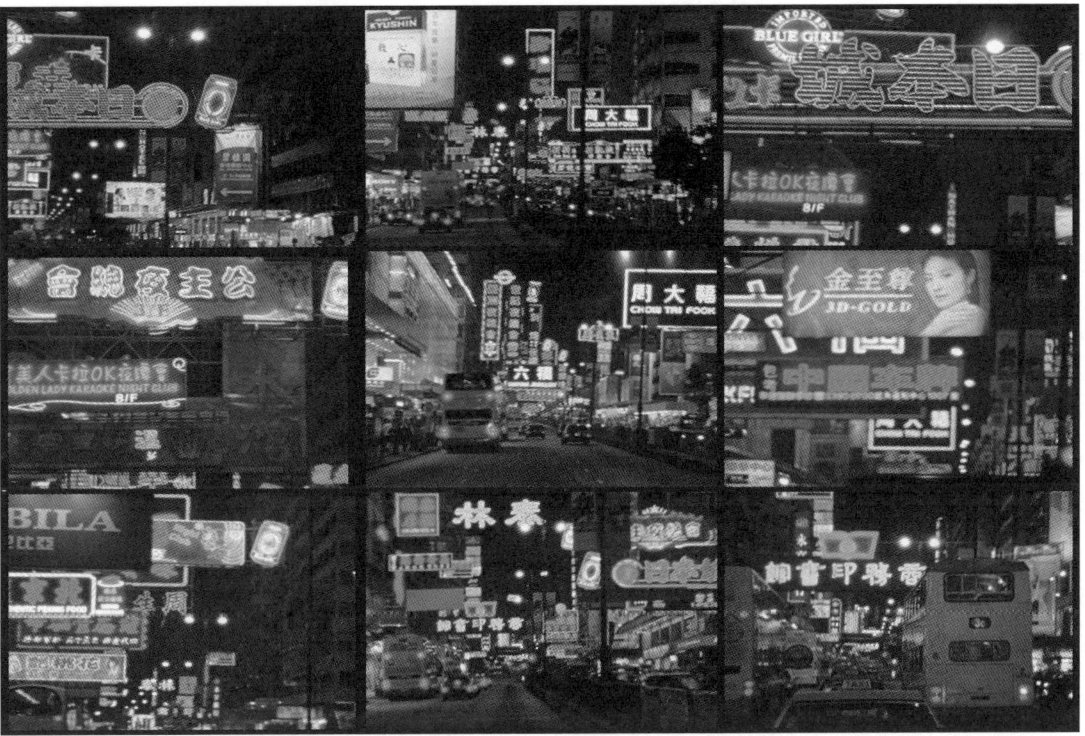

Figure 2. Super 8mm time-lapse, Nathan Road, Hong Kong. *Electric Signs* (2013), © Alice Arnold.

designed to create the sort of rhythms one feels in urban environments: a feeling of being in flow with traffic; moving en masse with a crowd of people; standing still, waiting for the light to change; or following in the footsteps of a nineteenth-century *flâneur*, the 'explorer of the crowd' (Benjamin 2003: 21), strolling with an all-consuming gaze.

Another visual strategy employed was to shoot with a moving camera in a way that relates to the tempo and character of each city. In Los Angeles, cars were used; in Hong Kong, the tram that runs through the centre of the Central District; and in New York, the camera was rigged to a unicycle and 'walked' through the city. This shooting method was often combined with 'jump cut' editing techniques to heighten the perception of the social and spatial dynamics of city space (within the two-dimensional cinematic space).

Manufacturing consent (Hong Kong)

Media saturation changes [...] people's experience of space so that it becomes abstract, dominated by signs and images that dispel meaning, history and presence.

Ackbar Abbas, *Hong Kong: Culture and the Politics of Disappearance*

Chung King Mansions, a block of dull, grey buildings, houses a warren of low-budget hotel rooms, cheap eats and small stores owned primarily by merchants from the Indian subcontinent. These shop owners, along with the many African traders and backpackers from all over the world, make Chung King Mansions one of the most ethnically diverse spaces in Hong Kong, which is 93 per cent ethnic Chinese. It is a well-known Hong Kong landmark and is famous to cineastes as the location of Wong Kar-Wai's film, *Chung King Express* (1994). But the building is noticeable on this bustling stretch of Nathan Road because of the 90-metre digital sign on the front facade, which is so active and colourful that one barely bothers to look up to see the rest of the building. This screen, which faces one of the busiest shopping streets and transportation corridors in Kowloon, 'influenced a lot of real estate developers', Ronald Lo recalled (Lo 2007). Lo's company, Join Merit Media, a marketing firm that operates a network of digital advertising signs in Hong Kong, installed the sign in 2005. Shortly afterwards, the building was put on the market and it sold at a very high price, which was attributed to the additional value that the screen added. 'So a lot of other developers actually picked that up,' continued Lo, 'and right after that installation there were at least 15 or 20 screens built afterwards.'

The Chung King sign and other large video screens like it are made from LED lighting technology. An LED, or light emitting diode, creates light by utilizing semiconductors to convert electricity into a light source. The first LEDs to be used commercially were red LEDs in the late 1960s. These were used mainly as machine indicator lights. By the

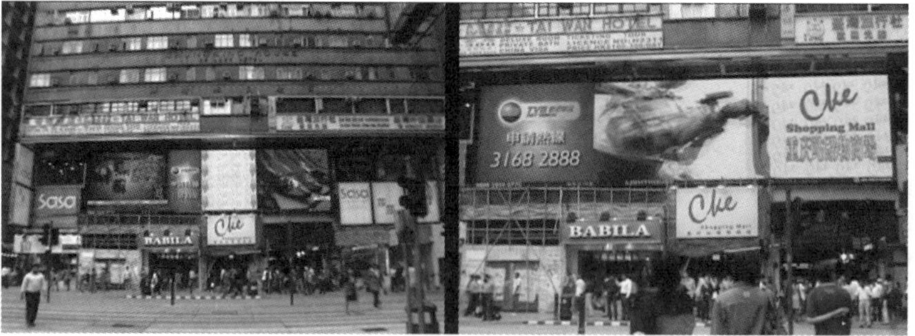

Figure 3. Chung King Mansions, 2007, © Alice Arnold.

1970s, there were also green and amber LEDs and they became cheap enough to be used in personal electronics, such as calculators and watches. The next evolution was the development of a high-capacity, inexpensive blue LED by Shuji Nakamura in 1994. With this invention, red, green and blue LED light sources could be clustered together to form a full spectrum lighting pixel – a phenomenon known in colour-theory terms as the Additive RGB system: adding together red light, blue light and green light creates white light, the visible light spectrum. This enables LEDs to be used as general lighting, a white lighting source that is more energy efficient than incandescent bulbs. LEDs are also 'smart' devices. They can be used with sensors and software to receive information as well as transmit data from them. This ability supports a synchronized grid of LEDs to become a programmable video platform, such as the large screen on Chung King Mansions.

The growth of the outdoor-screen culture in Hong Kong is due to several factors. As Ronald Lo mentioned, the screens can enhance real estate deals and add an income stream to property owners. LED technology is also relatively cheap and readily available in Hong Kong. The Pearl River Delta, located just to the north of Hong Kong in southern China, is one of the centres of LED and flat-panel-display manufacturing and many of these factories are financed and controlled by Hong Kong companies. Additionally, signs are an important part of the city's visual culture and built environment. People are accustomed to seeing buildings covered in signage and historically the government has had a loose regulatory policy about the size and placement of on-premise signs (i.e. business signs for that particular location). Many European cities, on the other hand, tightly control the size and placement of outdoor signage.

Another driver is media saturation, which fuels investment into technologically more sophisticated promotional systems. Ad spending in Hong Kong in January–February 2015 was 7 billion HK\$, and of this amount, 15 per cent was spent on outdoor advertising (Eaton 2015). Ted Lo, Ronald's brother, is an LED artist and lighting designer with offices in Hong Kong, China and New York. 'If you compare a static advertising poster to an LED screen, which has the motion graphics [with] the same branding design,' he points out, 'you'll know the platform that has the motion is a lot more attractive than the static sign. So I guess a lot of media and advertising people realize this and really try to push this projection technology to the masses.' (Lo 2007)

Some of the most heavily saturated screen areas in Hong Kong are in shopping malls, of which there are many in the city. In the newer, high-end malls, one large screen is typically featured on the facade, showing a mix of ads and promotional messages for the mall and for outside brands, along with some news or other entertainment or public-service content. Inside the mall there is usually one very large screen placed in a prominent position in the main atrium, as a focal point for people and activities in the mall (and individual shops within the malls also feature screens as part of their store design).

Hong Kong is a densely built city with very little public space in the commercial areas of the city. According to Hong Kong government statistics, Hong Kong's population in 2014 was 7.24 million (Hong Kong Special Administrative Region Government 2014),

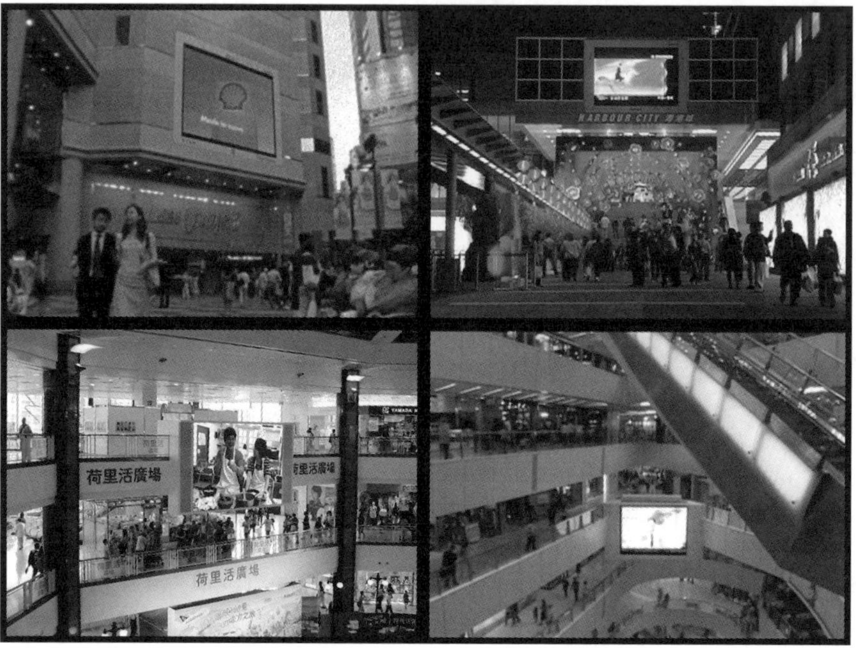

Figure 4: HK Shopping Malls (from top left, clockwise): Times Square, Harbour City, AMP, Hollywood Plaza, 2007, © Alice Arnold.

who live at an average density of 6,300 people per square km, which makes Hong Kong one of the most densely occupied cities in the world (World Population Review 2015). In this physically and visually crowded city, shopping malls provide an orderly, sheltered and climate-controlled environment for people. They are a cleaner, more leisurely, more controlled and organized version of the streets outside (Abbas 1997). But, as Mike Davis has shown in his analysis of downtown Los Angeles, shopping malls are only a simulacrum of public space and the values that those spaces embody (Davis 1992, 226). Shopping malls are controlled by private corporations, who can decide who is allowed in and who is not; they are under heavy surveillance, and their rationale for existence is to sell consumer goods and experiences (Zukin 1995). If you are not there to consume, whether that be clothes or food, a movie or a facial, you are not wanted in that space. The screens, with their bright, flashy, never-ending loop of images, are part of the experience that makes the malls a seductive space to people.

The growth of outdoor screens is also connected with the rise of mobile screens and the development of the mobile marketplace. Hong Kong has a large and sophisticated mobile-phone user base. According to Google research, Hong Kong has a 62.8 per cent smartphone penetration, placing it behind South Korea, in first place at 73 per cent, and ahead of the United States, 56.4 per cent (Think With Google 2013). Digital media producer Cedric Chan, who produces digital advertising campaigns, enjoys the challenge of creating content for outdoor and mobile screens because, he says, 'they offer new ways to interact or affect the public'. (Chan, 2007)

In 2007, Chan was at the forefront of working on strategies to connect mobile devices, the web and public screens. For example, an outdoor screen sends a message to your phone via Bluetooth or RFID, so that you can interact with the ad or the product on your mobile screen. The goal, says Chan, is 'to get people more involved in what the client wants to sell'. These outdoor screens are not broadcast television, he points out, so they are not truly mass market, but they are networked. (Chan, 2007)

So that allows you to use web technology, to give you a level of control of your narrowcast. To say at this time of day let's play this specific clip because we expect people getting off of work to be a certain demographic. So who's being targeted? Everybody, everyone's fair game. It's public spaces. Broad and narrow at the same time. Now we're getting to this level of control that we never had before. And that is a very different dynamic. (Chan, 2007)

This new dynamic is leading to a city where public spaces are diminishing and political power is concentrated in the hands of the financial elite. Mirana May Szeto, a professor in Comparative Literature at Hong Kong University and a political activist, thinks 'the city is very subtly controlled' (Szeto, 2007) . Key industries, such as real estate and the financial sector, have a lot of economic and cultural power in Hong Kong because they are the financial backbone of the media. 'And media, in order to survive really cannot antagonize their opinions, a consortium of this kind of financing.' Twenty years ago, Hong Kong had more newspapers than it does now: 'Other channels,' she says, 'where you could say something different or alternative.' Szeto thinks the theory of Manufacturing Consent explains how mass media operates under a culture of self-censorship in Hong Kong. 'So it isn't that there is nothing happening in civil society, but it is not recorded in mainstream media. So it's really about that, how media is really very highly and subtly controlled on all levels of its production.'

The increasing commercialization of public spaces, the high ratio of shopping malls to public spaces, where people can freely gather, and the growing economic and political power of the real estate and financial sectors are issues that surfaced in the Queen's Pier protest in July 2007. Queen's Pier was a public space pier on Hong Kong Island that the government decided to demolish, so that this prime waterfront location could be extended, through land reclamation, and developed into what the government considered a more productive use of the land (the original plan called for a highway, shopping mall and open green space). This development plan coincided with the rollout of a new marketing campaign for Hong Kong, branding the city as 'Asia's World City'.

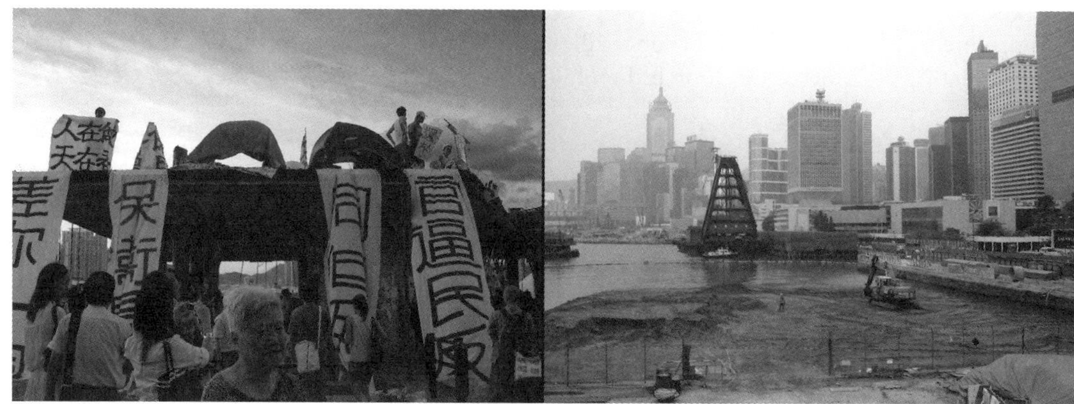

Figure 5. Queen's Pier protest (left); Queen's Pier demolition and harbour land reclamation (right), 2007, © Alice Arnold.

The protest, which used art and street-theatre tactics, such as writing love letters to the pier, sparked a critical dialogue in Hong Kong about the importance of public space and the lack of political power that ordinary Hong Kongers have over development decisions. Ultimately, however, the courts sided with the government, the protestors were forced out, the pier was torn down, and the redevelopment plans went forward.

Protests over public space and democracy issues have continued in Hong Kong, most noticeably with the Umbrella Revolution, an Occupy-style protest, which started in September 2014 when massive street protests ignited over the issue of open elections for the Chief Executive position, the top political post in Hong Kong (the government in Beijing controls the voting process and it opposes open elections). Police responded to the peaceful, largely student-led protests with tear-gas attacks and beatings, which brought even more people out into the streets. Tens of thousands of protestors occupied several major roads in Hong Kong, stopping traffic and shutting down businesses, for over two months (the final protest sites were cleared on 11 December 2014). The Umbrella Revolution's name is derived from the umbrellas that the protestors used to protect themselves against the tear-gas attacks. The Hong Kong people have transformed an ordinary, familiar object into a potent symbol of people power. It remains to be seen whether the protestors can unite more people and shift Hong Kong towards a more open society, but the occupation of public space was a good place to start.

Sign wars: Los Angeles

I think that I shall never see
A billboard lovely as a tree
Indeed, unless the billboards fall
I'll never see a tree at all.

Ogden Nash, *Song of the Open Road*

Los Angeles is often described as a postmodern city, because it does not have a unified centre. Instead, it sprawls horizontally, networked together by its freeway system. Given this geography of the built environment, driving is part of the fabric of life in LA, and people spend a lot of time looking out at the city through their windscreens. This is a very cinematic way to experience the city, because the history of LA is intertwined with the invention of images and lifestyles, through the production of films and television shows.

Anne Friedberg and other scholars have noted that the experience of a mobilized gaze, which starts with railroad travel in the 1820s, changed the way people experienced space and place. The landscape became a consumable view, a moving image framed through a glass window. This new way of seeing, of framing moving images, was also a precursor to the formation of cinema in the 1890s (Friedberg 1994). For Los Angelenos, traversing the city in their private cars, the mobile gaze is part of their everyday life activity, turning the city into a private image. Driving also heightens the cinematic experience through the perception of controlling speed, 'slowing down or speeding up time and of extending or

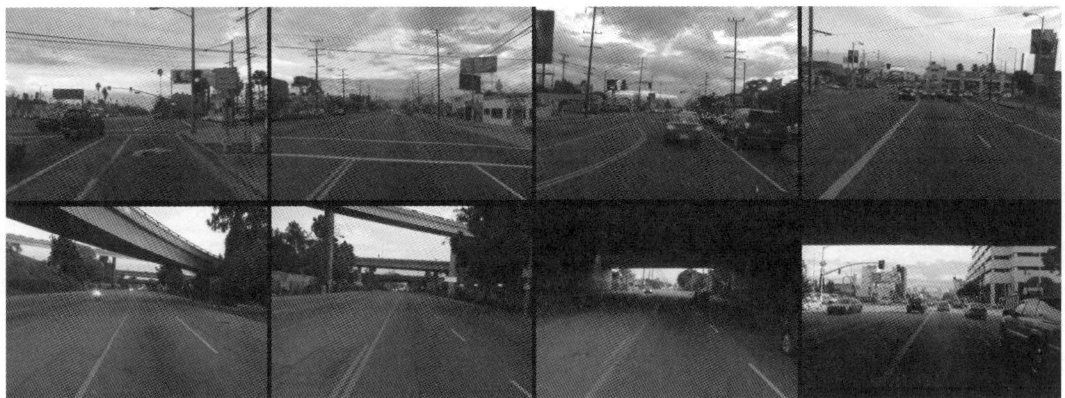

Figure 6. LA Driving College. *Electric Signs*, 2009, © Alice Arnold.

shrinking space at will' (Gudis 2004: 41). The presence of the billboards also turns the city into a 'consumerable landscape' (Gudis 2004: 6), encouraging drivers 'to window shop right through their windshield' (54).

Reyner Banham celebrated LA's billboards in the 1970s: 'Anyone who cares about the unique character of individual cities must see that the proliferation of advertising signs is an essential part of the character of Los Angeles' (Banham 2009: 121).[3] But 30 years later a significant proportion of Los Angeles's population considers them to be visual pollution. LA has an estimated 10–11,000 billboards and is known as the billboard capital of the United States.[4] There are two underlying causes for this shift. First, as the population and traffic increased in LA, cars could no longer zip through the city. Instead, drivers now spend a lot of time sitting in traffic, where they are a captive audience for the billboards. And second, in global cities such as Los Angeles, Hong Kong and New York, advertisements dominate the urban environment and people are saturated with media. Images are an increasingly important aspect of the way people communicate ideas, emotions and messages, but we generate them so cheaply and quickly that they can blot out other aspects of our visual, as well as mental, environment.

Dennis Hathaway, the director of the nonprofit organization the Coalition to Ban Billboard Blight, feels that this is happening in LA.

> I think that just giving this environment over, conceding it, to advertising, as just a big blank canvas to be filled, really diminishes us as citizens. And we've got a situation now where advertising is more and more dominating the visual environment. (Hathaway, 2009)

The sign wars in Los Angeles date back to the 1980s, when community groups tried to reduce the number of billboards in LA, many of which were put up illegally.[5] In 2002, the City Council passed a ban on all new billboards, but the billboard companies sued the city, citing First Amendment rights for commercial speech. The city ended up settling one of the lawsuits by allowing two of the billboard companies to convert 840 billboards to digital billboards. The activation of the first digital billboards in autumn 2008 set off an intense public debate about the visual landscape of the city and more lawsuits, which are still ongoing in 2015. A sign taped to a digital billboard in the Silverlake neighbourhood expresses the mood and sentiment of many Los Angelenos when the signs were first switched on:

> *Kill the Sign. It is visible from many of our living rooms. Its 50,000 watts of power flash a cavalcade of tacky advertisements at one per five seconds […] We have worked hard […] making Silver Lake a beautiful and desirable place to live, only to see all that work substantially devalued by a mega-corporation that cares nothing about our community.*

There was also public outrage over the way the city negotiated and implemented the deal. The digital billboards were installed without community district discussion, without complying with zoning regulations and under questionable legal conditions. The *LA Weekly* investigated what happened and concluded in the article, 'Billboards gone wild: Is city hall corrupt or inept', that 'the mayor and city council have let the billboard industry flout the law' (Pelisek 2008).

'The issues with signs is about money,' states Hathaway. 'These billboards are like slot machines for the industry. A single digital billboard can make up to 800,000 dollars a year in revenue.' Hathaway believes that the visual environment of the city belongs to the public and that private interests who use this space, such as the outdoor advertising industry, should not be making enormous profits from a public resource (Hathaway 2009).

'The problem of course is that many of these screens or billboards are controlled by corporations, for whom it is of course a form of big business,' adds Professor Erkki Huhtamo (Design Media Arts, UCLA). 'So the issue of access to those messages that surround us in public spaces is anything but simple. Public space is highly controlled space, so you just simply cannot put anything you want on that space, unless you chose to do it illegally' (Huhtamo 2010).

Pressure from community groups and media scrutiny convinced the City Council to pass a billboard moratorium in 2009, so that the city could rewrite the sign code. The billboard companies responded with more lawsuits. Filming for *Electric Signs* was completed in 2011, but the sign war continued through legal cases and new sign proposals. In one of the most significant cases, the California Court of Appeals upheld a ruling saying the original digital billboard deal was illegal, forcing those signs to go dark in April 2013. There is a surreal aspect to seeing these empty, black billboard screens while driving now in LA. But this situation could reverse. Another lawsuit over the city's ban on new digital sign permits was recently decided in the billboard company's favour, so there could be more digital signs installed in the future.

The trend in Los Angeles, and many other cities, is to raise revenue through selling space in the public landscape, such as on city buses and street furniture and in public parks. Currently, the city council has proposed creating special signs districts, so that certain areas in the city would become more 'Times Square' like. Signs have become a source of income for cities as well as for real estate developers and the advertising industry. Dennis Hathaway, however, does not think there is any public interest involved in allowing multinational corporations to push their products in the public sphere. 'That's kind of a hard sell because there are a lot of powerful interests behind that, who want that public space to be available to them. And they have the wherewithal to put a lot of pressure on the politicians.' Hathaway believes that people can counter that pressure with numbers: 'If enough people say, "No, we don't want that", the politicians are going to listen' (Hathaway, 2009).

Media city

Today, the most real, mercantile gaze into the heart of things is the advertisement. It tears down the stage upon which contemplation moved, and all but hits us between the eyes with things as a car, growing to gigantic proportions, careens at us out of a film screen.

Walter Benjamin, 'This space for rent'

Walking through Times Square, one is simultaneously distracted and charmed by the jumble of brightly lit semiotic displays that encircle this space, known as the 'crossroads of the world'. Times Square is not actually a square. It was named for the *New York Times* newspaper, which moved their headquarters there in 1905 (Sagalyn 2003). The area is formed by the crossing of Seventh Avenue and Broadway, from 42nd Street to 48th Street. Within these six blocks Manhattan's grid opens up and this creates a unique public space in the middle of Manhattan. The signs pull people into this stage, where they enter the spectacle of Times Square, a fantasy world created by the big brands, whose images dominate the screens. Because these screens are always in your field of vision, it is difficult to focus on just one ad, one message, one image. It is easier to let the colours, the motion, the crowds of people and the sounds of the street lull you into a dreamy state. It takes effort to concentrate and look critically at this phantasmagoria of light and colour.

Times Square developed into an urban spectacle and a media capital in the 1920s, when an assemblage of sign spectaculars, theatres, cinemas and other forms of media drew in crowds of people. Times Square remained an exuberant and popular entertainment centre for New Yorkers and tourists through the 1950s (Sagalyn 2003; Zukin 1995). By the 1970s, however, the lights had dimmed in Times Square. TV, shopping malls and suburban homes had shifted affluence and influence, away from the city to the suburbs (Cohen 2003). New York City was on the verge of bankruptcy, and in Times Square there were empty billboard spaces, vacant buildings and illicit activities. Revitalization plans for the area started to surface in the 1980s (Zukin 1995). One strategy unfolded organically through an investment in signs.

Some of the Japanese companies that had a consumer market in the United States, like Sony and Minolta, helped to revive business in Times Square by investing in outdoor advertising. For the Japanese corporations, putting sign spectaculars in Times Square helped broadcast their prominence to the world as global brands. For New York, this investment showed that the space was still valuable as a media channel (Starr and Hayman 1998).

Under the Koch administration (1978–89), the city proposed a redevelopment plan to turn Times Square into a cleaner, safer and more business-friendly environment. The main feature was a set of skyscrapers on 42nd Street by Philip Johnson and John Burgee. This plan, however, was widely disliked, because of its focus on commercial office space and its disregard for the cultural history of Times Square (Sagalyn 2003). The Municipal

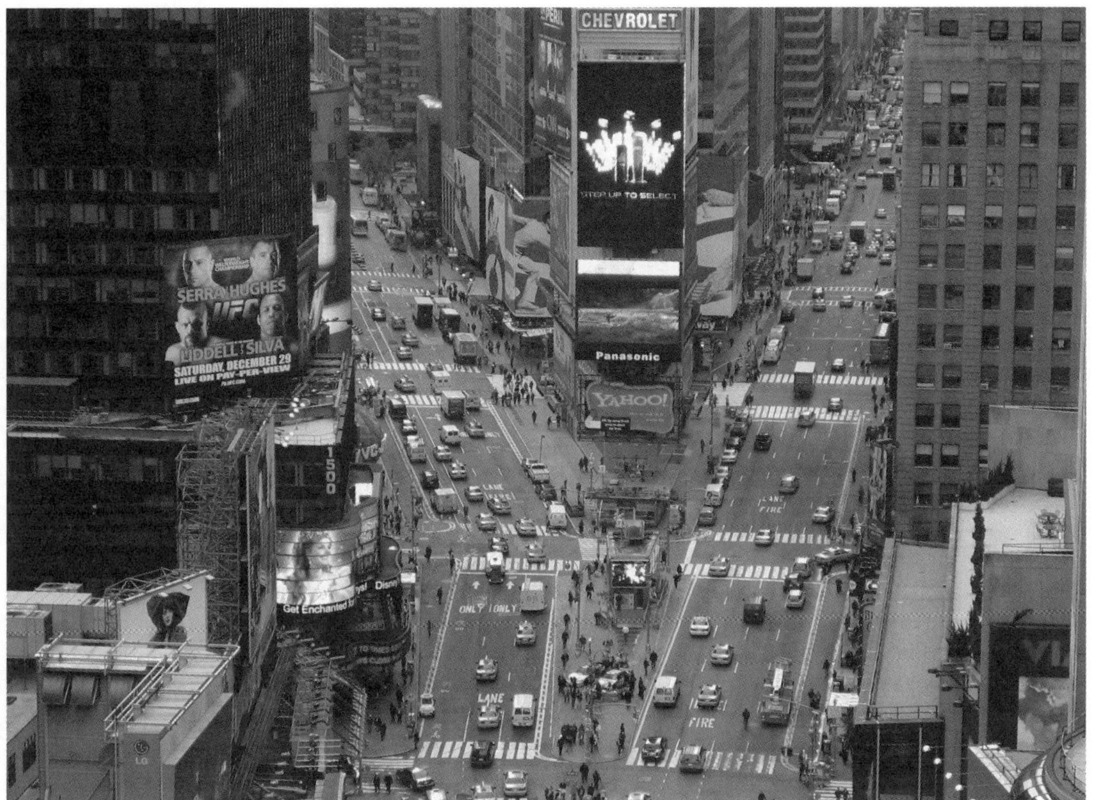

Figure 7. Times Square overview, 2008, © Alice Arnold.

Art Society (MAS), a nonprofit organization founded in 1893 to help create a more livable city, stepped into the fray with an alternative plan, to create a sign district in Times Square. MAS had a history of fighting to reduce advertising signs in the city, but they argued that what made Times Square successful in the past was its unique populist character. The city could reclaim the space and capture the feeling of excitement that Times Square was known for by keeping the visual character of the old Times Square (Gilmartin 1995). 'So Times Square was made a unique zone in New York City' [in 1987][6], explains urban sociologist Sharon Zukin, 'where electric signs are required by law. Every building in Times Square must be covered on the outside by giant electric signs'

Standing in Times Square with Sharon Zukin, we wondered, what would Walter Benjamin think about today's electric signs? 'Walter Benjamin would find the lure of commodities and goods too abstract in this space,' she immediately replied. 'Our visual field is overtaken by the signs and symbols of corporations. Not just by the immediacy of products, but by the immediacy of the brands.' But people do like signs, she continued. 'They may advertise something abstract like a brand, but they are visual, they are immediate, they are in your face. They are a form of public art that we all grow up with. The problem is when there is nothing but these signs.' (Zukin, 2010)

The sign-district concept was highly successful in attracting new investments and people back to Times Square. The area's business-improvement district estimates that there are over 300,000 visitors a day (Times Square Alliance 2015). Signs have become a sophisticated form of visual capital – they are worth millions of dollars to advertisers, real estate developers and to city governments. Currently, the largest sign in Times Square is on the facade of the Marriott Hotel, spanning a full city block and eight stories high. It rents for US\$ 2.5 million a month (Steel 2014). The value of these sign spectaculars is so exuberantly high because of their extended visibility. Times Square is a staging ground for television shows, news broadcasts, films and marketing promotions (e.g. the New Year's Eve celebration). And images of Times Square circulate widely through people's personal social media channels.

The relationship between media and the public city space is becoming more complicated with this increase in outdoor screens and networked mobile screens. Phones, tablets, cameras and wearable technology, in addition to the large screens overhead, are simultaneously competing for our attention. The screens draw us into virtual spaces where we can easily disconnect from the places we are in. For some, this is a welcoming experience and one that will be enhanced in the near future by new vision technologies, such as virtual-reality headsets. But this multiplicity of screens can generate mass distraction, which weakens the ties between people in public space.

Screens are also surveillance devices. The screen is an information surface, a window we view, but screens are also used to record our movements and collect data from us. Businesses use locative data from our mobile phones (and Internet browsers) to create targeted ads, so that they can appeal to us, as individual consumers.

And smartphones also are changing people's perceptual experiences. As people start to rely on machine-thinking to navigate their environments, they use their internal cognition skills less. For example, many people rely on Google Maps rather than looking at the environment with their own eyes. Perhaps this is because the virtual-map world is easier to understand than the real world. But what happens if there is no Internet service of if your battery dies and there is no way to recharge your device? During Hurricane Sandy (October 2012) many New Yorkers were without electricity and the Internet for several days, so these are not hypothetical what-ifs. Depending solely on smartphones to understand and or interpret the world for us can dumb us down.

Another way that mobile screens impact our perception is through image making. Visitors to museums often take quick shots of art objects with their phones, and then move on to the next photograph. It seems like the digital image, which can be shared on social media sites, is a better trophy to have than the experience of looking in real time at the original object – an encounter that is not as easy to share online. In the digital screen era, the aura of an original piece of art, which Benjamin wrote about in response to the reproduction of images in photographs and film in 1936, is further dematerialized (Benjamin 1969: 217-251).

Conclusion

For Benjamin, the loss of the aura of original art was not an entirely negative outcome, because it popularized the image. By the 1920s, new techniques and technologies had lowered the cost of image reproduction, disrupting the control over images by the traditional elite, the nobility and the clergy (Berger 1990). As images began to pass through more hands and before more eyes, this had a democratizing effect on the creation, content and interpretation of images. However, as Benjamin was keenly aware, photographs, advertising signs and films can also be used as propaganda tools, something that he experienced first hand as the National Socialism party rose to power in Germany in the 1930s. As Benjamin perceived, visual technology is a form of power, an exploding force that can 'burst the world asunder by the dynamite of a 1/10 of a second' (Benjamin 1969: 236). *Electric Signs* ends with a montage of images: people taking pictures in Times Square, a giant stock-market ticker sign, a girl on her cellphone in Tokyo, protestors with hand-drawn signs, a crowded Hong Kong street, a string of taillights and colourful signs on the Las Vegas Strip… These electric signs, they shine seductively with messages of modernity and freedom, of free consumer choice, but their luminous beauty masks the power that drives these signs. And that power is used to control our public spaces, dominate our public lives, and influence our private selves.

References

Abbas, A. (1997), *Hong Kong: Culture and the Politics of Disappearance*, Minneapolis: University of Minnesota Press.

Arnold, A. (2006), *To Be Seen*, USA: Icarus Films.

—————— (2013), *Electric Signs*, USA: Icarus Films.

Banham, R. (2009), *Los Angeles: The Architecture of Four Ecologies*, Berkeley: University of California Press.

Benjamin, W. (1969 [1936]), 'The Work of Art in the Age of Mechanical Reproduction', in H. Arendt (ed.), *Illuminations* (trans. H. Zorn), New York: Schocken Books, pp. 217–51.

Benjamin, W. (2003), 'Paris, capital of the 19th Century', in R. Tiedemann (ed.), *The Arcades Project* (trans. H. Eiland), Cambridge, MA: Belknap Press of Harvard University Press.

Benjamin, W. (2004 [1928]), 'This Space for Rent', in M. Bullock and M. W. Jennings (eds), *Walter Benjamin: Selected Writings, Volume 1, 1913–1926* (trans. H. Eiland), Cambridge, MA: Belknap Press of Harvard University Press, p. 476.

Berger, J. (1990), *Ways of Seeing*, New York: Penguin.

Chan, C. (2007), Interviewed by Alice Arnold for *Electric Signs*, 6 October.

Cohen, L. (2003), *A Consumer's Republic*, New York: Vintage.

Davis, M. (1992), *City of Quartz: Excavating the Future in Los Angeles*, New York: Vintage.

Eaton, M. (2015), 'CNY drives $3.3bn surge in Hong Kong ad spend', http://www.marketing-interactive.com/cny-drives-surge-hong-kong-adspend/. Accessed 26 March 2015.

Friedberg, A. (1994), *Window Shopping: Cinema and the Postmodern*, Berkeley: University of California Press.

Gilmartin, G. (1995), *Shaping the City: New York and the Municipal Art Society*, New York: Clarkson Potter Publishers.

Gudis, C. (2004), *Buyways*, New York: Routledge.

Harvey, D. (2004), *Conditions of Post Modernity*, Oxford: Blackwell Publishing.

Hathaway, D. (2009), Interviewed by Alice Arnold for *Electric Signs*, 17 January.

Helfand, J. (2001), *Screen: Essays on Graphic Design, New Media and Visual Culture*, New York: Princeton Architectural Press.

Hong Kong Special Administrative Region Government (2014), *Hong Kong: The Facts*, www.gov.hk/en/about/abouthk/factsheets/docs/population.pdf. Accessed 9 June 2015.

Huhtamo, E. (2010), Interviewed by Alice Arnold for Electric Signs, 21 May.

—————— (2012), *Illusions in Motion: Media Archaeology of the Moving Panorama and Related Spectacles*, Cambridge, MA: MIT Press.

Iveson, K. (2012), 'Branded cities: Outdoor advertising, urban governance and the outdoor media landscape', *Antipode*, 44: 1, pp. 151–74.

Kittler, F. (2010), *Optical Media*, Cambridge, UK: Polity.

Lefebvre, H. (2007), *Rhythmanalysis: Space, Time and Everyday Life* (trans. S. Elden and G. Moore), London: Continuum.

Lo, R. (2007), Interviewed by Alice Arnold for *Electric Signs*, 15 August.

—————— Interviewed by Alice Arnold for *Electric Signs*, 27 September.

Mathews, G. and Luim, T. (eds) (2001), *Consuming Hong Kong*, Hong Kong: Hong Kong University Press.

McDonogh, G. and Wong, C. (2005), *Global Hong Kong*, New York: Routledge.

McQuire, S. (2008), *The Media City: Media, Architecture and Urban Space*, London: Sage.

Nye, D. (1992), *Electrifying America*, Cambridge, MA: MIT Press.

Pelisek, C. (2008), 'Billboards gone wild: Is City Hall corrupt or inept?', *LA Weekly*, 23 April, http://www.laweekly.com/2008-04-24/news/billboards-gone-wild/. Accessed 24 April 2008.

Protalinski, E. (2015), 'Apple has sold 700M iPhones, sees 49% quarterly sales growth year over year', *VentureBeat.com*, 9 March, http://venturebeat.com/2015/03/09/apple-has-now-sold-700m-iphones-up-49-year-over-year/. Accessed 9 June 2015.

Sagalyn, L. B. (2003), *Times Square Roulette: Remaking the City Icon*, Cambridge, MA: MIT Press.

Schivelbusch, W. (2014), *The Railway Journey*, Berkeley: University of California Press.

Starr, T. and Hayman, E. (1998), *Signs and Wonders: The Spectacular Marketing of America*, New York: Doubleday Press.

Steel, E. (2014), 'Times Square's biggest and most expensive digital billboard is set to shine', *New York Times*, 16 November, http://www.nytimes.com/2014/11/17/business/media/times-squares-biggest-and-most-expensive-digital-billboard-is-set-to-shine-.html. Accessed 9 June 2015.

Szeto, M. (2007), Interviewed by Alice Arnold for *Electric Signs*, 9 November.

Think With Google (2013), 'Our Mobile Planet', http://think.withgoogle.com/mobileplanet/en/. Accessed 11 June 2015.

Times Square Alliance (2015), 'Pedestrian Counts', http://www.timessquarenyc.org/do-business-here/market-facts/pedestrian-counts/index.aspx#.VYXS_1VVhBc. Accessed 11 June 2015.

Venturi, R., Scott Brown, D. and Izenour, S. (1993), *Learning from Las Vegas*, Cambridge, MA: MIT Press.

Zukin, S. (1995), *The Culture of Cities*, Cambridge, MA: Blackwell.

—— —— (2005), *Point of Purchase*, New York: Routledge.

—— —— (2010a), *Naked City: The Death and Life of Authentic Urban Places*, New York: Oxford University Press.

—— —— (2010b), Interviewed by Alice Arnold for *Electric Signs*, 9 October.

World Population Review (2015), 'Hong Kong Population', http://worldpopulationreview.com/countries/hong-kong-population. Accessed 9 June 2015.

Notes

1. *Adbusters* magazine proposed an occupation of Wall Street to call attention to increasing political, social and economic inequality in the United States. *Adbusters*'s call to action can be seen here: https://www.adbusters.org/blogs/adbusters-blog/occupywallstreet.html. Accessed 6 January 2016.
2. Privately owned public spaces are city plazas and spaces controlled by real estate developers but required by law to be open for public use. For more information on this public–private partnership, see: http://www.nyc.gov/html/dcp/html/pops/pops.shtml. Accessed 6 January 2016.

3. Also of interest, Banham's BBC documentary on Los Angeles: https://vimeo.com/22488225. Accessed 6 January 2016.
4. This estimate is from 2008. Some of these billboards are legal and others were put up illegally. For more information, see: http://www.nytimes.com/2008/11/06/us/06billboard.html?_r=0. Accessed 6 January 2016.
5. The *Los Angeles Times* published an interactive map of unapproved city billboards: http://graphics.latimes.com/la-billboards/. Accessed 6 January 2016.
6. See Sagalyn (2003) p. 250 and Gilmartin (1995) p. 459.

Chapter 12

Public life and urban humanities: Beyond the ideal city

Luisa Bravo

Introduction

Cinema has often influenced the urban-planning discipline, as a tool for the documentation of the evolutionary process of the built environment and, providing a different knowledge, as a means to seduce and engage emotionally. Films are the conscience of the human eye, they have the ability to become a direct language with educational content: they can move the point of view from the overview perspectives of urbanists to the personal and subjective perceptions of individual observers, at eye level. The camera frames architecture and spaces, but mainly it offers human stories, evolutions of feelings; it captures details of social interactions, while the urban is moving around. The city, as seen through the lens, becomes a tale, open to multiple interpretations; a scenery of the collective consciousness, able to describe and disclose the changing urban identities and humanities, through space and time.

This chapter reports on the outcomes of 'Visioni Urbane/Urban Visions: Beyond the Ideal City', a film competition initiated by City Space Architecture in 2014, as part of the Italian festival Visioni Italiane ('Italian Visions'), promoted by Cineteca di Bologna. The competition brief sought to investigate the existing city, the connections, intersections and urban activities that take place inside it, seen through complex social issues, contexts and human geographies, with an emphasis on human relationships between individuals and the urban space in which these relations move. The aim was to collect stories addressing the urban environment in different film formats, such as fiction, documentary, experimental. 'Urban Visions' is the first film competition in the Italian context involving film-makers at a professional level on topics related to cities and urbanity, so it is a unique platform able to foster interaction and exchange between different disciplines, such as architecture, sociology, urban design and film studies, while offering spectators insights and meanings on daily urban life in cities.

In 2014, City Space Architecture, a nonprofit cultural association based in Bologna (Italy), joined the 21st edition of Visioni Italiane festival,[1] a well-known Italian film festival with a competition promoted by Cineteca di Bologna, a prime centre known globally for film studies, film archives and film restoration.[2] Starting in 1994, the festival has hosted those works made by young Italian film-makers that remain largely invisible, such as short films, documentaries, experimental films and debut films that need distribution, providing a place for discussion with other film-makers and the public. Several film-makers who took part in Visioni Italiane throughout the years are now known nationally and internationally.

City Space Architecture is committed to exploring the identities, meanings and complexities of the contemporary city, in different geographical contexts, through studies on public space. The association, based on an international academic and professional platform, promotes a critical reflection on our own world in a cross-disciplinary field of action. The aim is to spread knowledge and understanding of the urban and human environment for students, educators, designers, city managers and citizens.

Within the festival, City Space Architecture promoted a brand-new section called 'Visioni Urbane/Urban Visions: Beyond the Ideal City'.[3] This was an opportunity to develop a research field of activities intended to put urban theory and cinema studies in dialogue and to raise awareness on some contemporary urban issues. The competition brief sought to investigate the existing city, the connections, intersections and urban activities that take place within it, as seen through complex social issues, contexts and human geographies. Emphasis was placed on human relationships between individuals and the urban space in which these relations move. Focusing on the public realm, where public aspects, related to participation, sharing and social practices, mix up with private aspirations, related to individuality, diversity and lifestyles, 'Urban Visions' intended to collect stories of happiness or poverty, success or solitude, compliance or rebellion, beyond the seducing and reassuring shapes of the beautiful, ideal city.

Overcoming the stereotypes and well-known images of consumerism, 'Urban Visions' was looking for something that our eyes, deliberately or unconsciously, do not know or cannot see. Embedding artists and film-makers in the architectural and design practice is a consistent plus; cinema is the means to overlap cityscapes with mindscapes, engaging the discussion on a different level of interaction and enjoyment, based on feelings, emotions and personal experience, looking for mental fascination and enchantment.

The reference to films is a tool to open a new perspective, to explore new theoretical paradigms and research methods, establishing an effective understanding around urban humanities. This pedagogical approach has been already applied in the past decade in the academic context, through several courses and conference series, as well as in the professional context. Cinema, as the art of narrating spaces and their transformation, is becoming a powerful tool for architects and designers to describe their work to city planners and managers and to reach the hearts of citizens, functioning as a kind of meditation on our contemporary life. At the Venice Architecture Biennale in 2012, Jan Gehl, a Danish scholar and urbanist who has extensively researched the form and use of public spaces (Gehl 1987; Gehl and Svarre 2013), presented the documentary film *The Human Scale* by Andreas Dalsgaard (2012). Gehl has studied human behaviour in cities over four decades and has put his findings into practice in multiple locations throughout the world. *The Human Scale* – while describing major structural changes related to global cities, from political, social and economic points of view – questions our assumptions about modernity, redefining the role of people in urban planning, and suggesting that human needs for inclusion and intimacy need to be taken into account.

Some recent interesting books explore complexities between architecture, urbanism, landscape, cinema, perception and representation of urban space through the visual language of film, as a new field of study and research (Shiel and Fitzmaurice 2001; Lefebvre 2007; Mennel 2008; Penz and Lu 2011; Cairns 2013). One of the most relevant recent research programmes that links design activities with human and art studies, still underway, is the 'Global Urban Humanities Initiative', a joint venture between the University of California Berkeley Arts and Humanities Division of the College of Letters and Science and the College of Environmental Design. This initiative is based on the awareness that people shape the world around them and are in turn shaped by that same world. It sees social factors as playing a significant role in environmental design studies and practice.

The launch of the 'Urban Visions: Beyond the Ideal City' film competition

The 'Urban Visions: Beyond the Ideal City' film competition was announced at the *Past Present and Future of Public Space: International Conference on Art, Architecture and Urban Design*,[4] promoted by City Space Architecture, held in Bologna, Italy, in 2014, during a Cinema Session at Europa Cinema.

To an audience of about one hundred scholars, we presented, as a preliminary approach to cinema studies, three professional works: *I Tweet* (Parruccini, 2012), *Sotto casa/Right in Front* (Lauria, 2011), both award-winning short films in the Italian context; and *A Rua da Estrada/A Road as a Street* (Graça Castanheira, 2012), from the book of the same name by Alvaro Domingues (2010), geographer and professor at the Faculty of Architecture, University of Porto (Portugal).

I Tweet, filmed in New York, is the representation of a widely discussed phenomenon of our contemporary times: the lack of communication between individuals. An unexpected encounter between a young girl and a homeless man, both individuals in search of some emotional sharing, becomes an occasion to exchange thoughts about their loneliness that will help the young girl to redefine what a personal relationship means. *Right in Front*, set in a congested Italian city, is the hilarious story of a man who one night on his way home, finds a parking space right in front of his house: this surprising achievement completely changes his approach to life and his attitude towards the future.

Starting from common daily activities, both these two films are able to trigger reflections on a simple but relevant question: how can the urban environment and its dynamic changes influence our existence? In a growing urban complexity, where sometimes we can hardly understand the consequences of economic and political choices on our living environment, we need to establish a more conscious relationship with a world made of uncertainties and insecurities, outside our safe and comfortable place, and redefine our role as individuals. During a period as Visiting Scholar at IURD (Institute of Urban and Regional Development, University of California Berkeley) in 2012, the author developed a research project on the pursuit of happiness, dealing with urban living conditions. The

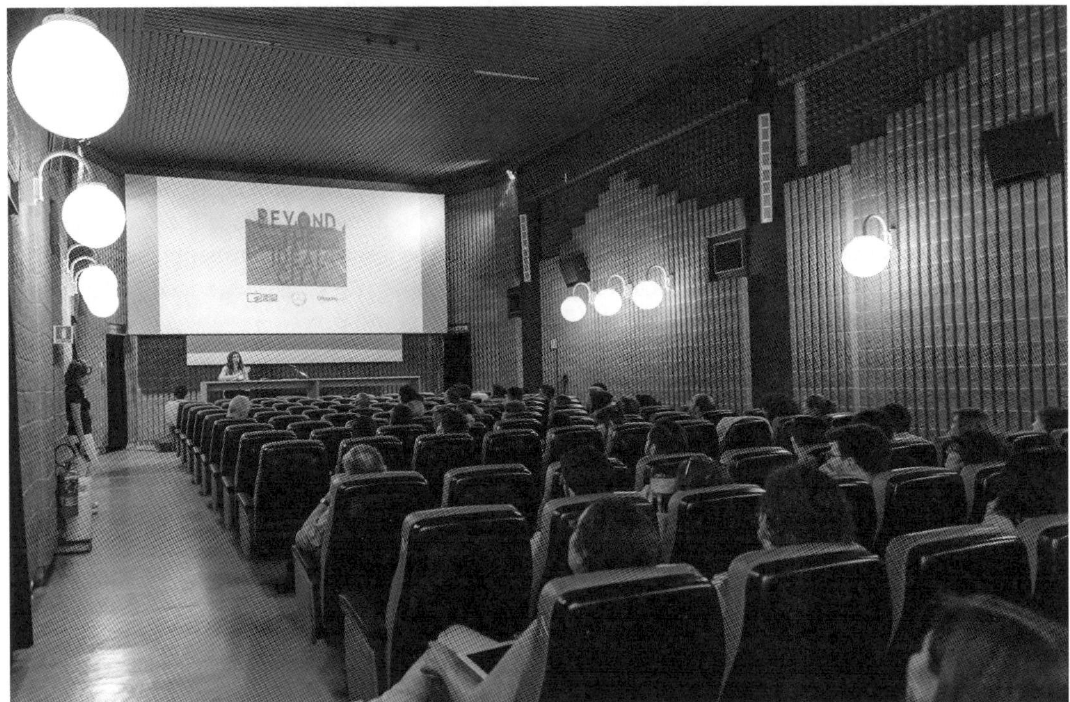

Figure 1. Luisa Bravo, President of City Space Architecture, introduces the 'Urban Visions: Beyond the Ideal City' film competition during the Cinema Session at the *Past Present and Future of Public Space: International Conference on Art, Architecture and Urban Design*, Bologna, 25 June 2014. Picture by Elettra Giulia Bastoni.

research was based on a public survey in order to understand how people live in the urban context, in terms of housing, working and leisure; how they experience, every day, space and distance in the city where they live; and how they create relationships with other people living in the same neighbourhood or in the same city. The survey was intended to be a tool capable of showing whether particular urban and town-planning design were successful, through evaluation and collecting comments from the public. Well-designed neighbourhoods and efficient cities in terms of walkability, public transportation, long-distance connections, urban spaces, public facilities and mixed-use density, should make people happy. The assumption is that the happiness of urban communities, together with well-planned settlements for urban daily life, should be the main goal of the urban planner. The first results of the research project were presented at the EURAU | Espaço

Público e Cidade Contemporânea conference, a European symposium on research in Architecture and Urban Design, held in 2012 in Porto (Portugal), and then published in the conference proceedings.

A Road as a Street is a poetic description of a trip on a road, along the Portuguese suburban landscape. Nowadays, urbanization progresses at an overwhelming pace and it is no longer exclusively dependent on the agglomeration and physical proximity between people, buildings and activities. Infrastructures, such as roads and telecommunication networks run through immense territories, generating our location patterns and forms of social organization. *A Road as a Street* questions the common idea that opposes the 'urban' to the 'rural'; namely, the densely constructed territory with a shape and a centre with perfectly defined limits, opposed to the agricultural environment.

More than a specific recognizable place, the road emerges as a result of movements and flows, and the city, grown up around it, is perceived as floating and unstable. If you want to make your business visible to anyone on the road, your problem 'is to make them stop!'

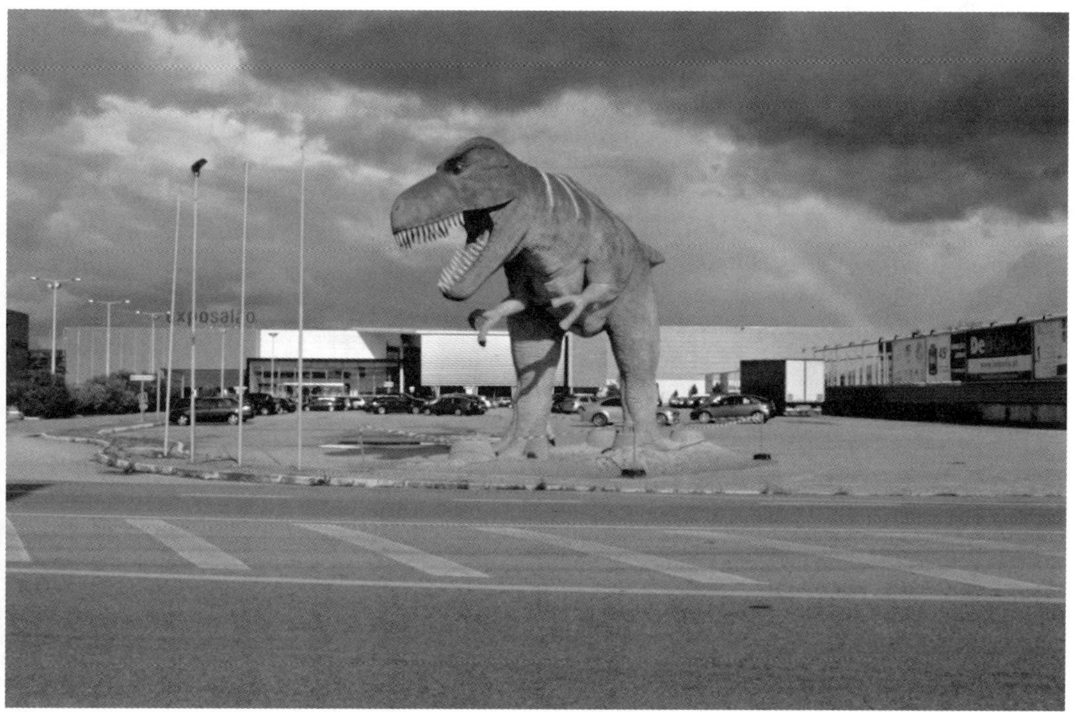

Figure 2. A frame from *A Rua da Estrada/A Road as a Street* (2012), © Graça Castanheira.

This film is able to clearly reveal a relevant relationship between the time and space of the suburban built environment, mostly dominated by cars: city-users move along corridors, such as roads or highways, experiencing their world through a kind of jump-cut urbanism (Ingersoll 2005: 34–39). This involves multiple perspectives, looking forward and backward, simultaneously using mirrors while driving, producing visual fragments in an accelerated montage at various speeds. Usually people do not look around, often they do not stop, they move from one point to a specific destination. *A Road as a Street* captures those fragments, as vivid images able to become metaphors of land and human consumption.

During the Cinema Session, the conference hosted two other short films, the results of research activities from architecture schools, *Magic Carpet: Re-envisioning Community Space in Sai Ying Pun* and *LuxCity*. It is becoming quite common that in architecture and urban studies courses, students are asked to behave as film-makers or to work in collaboration with film-makers. This encourages a multidisciplinary approach to their analysis and projects, giving emphasis to the creative design process and its results.

Magic Carpet: Re-envisioning Community Space in Sai Ying Pun is an outreach project combining the documentation of daily life, community engagement and urban design, initiated in 2012 by the School of Architecture and the School of Journalism and Communication at the Chinese University of Hong Kong (CUHK). The project team, coordinated by Professor Hendrik Tieben, collaborated with King's College, a secondary school in Sai Ying Pun. The participating students of the College interviewed people from the district of Sai Ying Pun in Hong Kong, capturing their life stories, their views on the district's development, and their proposal to change the neighbourhood for the better. The videos were shown at the *Magic Carpet* event in 2013, where the sloped Centre Street in Sai Ying Pun was transformed into an outdoor cinema during the Mid-Autumn Festival, the Chinese harvest celebration.

While enjoying films about the neighbourhood under the full moon, local community members and the general public were invited to reimagine the public spaces of one of the oldest districts in the city. Sai Ying Pun has undergone drastic changes in recent years due to urban renewal and major infrastructure projects; old buildings and traditional shop houses are disappearing rapidly, while high-end, westernized bars and restaurants, residences and hotels are starting to flourish – this transformation of Sai Ying Pun epitomizes urban gentrification across Hong Kong today. The portion of Centre Street, where the *Magic Carpet* event took place, has been made inaccessible to vehicular traffic, becoming a quiet yet underused area.

Employing the medium of community filming as a means of research, communication and community empowerment, and using outdoor screening as a way of community gathering and for the reinterpretation of public spaces, the *Magic Carpet* project re-envisions the city from the perspective of the grass-roots community and creates a heterotopia in the arena of urban life.

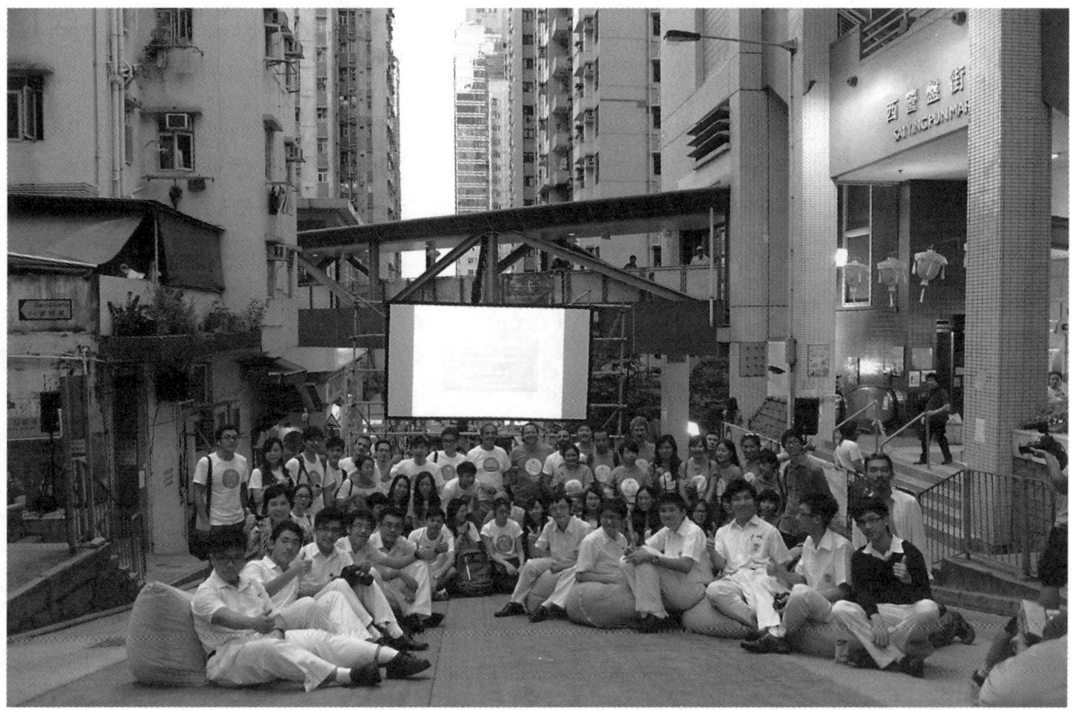

Figure 3. The 'Magic Carpet' project team in Centre Street, Sai Ying Pun, Hong Kong, just a few hours before the moonlight cinema event, Mid-Autumn Festival, 19 September 2013. © The Chinese University of Hong Kong.

The *Magic Carpet* initiative has since been extended in Taipei, through a collaborative project between the Chinese University of Hong Kong and the National Taiwan University (NTU), funded by Taiwan's Ministry of Culture and coordinated by Professor Min-Jay Kang. Using videos as a means of social empowerment and spatial investigation, this partnership aimed to compare the Hong Kong situation with that of Taipei, an Asian city that has taken important steps in regard to community-oriented urban regeneration, citizen participation and social activism. The historical district Wanhua was chosen as the site of investigation in Taipei, and was compared against Sai Ying Pun. Students from NTU's Graduate Institute of Building and Planning collaborated with Wanhua's cultural groups and individuals, activating the apparatus of community filming and screening as well as participatory mapping to catalyse a mechanism of self-regeneration and empowerment for the historical city. In the face of intensifying urban renewal and neoliberalist development, the inhabitants of Wanhua might assert their rights to the city through such direct spatial actions.

Videos and results from the two inner-city districts from the collaborative CUHK–NTU research project were presented and discussed with architects, planners, film-makers, citizens, social activists and city managers on a number of occasions in Taipei, Hong Kong and beyond. They were also exhibited at the 2013 Shenzen–Hong Kong Bi-City Biennale of Urbanism\Architecture.

Lux City is the film of a one-night urban installation event, held on 20 October 2012. It was led by Studio Christchurch as a joint project between New Zealand's Architecture and Design Schools for the Festival of Transitional Architecture (FESTA) in Christchurch in 2012. Studio Christchurch is a collaborative interdisciplinary teaching and research platform coordinated by Professor Uwe Rieger from the University of Auckland. It aims to facilitate partnerships between tertiary institutions, local industries, and professional and governmental bodies. After the devastating earthquakes of 2010 and 2011, this event attracted around 30,000 people to re-occupy a vacant city centre. In collaboration with Christchurch-based clients, approximately twenty design studios with over 350 students, organized in sixteen design courses and worked for over one semester in collaboration with demolition companies, local bars, restaurants and clubs to create temporary sculptural venues on demolished building sites. *Lux City* was both a proposal for future public spaces and an instant realization of urbanity. It addressed the potential of transitional projects to stimulate collaboration, explore a range of architectural possibilities, regenerate the central city and create excitement and hope for the city's burgeoning recovery.

All those films, both from film-makers and architecture schools, opened new perspectives on cities and public space –important as in a fast-growing and globalized world we need to re-establish a platform of values based on interaction and networking between individuals and social groups. As designers we should be more engaged with social and human issues, facilitating processes of sharing, defining strategies able to empower communities, working for inclusiveness and publicness. We need to do this while dealing with complex cities and metropolitan areas at all scales making full use of multidisciplinary analytical skills and an open-minded expertise. If cities are designed for people (Gehl 2010), the human scale should be part of the urban strategy.

The winner of the 'Urban Visions: Beyond the Ideal City' film competition

The winner of the 'Visioni Urbane/Urban Visions: Beyond the Ideal City' film competition was awarded on 1 March 2015, during the official ceremony of the Visioni Italiane festival at Cinema Lumière in Bologna. The jury assigned the first prize to Gianluca Abbate's *Panorama* (2014).

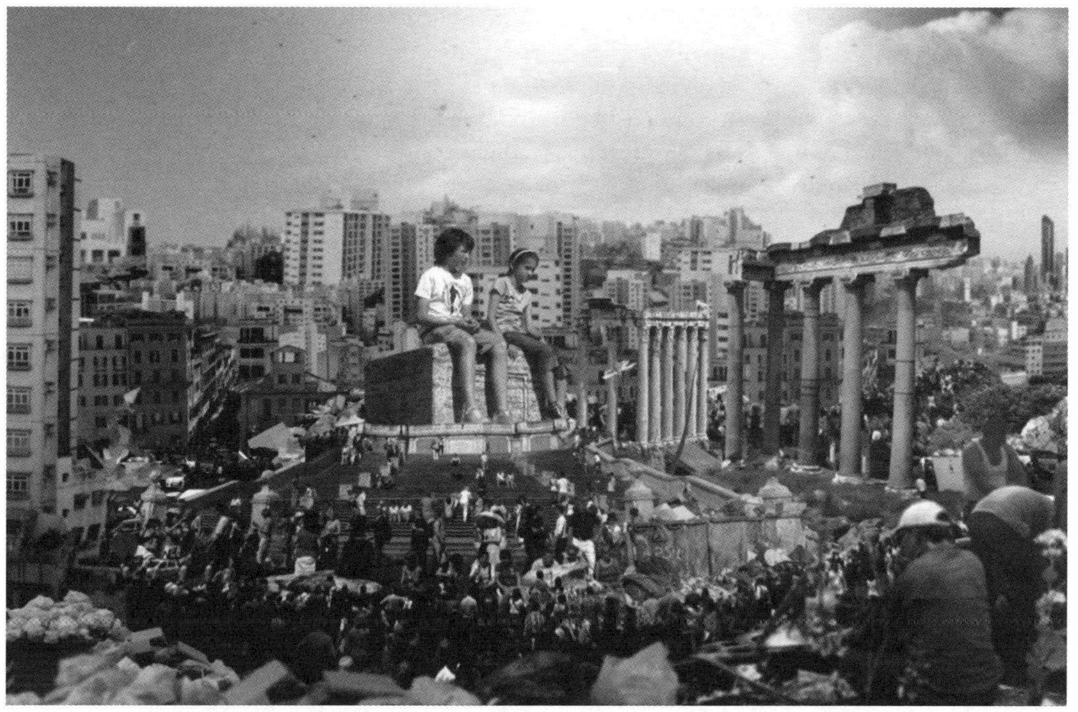

Figure 4. A frame from *Panorama* (2014), the winner of 'Urban Visions: Beyond the Ideal City', first edition (2015), © Gianluca Abbate.

The film, intended to be the first chapter of a trilogy on the city, is a contemporary reinterpretation of the ancient *polis*. The city is represented as an uninterrupted, extremely dense *continuum* of natural features, monuments, infrastructures and people that stretches away over an infinite, global space, with no uninhabited places or frontiers.

The cinematographic effect of creating a panorama of different foreground and background scenes and perspectives embedded in a large, unique moving sequence, is enriched with sound effects. These include an opening siren that fades to sounds of the city in streets and congested spaces, and then mixes with music, adverts and the sounds of nature. The scene is like a magmatic glue made of tall buildings, humans, trees and animals. The juxtaposition of gigantic butterflies over the built environment; the presence of over-scaled, poorly dressed humans sitting on top of buildings; and the dense, endless river of people in the public realm, from different ethnic groups, create a sense of anxiety and disorientation.

The moral entity embedded in the idea of *polis*, a holistic subject leading to the common good, is no longer identifiable nor depicted in this chaotic and over-crowded world. The boundary between reality and imagery is blurred. The built environment, beginning with the sea then ending in a quiet green forest, is a collage of recognizable pieces of different cities; it appears to be seamlessly mixed with nature, in a sort of hypnotic dream. Individuals are part of a multitude made of faces, bodies and languages; they become plural entities, moving in search of a place to call home. The film gradually builds to an emotional climax, a kind of vertigo, difficult to resist. Nature takes back possession of the city, overwhelming everything, becoming an apocalyptic prelude of a nightmare. Human beings are just survivors, frightened heroes of our contemporary times. 'If the city is the world which man created, it is the world in which he is henceforth condemned to live' (Park, Burgess and McKenzie 1938: 3).

Panorama tells the story of contemporary humankind, resembling the utopian and enigmatic heaven of *The Garden of Earthly Delights*, painted by Hieronymus Bosch (about 1500). We felt so much enchanted by mother nature that we were tempted to benefit from all its pleasures, hence becoming accidental sinners. We are nowadays experiencing the evil consequences of those sensual delights, made of corruption and greediness. We live in a false paradise, waiting for our punishment, but still feeling hopeful of regaining our innocence.

This film addresses several issues that are part of the current debate on urban culture: soil consumption due to a growing, suburban, high-density, infinite city; climate change; migration flows; widespread world poverty; demographic growth that will lead to a large increase of population in urban areas; the cultural transformation of society into multiple groups; respect for nature and its resources; and the globalization process. Some other reflections come to mind, even if they are not evident in the film: the new geopolitical configuration of the world; growing social injustice; and the search for identity and liveability for minorities escaping from disasters and wars. Thus it reminds us that urban complexity is also made of inequalities and false myths and that we should carefully read between the lines. In a powerful visual and sound narrative of just seven minutes, *Panorama* is able to shock and surprise. Nobody can feel emotionless.

The jury assigned honourable mentions to two other films: Chiara Zevi and Maria Laura del Tento's *Io li ho visti/I Saw Them* (2014) and Fabián Ribezzo's *A Tropical Sunday* (2013). *I Saw Them* is filmed in Rome, at Quartiere Trullo, a residential neighbourhood on the outskirts, built during the fascist period. It is the story of a peaceful protest promoted by a group of inhabitants complaining about a lack of facilities provided by the central government. They are called the Pittori Anonimi del Trullo (Anonymous Painters of Trullo) and carry out the protest by painting building facades, walls and steps with gaudy colours. Their action is illegal under Italian law, so they work only during the night and their gift to the neighbourhood is offered when the sun rises. The protest is a real do-it-yourself, tactical-urbanism action, a bottom-up attempt to actively contribute to changing urban living conditions, based on real and practical needs. The painters say that they do not want to leave their neighbourhood, so they will work to improve it for everyone. Their actions inspired many others: educators and kids at the local primary school participated in joyous craft sessions with their parents; young men from other neighbourhoods joined the anonymous painters late at night; and poets gave their rhymes, written in *romanesco*, the Roman dialect, to some of the beautiful street-art works. So inhabited urban spaces are currently becoming a common good, where everyone can be part of the urban regeneration process, by doing and sharing generously. This is a lesson everyone should learn.

A Tropical Sunday, filmed in Maputo, Mozambique, is the engaging portrait of four begging street kids, dressed in rags (Gito, Babu, Lisa and Nuno) at the Feira Popular, an amusement park in the heart of Maputo, on a Sunday afternoon. They want to eat and play so they beg the adults at the restaurants for leftovers and ask for tickets to get on the

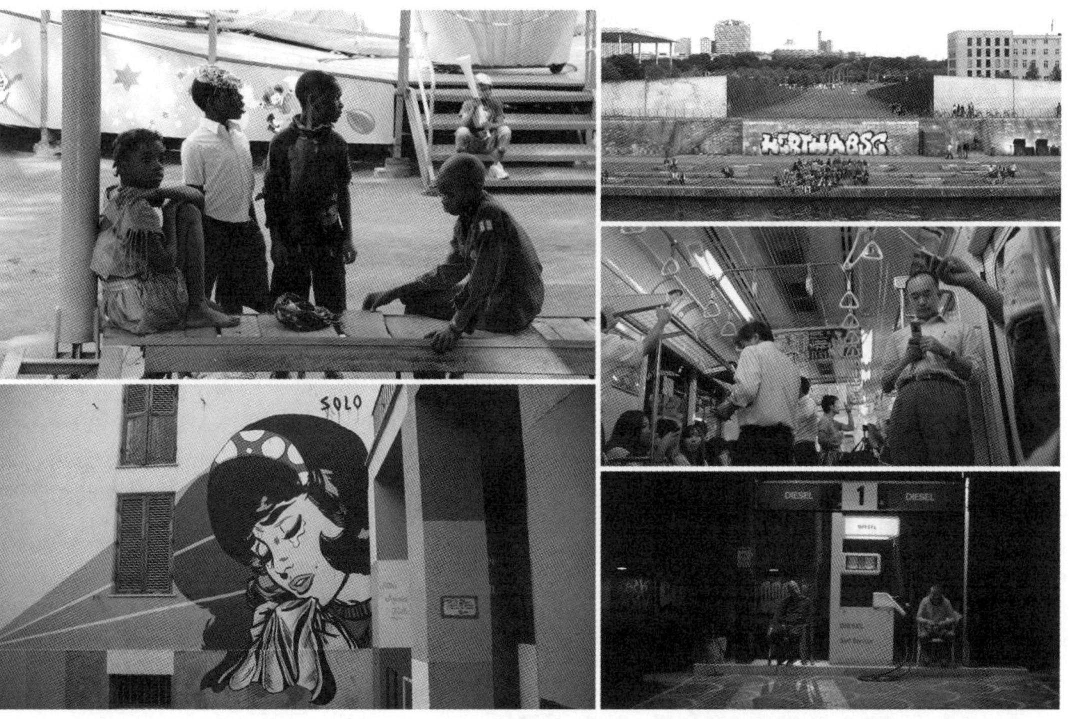

Figure 5. Left, top–down: frames from *A Tropical Sunday* (2013), © Fabian Ribezzo; and *Io li ho visti/I Saw Them* (2014), © Chiara Zevi and Maria Laura del Tento. Right, top–down: frames from shortlisted films *Capital* (2014), © Giulia Bruno and Lida Perin; *In cerca di un amico/Looking for a Friend* (2014), © Karma Gava and Alvise Morato; and *Gas Station* (2014), © Alessandro Palazzi.

Ferris wheel, the mini planes and the bumper cars. They wish to regain their childhood at least for a few hours, leaving behind their sorrows. The art of survival, collaboration and cleverness are what they learned on the street and are what they will use to gain amusement. This film is sad and happy at the same time. The very tough living conditions of these kids is touching, but their smiles and *joie de vivre* are overwhelming. *A Tropical Sunday* is an example of a common, simple life, as seen through the eyes of these kids from a city mostly unknown to the general public, characterized by poverty and exclusion, so far away that everyone can pretend it does not exist. But if we pay attention and look around in our own city, maybe we will see those same kids playing in the park in our own neighbourhood.

Other shortlisted films: Insights on contradiction, loneliness and illegality

Some other films submitted to 'Urban Visions' were shortlisted and evaluated by the jury members. Some of them placed important contemporary questions from different geographical contexts in the spotlight and provided profound insights so it is worth mentioning them.

Giulia Bruno and Lida Perin's *Capital* (2014) is set in Berlin, one of the richest and most vibrant contemporary European cities. Yet it hosts the first German favelas, as defined by *Der Spiegel*, along the Spree river, as a consequence of the European economic crisis and of the absence of a consistent political strategy for social housing, while new building sites for luxury apartments flourish nearby. There is a commonality that links such contradictions in their urban context, water. This natural resource is nowadays always present in our lives and in our homes. As a result it is often ignored. This film asks why. The film offers different answers through several interviews: from Arno Steguweit, the first hydro-*sommelier* of Europe and guru of mineral water; to Samuel Höller, a young researcher and a member of an environmental organization that promotes the use of tap water; to Rachel Raffaele Cutolo, daughter of the first generation of Italian immigrants, owner of a shop selling religious articles and holy water; and finally to the inhabitants of the newborn favelas, in the heart of the capital, who have no water connection.

Karma Gava and Alvise Morato's *In cerca di un amico/Looking for a Friend* (2014) is about loneliness in Japanese society. While the city, Tokyo, is a powerful, extremely modern, exciting environment, people walk as strangers along the streets, from the place where they work to the place where they live. They look for a friend, just to talk with someone. Some of them hire people from agencies for special occasions, even for wedding parties, to play the role of friend, husband, girlfriend, uncle, nephew, co-worker etc. For others it is easier to replace the emotional void with virtual friends on the Internet. Through interviews with the employees of those agencies, this film introduces an incredible, somehow frightening reality while in the background the city is still alive, a powerful presence.

Alessandro Palazzi's *Gas Station* (2014) is about Italy and illegal immigrants coming from Africa. Some of them are just passing through the country to their final destination in Northern Europe. For those who remain, their option is scraping some change by pumping gas at self-service stations at night. The two main characters of the film, Jamal and Rashid, stand in for the official gas station attendant all night long. Different kinds of people stop by: drug addicts, family men, independent girls, undercover cops. While waiting for customers to come and fill up their tanks, Jamal and Rashid spend their time reading sex ads and financial news in the newspapers left by customers, resulting in hilarious and silly comments being made. Even if lonely and desperate, they continue to dream of a different life. Jamal and Rashid are not professional actors and their story is true. Jamal, alias Kamal, is Moroccan and now works as a barman. Rashid, alias Mohamed, is Egyptian and is a writer. He lost an arm and currently pumps gas at night for tips.

Conclusion

The first edition of 'Visioni Urbane/Urban Visions: Beyond the Ideal City' was considered a success, not only in terms of participation but also for the quality and variety of works. The idea of addressing urban humanities as a research field to be developed in the urban planning and design sectors found fertile ground, already established in the Italian context.

Panorama, the winner, and the two honourable mentions, *I Saw Them* and *A Tropical Sunday*, were presented at the Urban Center Bologna on 9 April 2015, in front of an audience made of architects, designers, film-makers, photographers, academics, students and members of the public. This public session, intended to be a conversation on public space, received very positive feedback and stimulated discussion, promoting cross-pollination between sectors and peoples. The audience, looking at the city through the lens, felt seduced and engaged emotionally at multiple levels.

Films could be considered the 'conscience of the human eye'. They have the ability to become a direct language with educational content. They can move the point of view from the wide-scale perspectives of urbanists to the personal and subjective perceptions of individual observers. The camera frames architecture and spaces, but mainly it offers human stories, evolutions of feelings; it captures details of social interactions, while urban life moves around. Cities then become the scenery of the collective consciousness, able to disclose changing urban identities and humanities through space and time, providing a different type of knowledge.

The session at the Urban Center Bologna was included in the list of preparatory activities of the Biennale dello Spazio Pubblico/Biennial of Public Space, an Italian event promoted by the Italian Institute for Urban Planners and the National Council of Architects that took place at Università di Roma TRE in Rome, on 21–24 May 2015. 'Urban Visions' is part of a large research project on contemporary public space, *MaPS: Mastering Public Space*, which City Space Architecture is currently developing with a series of conferences, lectures, workshops and public meetings, in Italy and abroad. *Panorama*, the winner of 'Urban Visions', was presented during one of those events, 'MaPS@MAXXI', which took place at MAXXI B.A.S.E. in Rome, on 24 May 2015. MAXXI in the Museum of XXI Century Arts, a leading Italian institution, well-known nationally and internationally. City Space Architecture is currently working on the second edition of the 'Visioni Urbane/Urban Visions: Beyond the Ideal City' film competition, as part of the 22nd edition of the Visioni Italiane Festival, promoted by Cineteca di Bologna. The final event with the awards ceremony took place in Bologna at Cinema Lumière on 24–28 February 2016.

References

Abbate, G. (2014), *Panorama*, http://www.gianlucaabbate.com. Accessed 15 August 2015.

Bravo, L. (2012a), *Urban daily life and the pursuit of happiness*, www.bravodesign.it/urban_survey.html. Accessed 15 August 2015.

———— (2012b), *Public space and urban beauty: The pursuit of happiness in the contemporary European city*, in Pinto da Silva, M. (ed.), *EURAU12 Porto | Espaço Público e Cidade Contemporânea: Actas do 6° European symposium on Research in Architecture and Urban design*, Porto: Faculdade de Arquitectura da Universidade do Porto (FAUP), http://eurau12.arq.up.pt/sites/default/files/672.pdf. Accessed 15 August 2015.

Bruno, G. and Perin, L. (2014), *Capital*, short-film.

Cairns, G. (2013), *The Architecture of the Screen*, Bristol: Intellect.

Chinese University of Hong Kong (2013), 'Magic Carpet', www.magiccarpet.hk; www.facebook.com/magiccarpethk; www.youtube.com/magiccarpethk; www.flickr.com/magicarpet-hongkong. Accessed 15 August 2015.

Domingues, A. (2010), *A Rua da Estrada/A Road as a Street*, Porto: Dafne Editora.

Gava, K. and Morato, A. (2014), *In cerca di un amico/Looking for a friend*, https://vimeo.com/98036689 (trailer). Accessed 15 August 2015.

Gehl, J. (1987), *Life Between Buildings: Using Public Space*, New York: Van Nostrand Reinhold.

———— (2010), *Cities for People*, Washington: Island Press.

Gehl, J. and Svarre, B. (2013), *How to Study Public Life*, Washington: Island Press.

Ingersoll, R. (2005), 'Jump-cut urbanism: L'estetica dell'ambiente motorizzato', *Parametro*, 256: XXXV.

Lauria, A. (2011), *Sotto casa/Right in Front*, https://www.youtube.com/watch?v=x7ZlUMBSImA. Accessed 15 August 2015.

Lefebvre, M. (2007), *Landscape and Film*, New York and London: Routledge.

Mennel, B. (2008), *Cities and Cinema*, London and New York: Routledge.

Palazzi, A. (2014), *Gas Station*, https://vimeo.com/118772779 (trailer). Accessed 15 August 2015.

Park, R. E., Burgess, E. W. and McKenzie, R. D. (1938), *The City*, Chicago: University of Chicago Press.

Parruccini, M. (2012), *I Tweet*, http://www.rai.tv/dl/RaiTV/programmi/media/ContentItem-23954a34-e812-4640-a3c6-28dcbff4fb9d-cinema.html. Accessed 15 August 2015.

Penz, F. and Lu, A. (eds) (2011), *Urban Cinematics: Understanding Urban Phenomena Through the Moving Image*, Bristol: Intellect.

Shiel, M. and Fitzmaurice, T. (eds) (2001), *Cinema and the City: Film and Urban Societies in a Global Context*, Oxford: Blackwell.

Studio Christchurch (2012), *LuxCity*, https://vimeo.com/109651926; https://studiochch.wordpress.com/category/2012-luxcity. Accessed 15 August 2015.

Notes

1. Cineteca di Bologna (2015), Festival Visioni Italiane, http://www.cinetecadibologna.it/visioni_italiane_2015. Accessed 15 August 2015.

2. Cineteca di Bologna won the Golden Lion Prize for Best Film Restored – *Salò o le 120 giornate di Sodoma* by Pier Paolo Pasolini – at the 72nd 'Venice Film Festival' in 2015. This is just the last of a long list of prizes and successful collaborations with major partners in the film industries. With the New York-based Cohen Media Group, Cineteca di Bologna recently worked on the restoration of all Buster Keaton's silent films and previously dedicated over a decade to the restoration of Charlie Chaplin's entire work. In partnership with the Cohen Film Collection, Cineteca di Bologna has promoted, since 1986, the 'Cinema Ritrovato ['Cinema Rediscovered'] Festival', devoted to reviving old movies, and 'L'Immagine Ritrovata ['Image Rediscovered'] Lab' for film restoration, whose work is eagerly commissioned by major film organizations in Europe, such as Pathe and Studiocanal. Their archives hold a total of more than 18,000 titles.

3. 'Visioni Urbane/Urban Visions: Beyond the Ideal City' film competition, as a section of Visioni Italiane Festival promoted by Cineteca di Bologna, is coordinated and curated by the author, as President of City Space Architecture.

4. City Space Architecture (2014), 'Past Present and Future of Public Space. International Conference on Art, Architecture and Urban Design', http://www.cityspacearchitecture.org/?p=past-present-future-of-public-space. Accessed 15 August 2015.

Chapter 13

The mediating city: Towards a *mise-en-scène* for interaction online

Benjamin Koslowski

Introduction

This article examines the film set and filmic strategies as aides in the contextualization and the making-sense of social interaction online. It looks towards film and ways of conveying relationships on-screen that actively use the set and the guiding eye of the camera. *Mise-en-scène* will be interrogated as a mode of display – a tool to present action. It is argued that guiding mechanisms like the architectural construction of the film set are key in helping individuals understand their interaction with others across the boundaries of the physical and the digital, as online platforms do not map neatly onto physical settings of sociality. Can the city and an understanding of architectonic space help to augment the individual experience of the virtual spheres through which we 'move'? And can it help users of social media to construct and present images of identity more successfully at the same time as guiding their reception?

A range of films are used to exemplify ways in which architecture and its presentational role are key agents in framing action and how the notion of a *mise-en-scène* for social media might be used to test the spatialization of interpersonal relationships. *L'année dernière à Marienbad/Last Year in Marienbad* (Resnais, 1961) introduces the investigation into *mise-en-scène*; *Rear Window* (Hitchcock, 1954) positions the viewer and the camera; while *Dogville* (von Trier, 2003) is used to exemplify ideas on representation and miniaturization. *Factotum* (Hamer, 2005) is studied in relation to the perspectival urban images it deploys and the construction of mental maps.

Common to the films studied here are the architectural devices of scale, visibility and distance, which help to frame and moderate action. These variables are considered as key mediators of online interaction, which currently has no equivalent of *mise-en-scène* to frame it and to give it contextual qualities that are crucial to understanding and interpretation. Despite their clear architectural signification, these devices are lacking useful application in the post-perspectival space of digital sociality.

The aim here is to encourage a rethinking of the notion of mediation away from a focus on merely adding information onto the existing environment and towards using the legibility of physical contexts to shape the new settings of online sociality. While screen devices currently act as the lens through which informational overlays that augment the city and connectivity to others are perceived, can physical contexts, or sets, in turn offer clues for new ways of framing social interaction when this occurs in various offline and online contexts simultaneously? And can the relationship between the virtual sites of online sociality, such as Facebook, Twitter and Instagram, and the physical settings that frame offline interaction, be remapped to enable more human forms of interaction with others online? New ways of moderating – and indeed mediating – digital social interaction more effectively might enhance the understanding of relationships in hybrid social territories.

Setting the scene

The experience of online spheres has a short history of being understood, similarly to movement through physical space: the lone traveller navigates the database or the online archive in a similar way to which he might find his way through a building, or the city. The conception of the Internet as an agglomeration of information that needs to be mastered under a narrative of solitary experience (Dade-Robertson 2011: 3), however, stands in opposition to the ways in which online sociality is currently encountered. Communication with others is by its nature not a lonely experience, yet associated streams of information contain few guides to an understanding of relational dynamics. In contrast to the database and the comparatively static backdrop of the tectonic city, online exchanges are characterized by constantly shifting and evolving reciprocal interaction. Yet, the virtual domain offers few clues that help to frame the multiple viewpoints of the hybrid world of social networking. Further, unlike fleeting glances and passing moments that characterize the experience of the city, interaction online is traced and documented. It is often available, long after the moment that generated it, to future recipients that might differ from those initially intended as recipients; online audiences are therefore difficult to anticipate and manage.

Face-to-face interaction and its private facets clearly map onto physical settings: closing a door for a private conversation is as clear a spatial tactic as the figurative 'shouting it from the rooftops'. Contextual awareness, however, does not translate easily into the realms of online social interaction. In particular, privacy as a quality of interaction relies on degrees of contextual integrity (Nissenbaum 2010). Understandings of relationships between individuals and the wider network have shifted fundamentally with the arrival of mobile communication technologies and social media (Fuchs 2014). Emancipating users from a specific location, mobile devices have destabilized the notion of a virtual self that exists detached from a physical reality. In what philosopher Luciano Floridi refers to as 'onlife experience', digital online and analogue offline contexts are brought together: 'With interfaces becoming progressively less visible, the threshold between *here* (*analogue, carbon-based, offline*) and *there* (*digital, silicon-based, online*) is fast becoming blurred' (Floridi 2014: 43). Over the last few years, social media mishaps have illustrated a lack of awareness of audiences in online broadcast, frequently starting with the unknowing sharing of mundane – if potentially offensive – ramblings by people of generally little interest to a broad audience. A lack of perspective on the potential impact of comments and the scale of slippage between private communication with an understood audience of 'friends' and 'followers' and public broadcast to anyone in the network have led to dramatic events for some. In 2012, a photograph was tagged on Facebook, showing Lindsey Stone pretending to shout and giving the middle finger next to a sign at a cemetery that reads, 'Silence and Respect'. While it was taken jokingly, it went viral and earned broad disapproval; Stone eventually lost her job and avoided being in public for the better part of a year (Ronson 2015). This case was followed by just another example of how rapidly online postings can reach unintended audiences and can be read out of context: Anton Casey, a British expat-banker living with his family in Singapore, was effectively forced into exile in Australia in early 2014 as a result of a series of derogatory comments about the people of Singapore on social media. With these comments quickly going viral in their misjudged online contexts, Casey found himself out of work and he and his family received death-threats forcing them to leave the country (Tadeo 2014).

What these situations make clear, is that the interaction with others is not clearly framed in the 'post-spatial' environment (Vidler 2001: 235–42) of the online sphere. The use of social media across multiple networking platforms can make interaction with others highly complex and may result in unexpected consequences; crucially, audiences of content generated and shared on social networking sites can shift rapidly and therefore are difficult to grasp. The possible scales of engagement and levels of publicity people can attain are vast, and high levels of public visibility frequently are gained only unintentionally (Papacharissi and Gibson 2011). Social anxieties not unlike these were experienced already at the beginning of the previous century, as Anthony Vidler outlines, citing Georg Simmel: 'In the face of the crowded disorder of the modern metropolis [...], the "sensitive and nervous modern person" required a degree of spatial isolation as a kind of prophylactic against psychological intrusion' (Vidler 2001: 67). The close proximity and lack of distance and privacy experienced in the metropolis of the industrial age demanded clarification of the position of the individual; space began to be interpreted as an 'expression of social conditions', providing clues for the reading of new social dynamics where spatial relations might be read as symbolic of human relationships (Vidler 2001: 68). The social media mishaps occurring at the beginning of the twenty-first century may be attributed to a similar 'omnipotence of sight', exacerbated by the ubiquity of digital social interaction. Might a similar spatial, yet symbolic presentation of relationships in the sphere of mediated interaction help to communicate better individual standpoints in relation to others? A moderation of degrees of public visibility and the generation of a subjective sense of distance is crucial to enabling a better presentation of online relationships and to create greater degrees of psychological comfort.

This investigation into the role of architecture and the city in film is instrumental in helping to clarify contexts of social interaction, when this is no longer framed by shared physical surroundings. The analogous use of a language of space and movement in online settings, 'force[s] us [...] to understand the spaceless in spatial terms' (Vidler 2001: 236). It is suggested that the codes of architecture and the images it can create as a *mise-en-*

scène might assume a role in informing the mediation of sociality, in particular when this occurs both online and offline. 'Informing' here might be interpreted as a 'giving form to' the flattened and essentially non-perspectival realms of online interaction. William Mitchell notes: 'In much the same fashion [as the *mise-en-scène* in stage and film], by providing tangible, visible referents, the spaces of actual buildings and cities participate in constructing the meaning of the speech that unfolds within them' (2005: 4). Through its framing of behaviour, architecture in this sense is a form of etiquette that helps to specialize social expression (McCullough 2005: 39, 118). As such, it is 'a precondition, an invented and remembered fiction for something else' and may become a positioning device to spatially locate something not formerly part of this context, illustrating the escape and the seeking of refuge in spatiality that already characterized the arrival of cyberspace (Vidler 2001: 162).

The images of space presented in film do not require fully coherent settings, such as the ones experienced daily in the city; montage in film enables the construction of discontinuous sets that allow for the framing and reading of action. Both film and virtual environments, such as SecondLife, have in common their potential to be disengaged from physical constraints. Virtual settings have frequently been conceived of as standing in opposition to a lived physical reality, detached from a corporeal here-and-now (Gibson 1995: 67; Lister 2005: 38–47). As Marion Hamm comments in her paper, 'Reclaiming virtual and physical spaces': 'In the 1990s, [the Internet] was widely seen as a kind of parallel universe' (2006: 98). Platforms like SecondLife have explored the notional image of a landscape with architectural objects as the three-dimensional visual setting for the enactment of digital social interactions that users project themselves into, trying to emulate a sense of perspectival space. Platform-based social media, in contrast, have done away with the construction of an alternative layer of reality, on which to enact the meeting of avatars as removed versions of oneself. The notion of disparate sites and online environments catering for the potential development of a multitude of identities and distinct persona celebrated in the earlier days of cyberspace (Lovink 2011: 40), has advanced towards a more unified system of interlinking communication platforms. Instead of navigating discrete channels separately, users are continuously invited to share content with others, moving across platforms and thus creating a multifaceted picture of the same person, or a range of snapshots from various points-of-view. In contrast to the degrees of anonymity that the Internet promised in the 1990s, 'technologies of the self', and the way they enable the presentation of oneself, might ultimately have an impact on personal identity (Floridi 2014: 59–64). Social networking sites act almost as a running commentary on our lives, somewhat akin to the voice-over in film, and provide an informational overlay to existing social interactions and situated experience. It is important then, that the way online identities are received by others can be anticipated in their construction, regardless of whether relationships have been established offline and are resumed online as simply another site of interaction, or whether they have been generated entirely through interaction online, without a prior face-to-face encounter.

As overlays onto existing sites of sociality, online social media extend offline social engagement and enable 'broadcast' to a range of audiences – both known and unknown – beyond the physical constraints of distance and visibility. The concept of poly-social reality is the product of simultaneous interaction in various contexts of sociality, both virtual and co-located (Applin, Fischer and Walker 2012). Empowered by mobile communication technologies, users can engage with others in their immediate physical surroundings while projecting themselves into the virtual realms of online social media; they might engage with the person they are walking next to in the street in that moment, at the same time as with other people, who do not share the same physical setting. This overlapping interaction with hybrid audiences and the lack of guiding mechanisms that help to frame interaction risk the conflation of contexts of sociality, leaving sites, such as Facebook, Twitter and Instagram, without any guiding mechanisms. Physical settings are not qualified as distinct from the simultaneously inhabited virtual loci of interaction, making clear communication and projection of identity a great challenge, especially when interaction shifts between face-to-face and virtual communication.

Considering social media in relation to film allows for a more careful reading of the roles and positions users assume in digitally mediated interaction. As Erving Goffman already explores in his seminal work *The Presentation of Self in Everyday Life*, people in face-to-face interaction are positioned variously and at different times in the audience, on the stage or behind the scenes (Goffman 1971). Goffman argues that nuances of direct communication lie in the non-verbal, sometimes involuntary or less controlled aspects, such as body language and facial expression, requiring the individual's management of impressions upon others to present a consistent image of self. These facets are lacking entirely in mediated interaction; while communication through social media offers reasonably high degrees of control over verbal communication, it provides next to none regarding the space of reception and the impressions made upon an audience. There is no equivalent of body language that can aid the reading of content within a particular context. Emoticons, for example, are an attempt to overcome the lack of communication channels to support verbal communication, yet the online sites of interaction might be projected into many potential contexts of reception that are difficult to anticipate. More effective substitute mechanisms are required to enable a form of 'impression management'. The 'dramaturgical problems of presenting [...] activity before others' in face-to-face interaction that Goffman unpicks (1971: 26) are also encountered by the user of social media. Further, the positioning of participants in interaction seems particularly fluid in online social media and therefore is not always easy to gauge, while the relationship between performers and audience has shifted dramatically: users of digital social platforms are not just consumers of content, but performers, who try to create and convince their audience of a certain image of self, based on who they are offline, and how they want to be perceived online. However, they are not only charged with creating and maintaining their own profiles and sites, but also contribute to others' through commenting, liking, posting and sharing, effectively managing their own impressions on others, as well as those of other users of networking platforms. The online world of social media has expanded Goffman's 'presentation of self' to something more akin to 'presentation of self and others'. Does then the control over impressions on the part of the individual in turn become a form of control over the individual, if it is negotiated via the corporately owned social networking platform and impacted upon by a potentially large number of people?

'Impression management' seems barely possible in online sociality, as audiences in multiple platforms shift swiftly and do not map neatly onto physical settings of interaction. Guiding frameworks are instrumental in helping individuals understand their interaction with others across the boundaries of the physical and the digital. Despite dealing with at least partially known 'actors', online social media seem to struggle to successfully mediate relationships and interaction, and web-based platforms have to accommodate the additional challenge that relationships might shift rapidly and new 'roles' might be introduced at any time. The framing of action in film, in contrast, is inherently visual, and indeed spatial, using perspectival space to situate narrative and guide interpretation. In the following, four films will be studied to better understand the use of sets to construct images and to communicate a plot, to introduce and position characters and their interrelationships, and crucially, to guide and focus the viewer's attention.

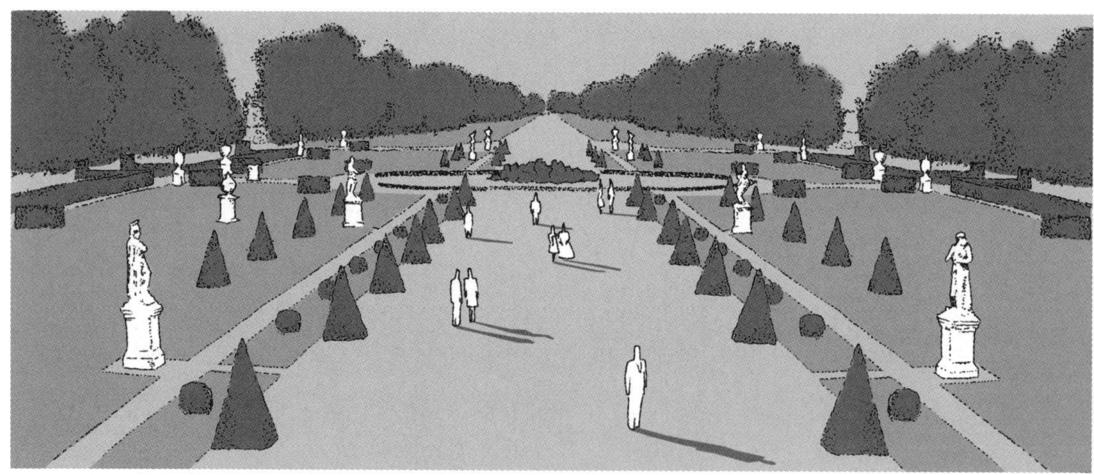

Figure 1. Motionless actors positioned akin to sculptures in the landscaped gardens of *L'année dernière à Marienbad*/*Last Year in Marienbad* (1961), © Cocinor.

Staging action

In Alain Resnais's film *Last Year in Marienbad* from 1961, the baroque interior of the seventeenth-century palace at Nymphenburg in Bavaria and its extensive grounds constitute a grand setting that offers an opulent backdrop to the unfolding of the relationship between two lovers (Cairns 2013: 53–61). Fiction and memory of the protagonists' encounter in the previous year, which is the mystery at the core of the plot, are explored from the two viewpoints of the protagonists. The film uses the actual architectural setting of the palace and interprets it to stage a plot that drifts between states of reality and fiction; for example, emphasizing the heavy baroque decor symbolically to highlight the artifice of the situation (Kawin 1978: 83). The labyrinthine corridors with their heavy detailing and gilded mirrors generate a strong sense of disorientation and isolation, underlining the uncertainties that the plot navigates, and are somewhat reminiscent of Walter Benjamin's Parisian arcades. Here, the urban wanderer is constantly reflected and refracted in shop windows and mirrors open up 'the perspective of infinity' (Benjamin 2002 [1999]: 538). Digital communication technology and the current experience of social media can create a similar sense of *mise en abyme*, or 'placed in abyss' – of standing between two mirrors, located neither here nor there.

The crowds of actors in the hotel lobby in *Last Year in Marienbad* resonate with anonymous crowds in cities, amongst whom the *flâneur* immerses himself, 'both immersed in the crowd but isolated from it' (Coverley 2010: 60). He never ever truly engages with this crowd and it remains a backdrop and part of his individual urban experience. Similarly, the hotel lobby itself might be viewed as 'epitomizing the conditions of modern life in their anonymity and fragmentation' (Vidler 2001: 72), rendering *Last Year in Marienbad* a useful example in the conversation about the coherence of online sociality. The setting of the film, as well as other actors positioned within it, help to frame the action: extras motionlessly scattered across the gravel paths outside are placed akin to the sculptures in the landscaped gardens with their long formal vistas, and merely serve as the backdrop to the interaction of the protagonists (Figure 1). Individuals and small muttering groups in the grand hall of the hotel are deployed like props and barely engaged with, highlighting the isolation of the couple from their surroundings and thus specializing their private and self-absorbed engagement with each other.

The voyeuristic viewer

In contrast to the actual place of the palace used as the setting for *Last Year in Marienbad*, Alfred Hitchcock's 1954 thriller *Rear Window* was shot on a designed indoor set. The familiar image of a New York city block with its typical architectural elements, such as balconies and escape stairs, produces a strong sense of place (Figure 2). Beyond merely creating an impression of a familiar setting, however, the film uses properties of the set symbolically, such as colour, to aid the viewer's orientation within the narrative (Jacobs 2011: 550). Windows are carefully positioned to offer glimpses of the unfolding story, presenting and representing particular qualities about each role that aid the reading of the storyline.

The representational interior set of the urban courtyard crucially brings with it codes and conventions of behaviour; the protagonist, L. B. Jeffries, who has been confined to a wheelchair in his apartment through an accident, is aware of his voyeuristic incursions into his neighbours' private spaces across the courtyard (Figure 3). The moment murderer Lars Thorwald notices the observer from his own apartment window in the build-up to the climactic scene of the film, the latter has been framed in his theatre-box of an apartment (Jacobs 2011: 554), literally 'caught in the act of seeing' (Colomina 1992: 82). He is spatially framed by the windows, which in such a dense urban setting demand an etiquette of not looking; these have offered him insights into the daily activity of this Manhattan city block, and indeed have allowed him to unpick the murder at the centre of the plot.

'Each window offers a view to a singular picture and the entire courtyard is a kind of urban equivalent of a cable television mosaic, with Jeffries (as well as the spectator) zapping between channels' (Jacobs 2011: 552). At a surface glance, social media operate similarly to the facade across the courtyard in *Rear Window*, allowing users to switch between different and sometimes interlinking narratives enacted within each window.

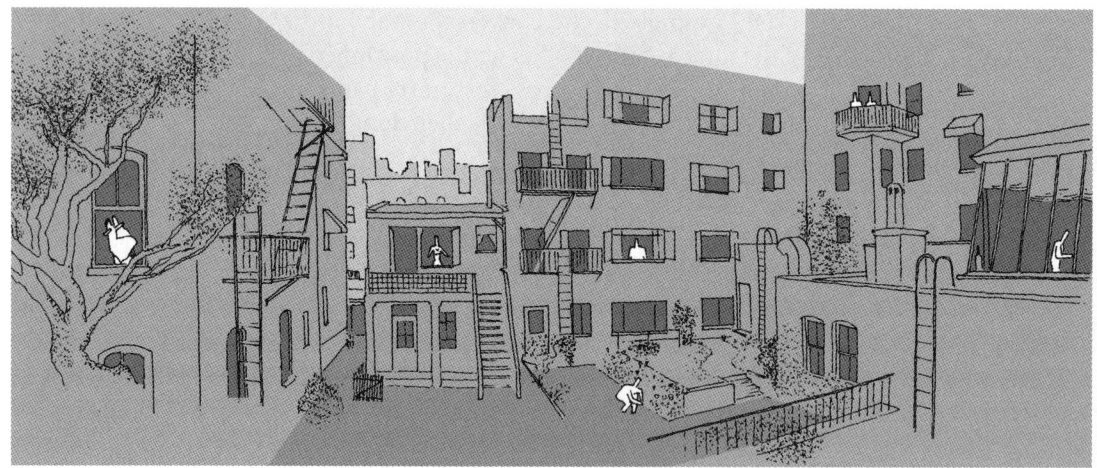

Figure 2. Windows offer glimpses into the lives of others and frame the narrative in *Rear Window* (1954), © Paramount Pictures.

Unlike situated experiences in the city, the distanced voyeuristic experience from Jeffries' apartment is not characterized by movement. The static protagonist, who watches the unfolding of a series of fragmentary events, is somewhat closely linked to the user of online social media, with a broad range of content delivered to the screen device. This mode of consumption counters the language of movement often used to describe online experiences, such as 'going to a page', 'surfing the web' or 'following' someone on Twitter, and its spatial associations.

New communication technologies have always augmented the perception of the here-and-now, as exemplified by Umberto Eco in his essay, 'The multiplication of the media' that explores ways in which individuals have become the curators of content, delivered to them via mass media, for example the television, simply by using the remote control (Eco 1987: 148). However, through the use of social media platforms, such as Facebook, Twitter and Instagram, users not only consume content and curate their individual mediated experience, but also create and contribute content themselves, to be shared with and consumed by others. As Anne Friedberg points out in *The Virtual Window*: '[Our new mode of perception] is "postperspectival" – no longer framed in a single image with fixed centrality; "postcinematic" – no longer projected onto a screen surface [...]; "post-televisual" – no longer unidirectional in the model of sender and receiver' (Friedberg 2006: 194).

Rear Window sets up fixed viewing positions in its spatial construct that draws parallels with Bentham's panopticon (Jacobs 2011: 556; Pallasmaa 2001: 161–62). Social media rely on mutual sharing, the 'framing in reverse' that Jeffries experiences only accidentally, operating as an inverse, or broken panopticon. Relationships between users shift rapidly, rather than being inscribed in a fixed model, or spatial construct, such as the panopticon, making it difficult to be solely a voyeur, or someone who is being observed. At the heart of the social media mishaps outlined above is the imbalance of control and visibility, with audience members 'hiding' behind their screens, remaining lurkers in the dark and violating the etiquette that interaction requires in the same way that L. B. Jeffries violates the privacy of others through his voyeuristic looking. It is key for users of online social media to be able to map their interactions with others in a mental construct that, if fragmentary, allows for the positioning of individual narratives.

With its 'repression of the fourth wall' and the static position of the protagonist in his particular viewpoint, the set of *Rear Window* functions almost as a theatre stage (Jacobs 2011: 553), while zooming and panning take on the role of opera glasses, reflecting Jeffries' use of his binoculars. Altogether, these spatial moves counter the liberation from a particular fixed vantage point in the theatre that film had given its audiences. Nevertheless, the illusion of an urban or interior space that is created for the screen only holds up from a particular viewpoint, which is considered at the outset and designed into the set as a representational device. The crucial role of the camera in upholding controlled viewpoints and the illusion of the set is underlined by Peter Wollen's analysis of the 'static space' of the scenery and the 'narrative space' of camera movement across this set, 'determined by the need to tell a story' (Wollen 2002: 203). *Mise-en-scène* as a contextualizing device depends

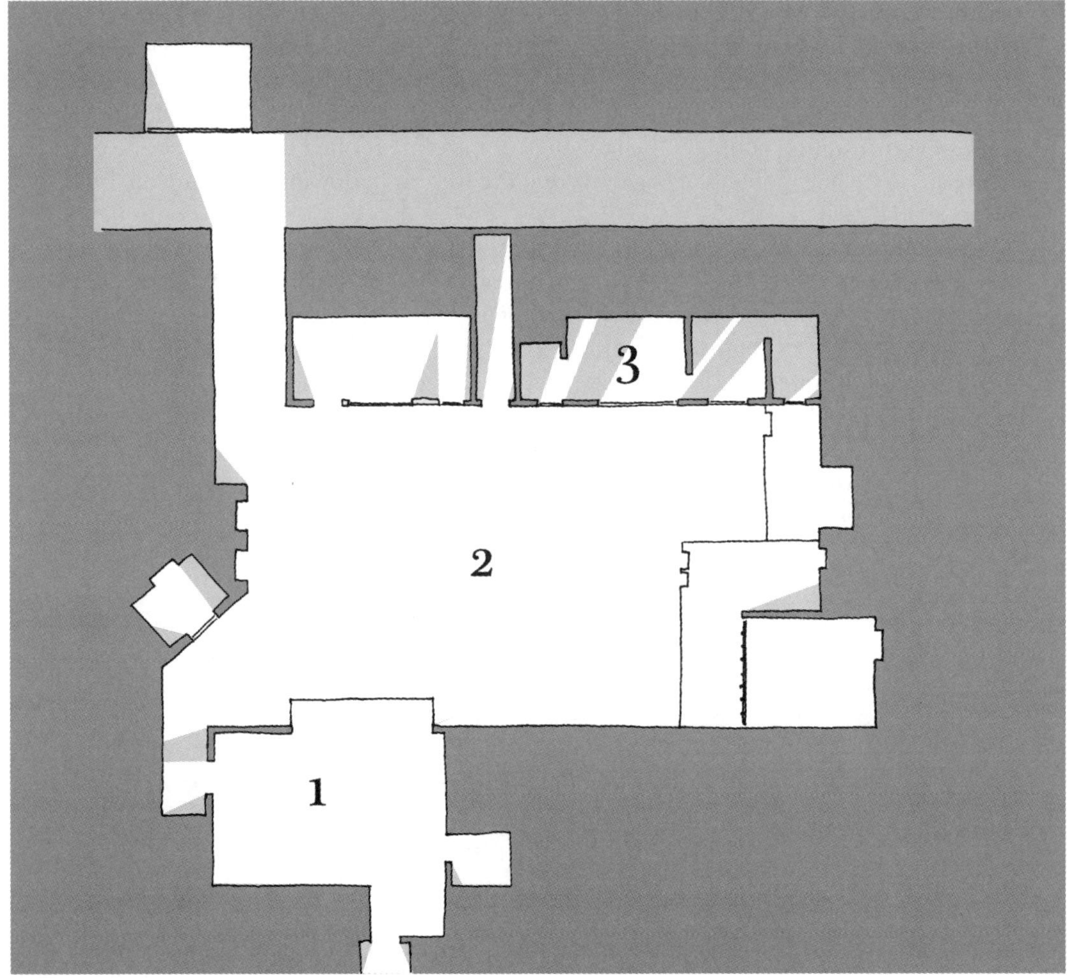

Figure 3. Drawing of the set of *Rear Window*, with sight lines from (1) L. B. Jeffries' apartment; (2) across the courtyard; and (3) into Thorwald's apartment. © Koslowski.

on the camera and its precise position; once the camera, and with it the viewer, leave their designated vantage point, the set risks exposing itself as an artificial construction. An analogous perspectival positioning is required in digital sociality to locate the subjective viewer, who plays an active role within the narrative engaged on the screen in front of him. This helps to establish a sense of distance, visibility and focus, and ultimately a clearer and more intuitive understanding of relationships to others.

The stage set

Similar to the indoor set of *Rear Window*, Lars von Trier's *Dogville* from 2003 plays out the whole plot across a single set that quite literally appears to be a theatre stage. However, here the camera is emancipated from the fixed viewpoint experienced in *Rear Window*. In what von Trier calls a 'fusion film', operating at the boundaries of film, theatre and literature (Björkmann 2003: 241), architectural orthographics and annotation are used on the black floor of the stylized stage to demarcate the various spaces of a small town; props are used to indicate programme, such as the clock tower suspended above the assembly hall that marks the space of congregation, the shop window or the entrance to a mine (Figure 4). The sound of an invisible door opening and the actors' respect for lines that indicate walls suggest an adherence to spatial conventions inscribed in the architectural elements of the set, even if they are not physically present. At the same time, action occurring in the background, such as the children playing in the street outside behind notional boundaries, is not acknowledged by the cast in the foreground. In contrast to the fragmented glimpses in *Rear Window*, the entire action taking place across the stylized theatre set is visible, yet the actors follow the guides to behaviour set out by the architectural frame of the set.

A visual flattening of background and foreground has occurred, which might be viewed as analogous to the visual experience of online interaction with others, where filters are lacking to moderate engagement and to give it some of the qualities of social relationships offline. However, there is a guiding mechanism in the film set, supported by the lens of the camera with its pan, zoom and focus, to control and help guide the viewer's reading of the action. The camera shifts between showing the whole set, with all action unfolding simultaneously, leaving the viewer to focus attention on the plot, and zooming in and selecting the view for the audience in close-up. This marks a break from a sense of the film being 'staged' in a theatrical manner with a fixed viewing position, somewhat subverting the initial impression the audience might get from *Dogville's* familiar appearance of a theatre stage with props.

Due to the way the film set is mediated by the lens of the camera, it is never experienced at full scale and remains a space that is also seen in fragments on-screen, at a distance determined by the camera and by the space between the viewer and the screen. The generation of scale-versions of a perceived reality, such as this film set, demand the careful consideration of what is represented and what is omitted. Any process of representation is to some extent one of miniaturization, and crucially an editing process. 'Values become condensed and enriched in miniature' (Bachelard 1994: 150), simultaneously giving greater significance to the elements that are shown rather than omitted, or edited in creating the miniature. The creation of a film set as a (re)presentational artefact requires such a focus on specific qualities, as the 'condensation of values' applies not only to the miniature, but also to the large-scale architectural object – the retained values of which are crucial to recognizing and understanding it.

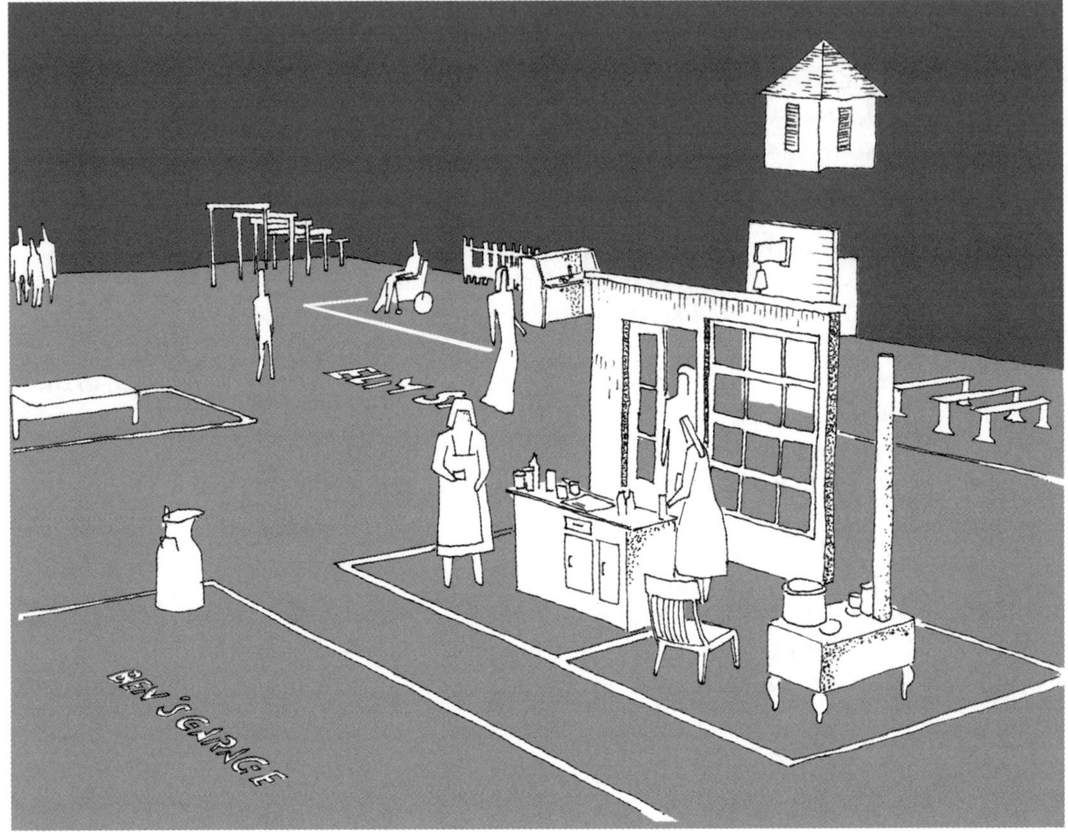

Figure 4. Sketch showing the stage set of *Dogville* with props, actors and orthographic drawings. © Koslowski.

The focus on particular qualities of the representation similarly applies to drawing, which becomes a process of drawing-attention-to, as is illustrated by the images accompanying this text (Figures 1, 2, 4 and 5). These are constructed in such a way that they highlight and support the particular elements of each set explored through writing and omit detail that is not seen as necessary in this. Architect Stan Allen's reflections on drawing and notation are useful in this context: 'An architectural drawing is an assemblage of spatial and material notations that can be decoded, according to a series of shared conventions, in order to effect a transformation of reality at a distance from the author' (Allen 2000: 32). The use of orthographic drawing in *Dogville* highlights the multiple viewpoints deployed to focus attention. The detached camera view from above is used to establish the set, giving a view of the drawings on the floor to help orientate the audience within the small mining town; in a sense, *Dogville* tells the story on the unfolded map (Björkmann 2003: 245). The abstracted two-dimensional representation folded onto the floor complements the three-dimensional recognizable architectural fragments as semiotic signs of use to form a coherent whole. 'The process of signification [in the theatre] is directed and controlled. Even if something has arbitrarily entered into the frame it is read as significant' (Aston and Savona 1991: 99). Commenting on the *mise-en-scène* in *Dogville* and its spatial conventions, Lars von Trier suggests: 'We're establishing an agreement with the audience under which these circumstances are accepted. If that agreement is clear enough then I don't think there are any boundaries to what you can do' (Björkmann 2003: 246).

The set generates tension between orthographic projection and perspectival viewpoints. Architectural representation, used here in the form of drawings on the ground, tends to take a removed position from the drawn object, placing the viewer at 'infinity', while perspective viewpoints – in this case in cinema – lock the viewing subject in a particular vantage point (Allen 2000). The use of perspective describes a shift from attempts to describe the city as a whole towards 'what one [sees] from a subjective, secular point of view' (Maki 2008: 92). This subjective mode of seeing is crucial to the discussion of individual perspectives in social media, as it allows individual experience to be positioned against a backdrop that positions and clarifies it. Testing the limitations of the 'unity of space' in *Dogville* (Björkmann 2003: 245), the range of viewpoints deployed – from close-ups to wide-angle shots showing the whole set and bird's-eye views of the whole town – are key to guiding the viewer across the set as the container for the story. This multitude of perspectives and the 'agreement' on how to read the plot framed in the *mise-en-scène* allows film and its 'pseudo-individual perspective' (Truninger 2012:131) to establish a point of view that is perceived as particular to the viewer. While this is actually experienced by the whole audience in the same way, online social media can contain highly individual interactions and perspectives. However, these currently are dominated by the uniform and inherently non-perspectival mechanisms of display of activity and interaction, such as 'timelines' and templates that offer little reflection on the nature or quality of the interaction of their users, or 'actors'. The linear representations of interaction lack meaningful hierarchy, and documented content is hardly differentiated based on the quality of engagement with others, which might range from flippant remarks to more meaningful exchanges.

Urban images

In contrast to the other films discussed here, Bent Hamer's *Factotum* of 2005, based on a novel by Charles Bukowski, is clearly situated in the open terrain of the city. Unlike the single contained sets of *Rear Window* or *Dogville*, for example, a series of images of familiar urban sites establish the setting of the story of Henry 'Hank' Chinaski, a hopeless drifter, who struggles to maintain his jobs, as well as his personal relationships. The American city and its familiar sites – or sights – of isolation and transience frame the aimless wanderings of the protagonist and operate metaphorically as filmic landscapes (Lukinbeal 2005: 13): the journey on a bus at night, the diner, the motel and the lowly lit bar and stripclub. Wollen's 'static space' of scenery – in this case the city itself – is captured in a series of shots establishing the sites of interaction. The frequent shifts in location create a sense of disorientation and distance that contrasts with the sense of intimacy experienced in Hitchcock's *Rear Window*. This distance and the surfacing at seemingly any point in the urban network resonates with the experience of expansive social media networks, which allow users to rapidly shift across a range of sites of interaction. Chinaski's transience gives a sense of being nowhere in particular, at the same time as the sets used to locate him and his story in a series of images rather paradoxically convey a strong sense of place. The notion of 'landscape as place' provides a sense of the action 'taking place', transforming film into narrative space; the particular 'geography in film holds the action in place', and prevents a sense of displacement in the viewer (Lukinbeal 2005: 6–7).

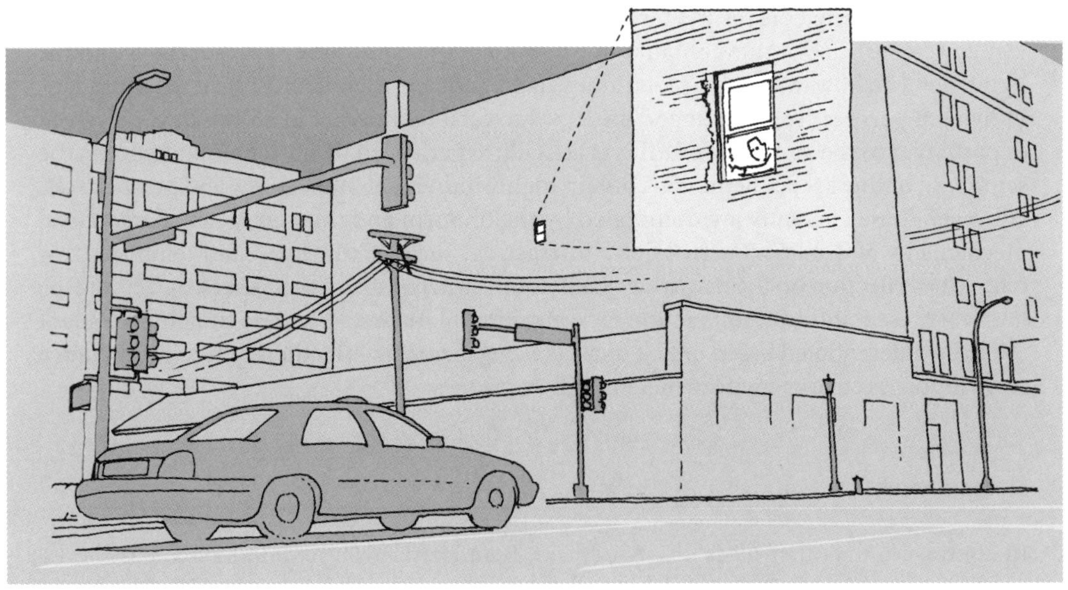

Figure 5. The camera zooms out from a close-up on Chinaski to show his isolated location within the urban context. *Factotum* (2005), © IFC Films.

In much the same way that *Learning from Las Vegas* invites the reader to consider the 'value of representational architecture' along the highway (Venturi, Scott Brown and Izenour 1977: 8), familiar urban images are used symbolically to locate the viewer, while urban settings and the architecture of the city simultaneously are representative of the state of mind of the protagonist. The plot seems to emerge almost randomly anywhere within the network of the city, relying on the familiarity of the urban settings to contain the narrative and to guide a reading of the story. Shots establishing new sets frequently show a building or a street corner, creating a strong perspectival viewpoint that positions the audience, both within the image itself, as well as within the city as the setting of the film. Nevertheless, these images shy away from showing any fragments of the city that might be highly recognizable; a sense of being in potentially any North American city remains.

Unlike the inhabited and directly experienced architecture of the city, the fictive sets of film do not need to form a coherent whole; what is seen on-screen offers a series of carefully constructed clues based on shared and 'agreed' conventions to help make sense of the space of the film and its plot. 'The filmic montage is thus an instrument for relating the "fluctuating" experience of routes taken. It creates small units as necessary for orientation', which guides through narrative over space (Truninger 2012: 131). In the city, at the theatre, as in film, shared understandings of clues, codes and conventions allow for a reading of environments and the construction of mental images of places. In this way spatial devices mediate between people occupying the same physical setting. Sets help to contain the action on-screen and allow the viewer to build a mental map of a range of places, even if these are never experienced in sequence (Pallasmaa 2001: 155) and instead manifest as an assemblage of images in the minds of audience members. In *Factotum*, the mental construct that helps to locate the viewer relies on familiar urban images, rather than the coherence of the set; no 'overview' is given regarding the here-and-now, as so strikingly exemplified in *Dogville*'s establishing shots of the stylized stage.

As architect Fumihiko Maki illustrates in his exploration of individual 'mental landscapes' of the city,

> people will get an opportunity to discover what parts of their separate cities they do in fact share. It is then that people will discover that possession by each individual of a city of his or her own provides a more stable foundation for the city as a community. (Maki 2008: 95)

A similarly clear cognitive – and perspectival – framing of the domain of online social networking, which by its very nature is shared, might afford users of networking platforms a more stable basis for interaction, somewhat connecting a sense of self to a sense of place. Online sites, however, currently do not present themselves as settings that contain a degree of familiarity, such as the urban images forming the contextual backdrop to *Factotum*. The landscape of perception of the digital age is one of high speeds and distance, and might benefit from a symbolic use of representational architectural space as a referent in the mediation of communication. Such communication strategies for the post-perspectival realm of digital interaction, like 'The Strip' in Las Vegas, might be viewed as an 'architecture of communication over space' (Venturi, Scott Brown & Izenour 1977: 8).

Conclusion: Staging interaction

The films studied here suggest ways of thinking about how the images and commentary distributed through social media can be brought together in a form of *mise-en-scène*. This literal placing on a stage, and the resulting framing of a plot through dialogue and spatial conditions, help to position action in film. *Mise-en-scène* is a device to frame action and has the potential to specialize, and indeed spatialize, interaction in online social networking. While the enhancement of urban experience through informational overlays allows users to deploy their mobile screen as a filter that includes additional contextual information to the architectonic backdrop of the city (Manovich 2006: 225–26), the discussion of the relationship between architectural sets in film and online social interaction suggests that a corporeal reality, the space of the city, could in turn augment the experience of the fluid information exchanges that have come to characterize sociality at the beginning of the twenty-first century. Familiar images of urban settings might then act as an informational overlay that helps to provide context to specialize the otherwise unbound realm of online interaction.

The participation in online social media is inherently more complex than watching a film, both in terms of the 'hybrid' spatial challenges it poses, as well as concerning clarity and the legibility of narrative. While this chapter attempts to draw comparisons between a mode of seeing in the cinema and the experience of sociality, there are key shifts in the move from cinema to online social media regarding the positioning and involvement of the viewer, as well as with respect to modes of reception. In cinema, the viewer is positioned as a voyeur (Colomina 1992: 90), without impact on the action: 'The viewer becomes invisible to anyone within the diegesis, the world of the film's narrative' (Lukinbeal 2005: 12). The segregation that has been established in the filmic viewing experience, has been broken down in online social media. Here, viewers participate in 'live' narratives, and are able to return a series of posts and comments recorded in the past to the present by sharing, liking and commenting. Crucially, however, viewers have become actors themselves, yet retain their original distanced viewing position behind the screen; the viewer in social networking effectively sees himself outside of himself, occupying multiple vantage points simultaneously. While the actor in film, however, is aware of the dynamics of reception, the role of the user-as-performer in online sociality is less clearly scripted. Here, he watches events unfolding in images and text at a distance on the screen, at the same time as being 'immersed' in the unfolding spectacle. Film and its *mise-en-scène* offer reference points to frame events, allowing them to actually 'take 'place' and to present individual identity in online social media in a way that aids their legibility.

The architectural film set and its urban referents are proposed as a key tool to devise a shift in thinking about enhancing the digital sphere of the social, beyond considering augmentation merely as a process of overlaying information onto the static physical environment of the city. The physical sets of film as well as two-dimensional modes of representation are useful devices in thinking about how tangible tectonic space and its depiction on-screen can help to clarify the interaction between 'actors' in mediated sociality. Forms of architectural presentation, as found in the film set and the images it creates, act as a contextual framing device. Such a context is required to 'stage' online sociality more successfully, and to help 'actors' and 'audiences' alike to interpret the plots, or the content, of online sociality. *Mise-en-scène* is an example of how spatial devices might be reintroduced into social engagement when this is virtually mediated. Constraints such as scale and visibility that are so crucial to the reading of action in film, help to better position online selves, grasp audiences and tailor behaviours more consciously: an architecturally informed communication design might become the virtual equivalent of the film set.

References

Allen, S. (ed.) (2000), *Practice: Architecture, Technique and Representation*, Amsterdam: G+B Arts International.

Applin, S., Fischer, M. and Walker, K. (2012), 'Visualising PolySocial reality (revised)', *Just-In-Time Sociology*, http://jitso.org/2012/12/03/visualising-polysocial-reality-revised/. Accessed 3 December 2013.

Aston, E. and Savona, G. (1991), *Theatre as Sign-System: A Semiotics of Text and Performance*, London: Routledge.

Bachelard, G. (1994), *The Poetics of Space* (trans. M. Jolas), Boston, MA: Beacon Press.

Benjamin, W. (2002 [1999]), *The Arcades Project* (trans. H. Eiland and K. McLaughlin), Cambridge, MA: Belknap.

Björkmann, S. (ed.) (2003), *Trier on von Trier* (trans. N. Smith), London: Faber and Faber.

Cairns, G. (2013), *The Architecture of the Screen: Essays in Cinematographic Space*, Bristol, Chicago: University of Chicago Press.

Colomina, B. (1992), 'The split wall: Domestic voyeurism', in B. Colomina (ed.), *Sexuality & Space*, Princeton: Princeton Papers on Architecture, pp. 73–130.

Coverley, M. (2010), *Psychogeography*, Harpenden: Pocket Essentials.

Dade-Robertson, M. (2011), *The Architecture of Information: Architecture, Interaction Design and the Patterning of Digital Information*, New York: Routledge.

Eco, U. (1987), *Travels in Hyperreality: Essays* (trans. W. Weaver), London: Picador.

Floridi, L. (2014), *The Fourth Revolution: How the Infosphere Is Reshaping Human Reality*, Oxford: Oxford University Press.

Friedberg, A. (2006), *The Virtual Window: From Alberti to Microsoft*, Cambridge, MA: MIT Press.

Fuchs, C. (2014), *Social Media: A Critical Introduction*, London: Sage.

Gibson, W. (1995), *Neuromancer*, London: HarperCollins.

Goffman, E. (1971), *The Presentation of Self in Everyday Life*, London: Penguin.

Hamer, B. (2005), *Factotum*, Norway/France/USA: IFC Films.

Hamm, M. (2006), 'Reclaiming virtual and physical spaces: Indymedia London at the Halloween critical mass', *Open 11: Hybrid Space*, http://www.skor.nl/_files/Files/OPEN11_P96-111%281%29.pdf. Accessed 11 November 2013.

Hitchcock, A. (1954), *Rear Window*, USA: Paramount Pictures.

Jacobs, S. (2011), 'The architecture of the gaze: Jeffries's apartment and courtyard', in L. Weinthal (ed.), *Toward a New Interior: An Anthology of Interior Design Theory*, Princeton: Princeton Architectural Press, pp. 546–58.

Kawin, B. F. (1978), *Mindscreen: Bergman, Godard, and First-person Film*, Princeton and Guildford: Princeton University Press.

Lister, M. (2005), 'Dangerous metaphors and meaning in immersive media', in J. Furby and K. Randell (eds), *Screen Methods: Comparative Readings in Film Studies*, London: Wallflower, pp. 38–47.

Lovink, G. (2011), *Networks Without a Cause: A Critique of Social Media*, Cambridge, UK: Polity.

Lukinbeal, C. (2005), 'Cinematic landscapes', *Journal of Cultural Geography*, 23: 1, pp. 3–22.

Maki, F. (2008), *Nurturing Dreams: Collected Essays on Architecture and the City*, Cambridge, MA and London: MIT Press.

Manovich, L. (2006), 'The poetics of augmented space', in C. Jewitt, T. V. Leeuwen and T. Triggs (eds), *Screens and the Social Landscape*, 5: 2, pp. 219-240.

McCullough, M. (2005), *Digital Ground: Architecture, Pervasive Computing, and Environmental Knowing*, Cambridge, MA and London: MIT Press.

Mitchell, W. J. (2005), *Placing Words: Symbols, Space, and the City*, Cambridge, MA: MIT Press.

Nissenbaum, H. (2010), *Privacy in Context: Technology, Policy and the Integrity of Social Life*, Stanford: Stanford University Press.

Pallasmaa, J. (2001), *The Architecture of Image: Existential Space in Cinema*, Helsinki: Rakennustieto oy Helsinki.

Papacharissi, Z. and Gibson, P. L. (2011), 'Fifteen minutes of privacy: Privacy, sociality, and publicity on social network sites', in S. Trepte and L. Reinecke (eds), *Privacy Online: Perspectives on Privacy and Self-Disclosure in the Social Web*, London: Springer, pp. 75–89.

Resnais, A. (1961), *L'année dernière à Marienbad/Last Year in Marienbad*, France and Italy: Cocinor.

Ronson, J. (2015), '"Overnight, everything I loved was gone": The internet shaming of Lindsey Stone', *The Guardian*, 21 February, http://www.theguardian.com/technology/2015/feb/21/internet-shaming-lindsey-stone-jon-ronson. Accessed 23 May 2015.

Tadeo, M. (2014), 'Anton Casey fired and flees Singapore in economy class over "poor people" comments', *The Independent*, 27 January, http://www.independent.co.uk/news/business/news/anton-casey-fired-and-flees-singapore-in-economy-class-over-poor-people-comments-9088199.html#. Accessed 26 August 2015.

Trier, L. von (2003), *Dogville*, Denmark: Lions Gate.

Truninger, F. (2012), *Filmic Mapping*, Berlin: Jovis.

Venturi, R., Scott Brown, D. and Izenour, S. (1977), *Learning from Las Vegas: The Forgotten Symbolism of Architectural Form*, Cambridge, MA and London: MIT Press.

Vidler, A. (2001), *Warped Space: Art, Architecture, and Anxiety in Modern Culture*, Cambridge, MA and London: MIT Press.

Wollen, P. (2002), *Paris Hollywood: Writings on Film*, London: Verso.

Epilogue

Ari Mattes and Mirko Guaralda

In *Understanding Media: The Extensions of Man* (2001 [1964]), Marshall McLuhan famously argued that the content of any medium is another medium. The content of a movie 'is a novel or a play or an opera' (p. 19). Its 'effect' is not determined by or in relation to its 'content', but is the product of the medium itself. Even if McLuhan's separation between form and content does not quite hold up to ontological scrutiny, falling back, as it does, on the old form-content dichotomy that dominated aesthetic criticism from the ancients to the moderns, there is something remarkably compelling (and productive) about this formulation in the context of the current collection, a book of essays about film.

This is then magnified if we consider Friedrich Kittler's argument in *The Truth of the Technological World: Essays on the Genealogy of Presence* (2014), that the city itself is a medium. Kittler designates the city as a space and term incorporating its own mapping, infrastuctures, technologies and informational and physical communications pathways (including those peculiar and unpredictable communicating vessels: people). Media, Kittler argues, constitutes the 'storage, transmission, and processing of information', and includes 'old-fashioned things like books, familiar ones like cities, and new ones like computers' (p. 144). This notion of the city as medium – as well as the media city – is beautifully unpacked by Shannon Mattern in her short but provocative book, *Deep Mapping the Media City* (2015), in the context of her development of new forms of archaeological exploration and mapping of urban experience.

If we take Kittler at his word, we find we have, in *Filming the City*, then, a kind of triadic structure: a medium (book) about a medium (film) about another medium (city) – 'media cubed'?

Yet there is another medium – in fact the most dominant – that is absent from this schema, hidden even though its actual presence, as the agency, the 'law' that is 'beyond the law', is definitive – the human: the subject, the author, the hermeneutic medium channelling these reflections on urban space and film.

This authorial subjectivity becomes increasingly, in the contemporary spectacle age, 'subject to' as opposed to 'subject of' urban experience. Our experience of urban space, in the mediated city, is endlessly filtered through and fed back into our experience of urban spectacle – and we should never forget that these urban spectacles are usually controlled and administered from above by powerful corporations.

Whilst the essays in this collection have focused principally on representations and constructions of urban space in cinema, a future collection could just as easily focus on a theme latent in some of these texts: the interpretation of urban phenomena as filtered through and overlaid by imaginative constructions derived from cinema – looking at the way our experience of the urban is subjectivized and vitalized (or de-vitalized) as a product of cinema. This perhaps more closely maps onto the experience of those of us growing up and living in contemporary 'spectacle' societies where vitalities and subjectivities are endlessly mediated and remediated through (and as) other phenomena.

For example, as a teenager growing up in Sydney, Australia, in the 1990s, Mattes's suburban reality was always first and foremost overlaid by his imaginings of Los Angeles, garnered from watching *Beverly Hills 90210* (Star, 1990–2000) and *Melrose Place* (Star, 1992–99) – Hollywood television beamed into the Sydney suburbs, courtesy of executive producer Aaron Spelling. His understanding of space in the city-proper was likewise contingent upon his a priori experiences of Scorsese's New York – urban Sydney rapidly developed as the product of, and in lieu of, Scorsese's depictions of the urban in *Mean Streets* (1973) and *Taxi Driver* (1976).

In any case, cities, with their complexities and vibrant environments, have always inspired artists. Painters, writers and musicians have described and celebrated urban spaces, and have taken inspiration from the narrative of cities to construct their visions of urban societies. Italo Calvino in *Invisible Cities* (1997 [1974]) renders different surreal cities, each one representing a human condition or a system of relationships, often sourcing inspiration from real-world settlements. Calvino celebrates cities as a way to reveal the contradictions of contemporary society, bringing the reader into a fictional world in which everyday architectures and activities become sources of wonder and amusement. Readers are carried away even as their fantastic journey is grounded in their own experiences of urban environments.

As we have seen in this collection, city spaces have inspired film-makers whilst providing the settings for their work, but film-makers have also provided a privileged perspective on cities. While other arts build on one's experience of urban environments, films not only immerse viewers in new and exciting spaces, but also unravel different perspectives on our cities.

Film can use architecture to underline a storyline and to illustrate a specific state of mind or set of moods in its narrative, but the cities depicted on the screen are ideal and idealized environments. Cities in film are, of course, much more homogeneous than in 'real life', with the potential of crafting perfect scenery allowing film-makers to select congruent parts of built environments to describe ideal cities as if they were coherent entities like a character in a plot. Even so, the idyllic suburb often presented in films became an aim for many supporting the popularity of New Urbanism in the 1980s.

One of the often cited outcomes of this urban design approach is Celebration in Florida. Developed by the Walt Disney Corporation, this town was designed and branded so that potential customers would feel like they were buying and moving into a Disney film. The strict control on the urban form and aesthetics of the city and the selection process of its inhabitants, more or less like a casting, have not allowed Celebration to escape the common issues of many suburbs – inhabitants were shocked, for example, by Celebration's first murder in 2010. The notion of 'experience', which is crucial in film, is a more and more debated area for designers and developers, who often indulge in promoting a lifestyle more than the actual qualities of a community. Trailers are today used to promote future developments, future cities promising vibrant environments and an ideal life. The experience of new cities, of new developments, is promoted using familiar features that the public has come to appreciate through their exposure to film.

In a reversal of Calvino's *Invisible Cities*, the narratives of cities are influenced by the narratives of films. The public seeks in the physical world pre-existing experiences created, transmitted and packaged by the magnates of the screen. In the age of cinematic (or post-cinematic) affect, our envisionings of urban space become mapped against a multidimensionality of cinematic experiences and memories. The city streets we walk are also the streets James Dean and Marlon Brando walked – perhaps, in fact, they are more so.

Notes on Contributors

Series editor

Graham Cairns has taught at Universities in Spain, the UK, Mexico, South Africa and Gambia. He has worked in architectural studios in London and Hong Kong and ran a performing arts company, Hybrid Artworks, with a specialism in video installation and performance art. The author and editor of five books, he has presented papers at international conferences and has published on architecture, film, interior design and advertising. Currently, he is Principal Editor of the scholarly journal *Architecture_MPS* and director of its research arm AMPS (Architecture, Media, Politics, Society). He is also Senior Honorary Research Associate at the Bartlett School of Architecture, University College London.

Editors

Edward M. Clift is President of Brooks Institute, a private and independent visual arts college located in Ventura, CA. Prior to joining Brooks, Clift was a communication professor and founding dean of the School of Media, Culture & Design at Woodbury University. He is a graduate of the Master's degree programme at the Annenberg School of Communication (U. Penn) and holds a Ph.D. in communication from the University of Utah. In addition, he holds a Master of Fine Arts (MFA) degree in photography from the Savannah College of Art and Design and a BFA from the Tisch School of the Arts in New York City. He has published articles on the rhetoric of economics and edited a book on the subject, *How Language is Used to Do Business* (2008). In addition to his work as an educational entrepreneur, he has served as Chair of the Burbank Cultural Arts Commission and as Education Director for the Burbank International Film Festival. Clift is a graduate of California Connections, a professional development programme sponsored by the Southern California Leadership Network.

Mirko Guaralda is Senior Lecturer in Architecture at the Queensland University of Technology (QUT); his background includes experience in architectural design, landscape architecture and urban design. Before joining academia full-time, Guaralda had been working in industry and local government, and has been involved in a wide range of projects at different scales, from small dwellings and gardens, to new estates and urban strategic planning. He is currently research associate with the Centre for Subtropical Design, the Urban Informatics Research Lab and the Children and Youth Research Centre at QUT. Guaralda's research investigates people–place interaction with a focus on unstructured activities that support the development of resilient and strong communities. The use of social media is evaluated as a more and more relevant strategy to structure not only interpersonal relationships, but also the way people relate to the built environment. Guaralda's work studies how communities can customize and appropriate the urban landscape through unplanned uses, guerrilla techniques and bottom-up approaches; in this approach to our cities, media often provide platforms to share ideas, connect and organize interventions. Smart technologies also support the navigation of the urban landscape, superimposing new meanings onto consolidated environments.

Ari Mattes is Lecturer in Media Studies at the University of Notre Dame Australia (Sydney). He has published scholarly articles on popular film – and visual culture more generally – in Australian and international journals, and writes a regular column, 'Vision Culture,' for *TheConversation.com*. Current research projects include media use in sacred spaces, Nietzsche and film aesthetics, theories of Accidental Cinema, and serial killing in new media. Mattes holds a Ph.D. from the University of Sydney in American literature and film.

Contributors

Alice Arnold is a nonfiction film-maker and an educator. In 2002, she was awarded an NYFA Fellowship for her photographic work, which examines city life and the urban environment. Her first film, *TO BE SEEN*, a documentary short about street art, was broadcast on REEL/NY, WNET/PBS, screened at MoMA and is distributed by Icarus Films. Her second film, *TEETH*, also distributed by Icarus Films, premiered at MoMA's Documentary Fortnight (February 2008). In 2007, she was awarded a Fulbright Fellowship in Filmmaking (Hong Kong) for *ELECTRIC SIGNS*. In addition to making media, she teaches media studies and media production and was a visiting professor in the School of Communication at American University in 2013.

Gemma Barton has ten years academic teaching experience in architecture and interior architecture. With four years experience as a freelance architecture and design critic Barton has had essays and features published in many of the leading industry magazines, journals and websites, including *Mark* and *Blueprint*. Barton's practice-based research includes curatorial and exhibition projects, undertaken through her design and production company, representing hundreds of artists around the world and working with clients such as RIBA, the Fringe and the Tate Britain. Barton is considered an active and challenging influence within the industry. Her grounded commitment to design and conceptual drive make her an ideal voice for exploratory research and a champion campaigner for the recognition of innovative strategy. She teaches at the University of Brighton.

Luisa Bravo is Charter member and President of City Space Architecture, a nonprofit cultural association based in Bologna (Italy), which works as a multidisciplinary research platform, involving more than one hundred scholars as affiliated members all over the world. Bravo is an Architectural Engineer, she received her education in Italy, France and the UK. She holds a Ph.D. in Building and Territorial Engineering, from the University of Bologna, with a thesis on Contemporary Urbanism. Bravo is currently a postdoctoral research associate at University of Bologna, and Adjunct Professor in Urban Planning and Design at University of Florence in Italy and Visiting Assistant Professor in Architecture at Lebanese American University in Lebanon.

In 2005 she founded her own professional studio, Bravo Design, in Bologna, where she currently works. Bravo was the Chair of the *Past Present and Future of Public Space: International Conference on Art, Architecture and Urban Design*, held in Bologna (2014), and is currently co-ordinating *MaPS: Mastering Public Space*, a collaborative research network on cities and urbanity; *Pop-up City*, a photography research project on instant urbanity; and 'Urban Visions: Beyond the Ideal City', a cinematography competition for short films. All these projects are promoted and supported by City Space Architecture.

Jarrad Cogle comes from a background in English and literature studies. He is on the steering committee for the Novel Studies postgraduate reading group based at the University of Sydney, where he is completing his Ph.D. His research is focused on Fredric Jameson's relationship to the nineteenth- and twentieth-century novel. Other research interests include subjectivity in the postmodern novel and global cinema space in contemporary Hollywood film.

Carmen Elisa Gómez-Gómez studied communications and earned an MA in film studies at Ohio University (Athens), and a Ph.D. in Latin American studies at the Ohio State University (Columbus). She is a specialist in Mexican cinema. She teaches topics related to the study of cinema and the city in graduate programmes, and the history of art to undergraduate students, both at Universidad de Guadalajara. She is the author of the books *María* Félix *en imágenes* (2001); *¿Verdad o ilusión? El cine fantástico y los géneros* (2002); and *Familia y estado: Visiones desde el cine mexicano* (2015).

Ayşegül Akçay Kavakoğlu teaches at İstanbul Kemerburgaz University, Department of Architecture. She previously worked at Eskişehir Osmangazi University and taught on the architectural design studio and urban design courses. Akçay graduated from Dokuz Eylül University, with a Bachelor of Architecture degree. She studied for her Masters at Middle East Technical University (METU) and Ecole Nationale Supérieure d'architecture de Paris Belleville, graduating from METU in 2008 with a thesis about representation of city images in cinema. She is currently finishing her doctorate at METU. Her research is devoted to the understanding of the contribution of moving images to the design process.

Benjamin Koslowski is a designer and researcher and has a background in architecture with an MA from the Royal College of Art. He has previously worked in architectural practice on projects ranging from small-scale interior design to the masterplan for London's Athletes' Village for the 2012 Olympic Games. From 2011 until 2013 he was Research Associate at the Helen Hamlyn Centre for Design, where his work was focused on analysing and improving the use of work environments through in-depth user research; this work has been tested in the mental health unit of a large British hospital, and at the headquarters of a large British bank. Koslowski is currently conducting doctorate research with the Creative Exchange, an AHRC initiative to bridge the gap between academic institutions and the creative industries, where his work focuses on how communication technology changes our cities, and in particular the way we relate to other people in digital and physical environments. In addition to his research activity, Koslowski is Visiting Lecturer in Interiors at Middlesex University, and has been a visiting critic at institutions including the University of Greenwich and UAL Central Saint Martins.

Lisa Landrum is an architect, artist, author and educator, with design and teaching experience in Canada, the United States and Europe. She is currently Assistant Professor of Architecture at the University of Manitoba in Winnipeg, Canada. Landrum's research into the dramatic agencies of architecture has been presented internationally and published in two recent books by Ashgate in 2013: *Architecture as a Performing Art* (eds Marcia Feuerstein and Gray Read); and *Architecture and Justice: Judicial Meanings in the Public Realm* (eds Jonathan Simon, Nicholas Temple and René Tobe). Landrum holds a Bachelor of Architecture degree from Carleton University in Ottawa (1995), as well as a post-professional Master's (2003) and Ph.D. (2011) in the History and Theory of Architecture from McGill University in Montreal. She is a registered architect in New York State and in the province of Manitoba. Since 1997, Landrum has also been exploring the performative potential of architecture and urban space by making collaborative group costumes for public parades.

Joern Langhorst is currently Assistant Professor of Landscape Architecture at the University of Colorado Denver. Previously he has held faculty positions at the University of Oregon and Iowa State University. His research and teaching focus on landscape architectural theory; on issues of visualization and representation, emphasizing film; and on post-industrial and post-disaster sites with a focus on the cultural production of space. A particular emphasis is on post-industrial and postcolonial cities and their mechanisms of de-development and redevelopment. He has been consulting on the recovery and redevelopment of post-disaster and post-industrial sites nationally and internationally, and has worked extensively in post-Katrina New Orleans.

Gabriel Solomons is both a practising graphic designer and senior lecturer at the University of the West of England's Faculty of Arts, Creative Industries and Education. Alongside lecturing, he is currently innovation manager and book series editor at Intellect, a UK-based publisher specializing in the fields of creative practice and popular culture. His current projects include both editing and art directing the World Film Locations book series that explores the relationship between the city and cinema, and Fan Phenomena, a book series that decodes icons of popular culture. Born in the UK but brought up in the Middle East and the US, Solomons received his BA in Graphic Design from the University of the West of England in 2000. Solomons has worked with a range of clients in both the arts and media over the past ten years and has delivered papers, lectures and speeches on design, film and book production at various venues worldwide.

Maciej Stasiowski is a researcher based at the Institute of Audiovisual Arts at Jagiellonian University, Poland. Previously, his research focused on the experimental literature underpinnings (postmodern novel, *nouveau roman*, metafictions) of Peter Greenaway's cinema: 'Atlas of All Things Inconstant'. His current research is centred at the convergence of cinema and architecture in the theoretical projects of deconstructivist architects, and cinematographic strategies in films. He has a Master's degree in cultural studies (specialization: film studies) and is currently completing his doctoral studies. He is associated with film and new media academic magazine *EKRANy* and amongst his previous publications are essays on the architectural attributes of Terry Gilliam's *Brazil* (1985) and *12 Monkeys* (1995) (in *Wunderkamera: The Cinema of Terry Gilliam*); the concept of spatial memory in Pedro Costa's *Letters from Fontainhas* trilogy; and the tradition of speculative drawings and utopian projects in the architecture of Piranesi, Sant' Elia and Abraham (*Film Quarterly* vol. 79 [2012] and vol. 82 [2013]).

Index